Miss Houghton

Evenings at Home in Spiritual Séance

Welded Together by a Species of Autobiography

Miss Houghton

Evenings at Home in Spiritual Séance
Welded Together by a Species of Autobiography

ISBN/EAN: 9783337120450

Printed in Europe, USA, Canada, Australia, Japan

Cover: Foto ©ninafisch / pixelio.de

More available books at **www.hansebooks.com**

EVENINGS AT HOME

IN

SPIRITUAL SÉANCE.

Ballantyne Press
BALLANTYNE, HANSON AND CO.
EDINBURGH AND LONDON

EVENINGS AT HOME

IN

SPIRITUAL SÉANCE

Welded together by a Species of Autobiography

BY

MISS HOUGHTON

AUTHOR OF "CHRONICLES OF SPIRIT PHOTOGRAPHY"

SECOND SERIES.

LONDON
E. W. ALLEN, AVE MARIA LANE
1882
[*All rights reserved*]

EVENINGS AT HOME

IN

SPIRITUAL SÉANCE.

CHAPTER I.

On the 6th of October 1870, I held my first séance after the return of Mrs. Guppy from her prolonged visit to Italy. It was of course a dark séance, and there were present at it Mrs. Ramsay, Mr. and Mrs. T., Miss S., Mrs. Varley, Mrs. Guppy, accompanied by Miss Neyland (whose mediumship in several phases was rapidly developing), Mrs. Pearson and myself. After beginning as usual with The Lord's Prayer, I was influenced to offer up a brief petition that our re-assembling might enable us to receive a fuller measure of spiritual gifts; that we might thereby become more fitted to do The Lord's work, and to shew forth His great Love to the world.

In a short time Miss Neyland exclaimed, "Oh! there is an angel:—it is Gabriel,—and he will soon make his presence known." We then all heard a sound like the rustling of large wings, not as if flying, but a gentle quivering motion, which ceased after a time; and I may as well mention here, that later in the evening she again saw Gabriel, and the same sound was then observable. . . . She then saw Mamma, my brother Clarence, and my nephew Charlie dripping with water, all of whom she had seen when I had been at Mrs. Guppy's séance on the 13th of September. After which she described a gentleman standing between Mrs. Guppy and Mrs. Ramsay, whom we recognised as General Ramsay. She also saw "James" in letters of light, which was yet another proof; and he beat the military call on the table with one of the paper tubes. She next saw a fair young girl, and her name, Môtee; she was holding a harp, and in illuminated letters were the words, "He gathers His lambs into His arms, and carries them in His bosom." She heard Môtee sing, accompanying herself on the harp: we none of us shared the privilege, but she repeated to us the words of the hymn as they came:

> "Happy birds that sing and fly
> Round thine altars, O most High;
> Happier souls that find a rest
> In a heavenly Father's breast:
> Like the wandering dove that found
> No repose on earth around,
> They can to their Ark repair
> And enjoy it ever there."

After that she described Papa with great accuracy, and then she saw the sentence, "Cast thy burthen upon The Lord, and He will sustain thee: His arm will uphold thee, so that the deep waters shall not cover thee."

To several of those in the circle were now brought bunches of white grapes, and to me was brought a very large cluster of purple grapes, and then Miss Neyland read, above my head, this text, in glowing letters, "I am the Vine, ye are the branches, and My Father is the Husbandman;"—thus shewing us that the grapes were to typify that we must be fruitful branches.

Mrs. T. said, "I feel as if an effort were being made to raise me, but you must not speak to me, nor touch me." The darkness being complete, we could not see how much she was raised, but she spoke occasionally, and her voice sounded very much above us, and when she had been gently lowered to her place, Mrs. Guppy said she had seen her feet above the level of the table, and the spirits immediately rapped in the affirmative, which they reiterated three or four times while we were discussing the subject. She said she had felt herself supported under the arms. Miss Neyland saw the letters M. E. S. T. before this circumstance took place, and thought they were the beginning of a word, but they were Mrs. T.'s initials, with the interpolation of that of her maiden name. This class of manifestation is habitually spoken of as *levitation*, but when we realize that a person is thus lifted up by spirits, by the means of their own spirit-substantial hands, I do not see that the word is more needed than when we see an infant carried by its nurse. It also often amuses me when people say that it is "contrary to the laws of gravitation" when a table is raised in the air without visible contact, but they do not imagine that they break a law when they lift up a light table with their own hands, and yet that is an exercise of a precisely similar power.

Mrs. Ramsay's handkerchief was gently withdrawn from her hands; it was afterwards knotted into the form of a figure, and tucked into the front of her dress. There were several attempts for direct writing: on one sheet of paper Môtee wrote (and Miss Neyland not only saw her while doing so, but she read each word aloud as it was written, and as we afterwards read it for ourselves), "Believe on The Lord, and you shall be saved." On another sheet were the words "good daughter," which I believe were written by Papa. We were then desired to have a light for the remainder of the séance, when Mrs. T. and Mrs. Varley saw a figure standing behind me whom they described very clearly, as also that he had on a blue coat with metal buttons, and Mrs. Varley especially noticed the ring on his finger, which she at first thought was only a thin gold one, but she then discovered that there was one small stone. The description was in all respects perfectly accurate of a friend who had passed into spirit life on the 6th of January 1861; the ring had been his mother's wedding-ring, into which he had had a small diamond set, so as to make it more suitable for a gentleman's wear, so that she saw it in both its phases, thus identifying it the more completely. I now brought my photograph albums for them to look at (which I had been forbidden by my spirit friends to do before the séance), and the moment Mrs. Varley came to one of the portraits, she exclaimed, "Why there is the gentleman I saw standing behind you, and that is the very coat, with its metal buttons." While she was speaking, both she and Mrs. T. again saw him. Miss Neyland also recognised the likenesses of several of the spirits she had seen, which gave an additional interest to the latter part of our séance, which we closed with a few words of thanksgiving.

On the following Sunday I accompanied my sister to Westminster Abbey, where for the first and only time I heard Dean Stanley preach, and I am induced to speak of it now, as he has been so lately withdrawn from the earth-plane to enter upon the realities of the world beyond, of which I believe him to have had some foregleams, although he may not have had the courage to proclaim the new truths that had come to him. It is a marvel to me what such a man could dread; for his position in life was unassailable, and his testimony, however slight, might have been as a tower of strength to those whose worldly prospects would risk being shaken by such an avowal. If all those who lean towards our side would boldly say, "Such and such *proofs* we have ourselves received,"—the voice of scorn would soon be shamed into silence. But the thorns are *not* to be thus removed from our path; nevertheless, I believe that such reticence will meet with its penalty in the hereafter, and there *may* come the words, "Whereas ye have *not* lightened the burthen of My suffering servants, ye cannot yet enter into the joys prepared for the faithful."

My next séance was in honour of Mamma's birthday, on the 22nd of October, and the circle was composed of Mrs. Ramsay, Mrs. Guppy, Mrs. Pearson of Harpur Street, Mrs. Beresford Scott, Miss Williamson, Miss Neyland and myself. As we concluded The Lord's Prayer, the table was gently tipped three times, as a sign that our invisible friends had united with us, and they have frequently on other occasions given us a token to the same effect.

The first spirit Miss Neyland saw was Mamma, looking especially radiant, then with her she saw many others of the family, but she could not separate them sufficiently in her vision to describe them. She then saw a young girl (Môtee) by the side of Mrs. Ramsay, and she was accompanied by a number of Indians, some of whom had white cloths tied round them, but some had not. General Ramsay, dressed in uniform, then became visible to her, taking Môtee by the hand; also many more Indians. She saw an angel behind me, and upon my asking the name, saw "Gabriel."

We heard rustlings of leaves, and felt that upon the table there was a mass of something, wet with rain, and we also heard the fluttering of a bird's wings: gradually we each felt that a wreath of some kind was placed upon our heads, except upon that of Mrs. Pearson, whose wreath was laid upon her hands, under which she had laid upon the table a pocket-handkerchief I had given her that had been embroidered by Mamma. "Light" was then spelt out, and we found that we had been crowned with garlands of ivy twined into wreath-forms. When again in darkness, Miss Neyland said that Mamma was writing on the wall, and the words were: "We have crowned you all with blessings, that you may do The Lord's work upon earth."

. . . She then saw a tall lady standing between Mrs. Guppy and me, but she could not distinguish all the name :— she saw a C and then Mole, and Mrs. Pearson asked her to go round to her (she was her sister, Clara Mole), which she immediately did, and answered a few questions by raps. . . . Miss Neyland saw Mamma write the message, "Dear daughter, I thank you for glorifying the remembrance of this day as much as while I was on the earth." She said Mamma seemed to be very busy indeed, and a message was spelt, "Put six glasses under the table." I did so, and we heard a ringing sound from them several times, but they did not succeed in producing music, which I think was what they had wished. Mrs. Scott saw many lights and stars, some of which were visible to Mrs. Pearson, and we all saw one in the centre, but only rather faintly, while Mrs. Scott was struck with its brilliancy. I had placed a sheet of paper and a pencil under Mrs. Ramsay's chair, which we heard moved away and written upon, and Miss Neyland saw Môtee doing it, and we afterwards read the message, "Dear Mother, I am very happy;" and Mrs. Ramsay took it home with her.

The alphabet was asked for, and we received the directions to "Eat, and sit again." This was so contrary to the usual custom of our séances here (for it was not quite nine o'clock), that we could not help wondering at it, but when we asked whether they wanted to gain physical power for an especial purpose, they answered in the affirmative. Of course we did their bidding, and when I had lighted the candle, we found a white feather on the table, which looked like the wing-feather of a white dove, and must have fallen from the bird whose fluttering we had heard.

On our return from supper, Mrs. Ramsay asked, as I came to my place after extinguishing the candles, whether I had touched her, which I had not, but she had felt something like a veil passed across her face. The alphabet having been again requested, they spelt out, "We will bring Sacha Home's pocket-handkerchief," and I immediately felt a handkerchief laid on my hands for a moment, after which it was given to Mrs. Ramsay; we were then told we might have a light, and lo! in front of her there was a small cambric handkerchief with a very broad hem, with the name of Sacha Home written with marking ink in small letters in one of the corners. When again in darkness, Mrs. Ramsay, who was much struck by what had taken place, asked if Sacha were present, and she answered "Yes." Miss Neyland saw and described her so accurately that Mrs. Ramsay, who was the only one present who had known her, recognised all the details. She then asked Sacha if she remembered something in connexion with this manifestation, and she rapped out, "In Regent's Park, I think."

Mrs. Ramsay then narrated that at a séance with Mr. Home at the house of Mrs. Crawford Parks, in the Regent's Park, not long after his wife's death (which took place in 1862), Sacha made her presence known, and she told Mrs. Ramsay she would give her one of her pocket-handkerchiefs; the séance was, however, concluded without its having been brought to her, and Mr. Home expressed his surprise that she should have made a promise and not have fulfilled it;—and now, after a lapse of upwards of eight years, she had been enabled to perform what she had then promised!!! The tubes had been moved about many times in the course of the evening, and Sacha was now making an effort to use one; at length, in a very gentle voice, she said to Mrs. Ramsay, "I never forget you;" and they held a little conversation, but as Sacha had not much power, she soon said, "Good-night;" but upon being asked if she had any message for her little boy, she answered, "I love him."

Some delicious perfume was sprinkled upon us, and at that moment Ann came to the door to enquire if Miss Leith might be admitted; to which an immediate consent was given. I had invited her to the séance, which to her mortification she had had to decline, as there was a dinner-party at home, but when she could make her escape, she thought she would come and plead for admission, so as at any rate to enjoy some portion of the séance, and she was much amused to see us all with our ivy crowns. Miss Neyland beheld an elderly lady, not very tall, standing behind her, but she could not see her with sufficient distinctness to describe her, in consequence of Miss Leith's atmosphere not having been harmonised into the circle by sitting with us from the beginning, but my spirit friends told me that it was her grandmother. Mamma had always been very fond of her, and expressed her pleasure at her having managed to come for her birthday fête. Môtee, too, who had several times been carrying her Mamma's little silver bell about and ringing it, now rang it again, and took it to Miss Leith. They were now very busy with the tubes, especially in the neighbourhood of Mrs. Pearson; they then brought one to me, and laid it across my arms. "Light" was then spelt, and we found that upon the tube was written "Look inside." There was also some writing *within* it, but too far up for us to do more than see that it was there; so I had to cut the paper and unroll the tube, and withinside were the words, "Dearest Mary," which were meant for Mrs. Pearson, and were written by her mother, my Aunt Sarah. We all felt the touch of hands very distinctly, and once I was allowed just to catch the hand touching me, which was that of Môtee, who then fingered for some little time my pearl ring as her own memorial. At length, after many caressing touches to each of us, "Good-night" was spelt, and our interesting séance was terminated in the usual way.

I was with Mrs. Guppy on the 3rd of November, when she told me that as they were going home, Miss Neyland mentioned that she had seen an additional crown hovering in the air, which they supposed had been intended for Miss Leith, but that the spirits had probably not been able to bring it to her when she joined the circle, because of her not having been present during the whole séance. But to Mrs. Guppy's great surprise, when she went up to her room, she found the said ivy-wreath on Mr. Guppy's pillow.

I generally think it best to leave calumny alone, to die out of itself, but for once I must depart from my own rule, as the publication of this séance may stir the wrong into fresh life, so I will as briefly as possible relate the facts upon which a false accusation was grounded. Mrs. Guppy's grandfather, Mr. Nicholl, was, as I have previously mentioned, a sculptor, and a model who came to his studio left behind her a pocket-handkerchief on which was the name of Sacha Home. How she had come by it I know not, perhaps she might have been a laundress as well as a model, and the handkerchief may have been forgotten to be sent home. It had, however, remained among Mrs

Guppy's things, and she had mentioned the fact to several friends. One of those *soi-disant* friends, who ought to have known Mrs. Guppy better, when she heard what had occurred here, immediately took it into her head that *that* was the handkerchief that had been produced at this house, and whispered her suspicions of trickery around, until, through my cousin, they reached my ears; and as I like to clear away all mysteries, I told Mrs. Guppy the next time I went to see her of the rumours afloat, thinking it possible that her powerfully mediumistic element might have enabled Mrs. Home to convey that identical piece of cambric into my room. "Oh dear, no," was her immediate reply, "*that* handkerchief is still in my possession: we will go up together, and hunt for it at once, for I know I put it into the drawer with Tommy's things." Sure enough, there we found the handkerchief, which was very different from the one that had been brought here, for instead of the delicate marking with indelible ink, the name was embroidered with red cotton in large fancy letters. I must still fight out the question a little farther, for even had it been the self-same handkerchief, that would not have touched the circumstances, for it was given here in fulfilment of a promise made so long before that it had slipped out of Mrs. Ramsay's memory, and no one else had known anything about it at all.

November 11th, I was present at a séance on the afternoon of yesterday, at Mrs. Guppy's, the circle consisting of ten persons, among whom were Mrs. Ramsay and Mr. Coleman. The spirits, after having requested us to wish for something, brought us a quantity of freshly gathered violets, mignonette, geranium leaves and fern leaves, all wet with rain. There were other manifestations, in which were given decisive tests of Miss Neyland's clairvoyant powers, but those personally interesting to myself referred chiefly to Mamma and Clarence. . . Then there was a certain undulatory movement of the table, like that of a vessel at sea, which gradually became more vehement, the strangers present finding out the similitudes, and suggesting that they referred to some one who had been drowned, assenting answers being given by the tippings of the table, and at the same time Miss Neyland saw behind me the youth dripping with water whom she had before described. He then traced in letters of light:

> " In vain your fancy strives to paint
> The moment after death;
> The glories that surround His saints
> Beyond the parting breath."

She says the writing is difficult to read in such cases, because it seems to appear and then disappear. I have heard in other instances, of the writing coming letter by letter, the first fading as the next shines forth.

After the séance was over, while we were chatting, I regretted that I had not fulfilled a previous resolution, which was that when the spirits should desire me to wish for something, to ask them to bring me a stone, for not being a perishable article, I could always keep it, adding that their bringing it to me would make it a *precious* stone.

I am now just returned from another séance at her house, which has been the most extraordinary I have ever attended. Mrs. Chevalier and a lady friend of hers were the only visitors besides myself, and we went down to the sitting-room, with the intention of having tea, but Mrs. Guppy had just heard some powerful raps, desiring that we should not have tea *before* the séance; so we walked up again into the room where it was to take place, and Mrs. Chevalier's lady friend, who had never before been at any séance, was requested by Mrs. Guppy to make a strict examination of the room, which she did most thoroughly, finding nothing but the simple furniture of table, chairs, sofa, and piano: the door was then locked and the key given into her possession. On the table were some sheets of paper, a pencil, a tambourine and a bell; and the circle consisted of Mr. and Mrs. Guppy, Miss Neyland, the two ladies I have mentioned, and myself. The gas was turned out, and when we had united in saying The Lord's Prayer, our invisible friends made an affirmative signal at the conclusion to imply that they also had joined with us. The alphabet was then asked for, and they spelt out the message: "We will bring you a precious stone," which led to my repeating yesterday's conversation, and after a short time Mrs. Guppy said, "They are trying to move my hand round, so as to turn the palm upwards;" and then she added, "Here is something small; am I to give it to Miss Houghton?" "Yes," was the response. When I had received it, we wished to light the candle, which they negatived, but allowed me to tie the small article into a corner of my handkerchief. We were then desired to hold hands all round. The tambourine was then played rather noisily, being carried to different parts of the room over our heads. Something cold was now placed on my hand, which felt like a saucer, and we gradually heard unmistakable sounds of crockery, the table being all the time in considerable motion. Mrs. Guppy began to fear that they had brought her best tea-service, which had been laid out in the lower room in readiness for the repast, but she was left in her anxiety, for our request for a light was again refused. The clatter of cups and saucers became still stronger, and we each felt something thrown into our laps, but we continued to obey the injunction not to unclasp hands, and at length received the welcome permission to strike a light, when we found that to each of us had been given a table-napkin, another having been spread on the table, upon which were seven cups and saucers (*not* those she calls her spiritual ones, from having been our gift to her), six small plates, a larger one (empty) for bread-and-butter, a jug of milk, a glass sugar-basin containing sugar, with sugar-tongs, and some biscuits. After we had investigated all, and remarked that the tea only was wanting, we were desired to extinguish the light, and almost immediately Miss Neyland made a sudden exclamation that something had burned her cheek, so we begged leave to light the candle, which was at once granted, and lo! there was the teapot, containing some very strong tea, and the no longer empty plate had on it a portion of the cake of which we had partaken the evening before, and a knife to cut it with. Of course we had our tea, and enjoyed it. I then examined my gift, which was a beautiful ruby, rather larger than one for which I had given £3 about five years ago, and also more exquisite in colour, so that my stone is *literally* precious. When we were again in darkness, Miss Neyland distinguished some of my spirit relatives, also Mrs. Chevalier's little girl, and others belonging to her. We were tenderly touched by the loving fingers of those so dear to us, Mrs. Chevalier feeling her child's hand very distinctly. A Neapolitan tortoise-shell dagger (a gift from Mrs. Guppy) that I wear in my hair, was gently withdrawn, and taken to Mrs. Chevalier, who was allowed to hold it for a time, but it was then brought back and replaced in my hair. Something was heard to fall into the cup near Mrs. Chevalier that sounded like money,—it was a shilling, which she was desired to keep, and Mrs. Guppy afterwards made a hole in it, to enable her to hang it to her watch-chain. Dear Môtee felt on my finger for the ring which is her emblem, and gave me a little tap of reproach for not wearing it on this occasion. "No more," was then spelt, but even after the door had been widely opened, so that there was a good deal of light, Mrs. Chevalier again felt the touch of her little girl's hand.

I then went to the kitchen to ascertain whether the servant had made the tea that had been brought to us, but she knew nothing whatever about it, and thought I was reproving her for not having made it in readiness for us. Miss Neyland then looked into the caddy, where there had been nearly half a pound of tea, but it had all vanished, so it was no wonder our tea had been so strong. The table-napkins had been brought from a linen press upstairs, and the teapot was also brought from an upper room, being one they were not in the habit of using.

In talking afterwards over that marvellous séance, Mrs. Guppy said how glad she would have been if any such manifestations would have come on the previous day, when there were visitors of importance present,—but it was the very fact of our being such a small circle, composed of strong mediums, with only one single stranger in our midst, that rendered it possible for such evidences of spirit power to be given. The tea itself must have been made in the sitting-room, where our meal was to have been taken, for there was a good fire, and the kettle was on the trivet in readiness for use. The room also was, so to speak, *full* of Mrs. Guppy, so that there was plenty of her atmosphere to be gathered for their purposes. Such conditions are well understood by Spiritualists, who know that they may therefore reasonably expect more striking séances at the medium's own house than elsewhere, more especially if there is additional power among the members who form the circle.

She invited rather a large party for November 25th in honour of Mr. Guppy's birthday, the circle consisting of eighteen persons, of whom (by the direction of the spirits) only four sat at the table, Mr. and Mrs. Guppy opposite each other, Miss Neyland and myself between them ; the others being arranged in two semi-circles beyond. I had heeded the reproach given by Môtee on the previous occasion, and had duly put on my oriental pearl, and as we commenced The Lord's Prayer, I felt her take my hand with her warm living fingers, and at each petition she signified her concurrence, either by stroking my hand or patting the ring. At the conclusion, I asked Miss Neyland if she saw any spirit touching me, and she answered, " Oh ! yes, the fair young girl, Môtee."

Some musical instruments were on the table, and among them one composed of eight metal cups (forming the scale), one above another on a handle, which emit a bell-like sound when struck. Upon this the spirits played " The last rose of summer " : —they then struck one single note, and carried the instrument round and round the room until the sound had faded away, and so on with each note :— after which they produced the most harmonious effect I ever heard ; they struck the deepest note, carrying it *once* round, above our heads, so that the room was filled with the vibrations, then the second in the same way, until at last we heard the vibrations of the whole eight, softened and blended into one another, forming, if I may so express it, a perfect *rainbow* of sound.

We were all freely sprinkled with perfume. The message was then spelt, "Faithful must wish," (for fruit), and afterwards, "Each must wish." I had asked for a banana, and each of the others requested fruit of some kind; almost all the wishes being complied with, sometimes instantaneously, and sometimes with a little delay; one friend having a cocoa-nut weighing a pound and a half, and one a watermelon that weighed four pounds. At length we were told to leave off, and return in an hour, so we retired to the adjoining room to have supper.

There were present two members of the spiritual press, who took down the depositions of each person's requests and the result, and I must quote one item of the report, as being so characteristic of Mrs Guppy, whose great weakness it always was, as she termed it, to "eat the manifestations." . . . . "I asked for some barberries, a pear for my little boy Tommy, and a quince, all of which were brought immediately. I began to eat the fruit, so Miss Houghton said, 'It would serve you right if they put a capsicum in your mouth,' and instantly it was done. ELIZABETH GUPPY."

Shortly after our re-assembling, they commenced rocking the table in a very peculiar manner, as if to represent a vessel at sea, gradually increasing the speed as if racing, and the movement became so vehement that we feared the table would be broken, upon which Mr. Guppy said they were quite welcome to break it, when they immediately took advantage of his permission, making a complete wreck it! We asked Miss Neyland what she saw, and she said it was the young man with the water streaming from him whom she had on other occasions seen near me. She also saw a steamer partly under water, and another in the far distance, and at last, at the final plunge of the table, her dress and petticoat were drenched with water, and remained quite wet all the rest of the evening: some of the water fell likewise on my skirt, although I was not near her, but I was not soaked as she was : there was no sound of water flowing, but suddenly it was upon us. She afterwards told me that she could not make out the name of the vessel, but she saw first a C and further on a T.—The *Carnatic* was lost in the Red Sea, through racing with a French steamer, and my nephew, whom she saw, was one of those who were drowned.

Miss Neyland (chair and all) was suddenly brought across to my side, and Mrs. Guppy exclaimed that they were tying something round her throat, Miss Neyland said they were doing the same to her, and I felt something being passed over my head round the back of my neck, but when I put my hand up to feel what it was, thus taking hold of it, they brought it in front of me, and then said we might have a light, when we found that we three were united together by a woollen band of drugget. There was then a little discussion about the Davenport manifestations, and one gentleman said he would be very willing to have his hands tied behind him, for the spirits to try to take off his coat under those conditions, but when we asked if they could do so, the answer was doubtful, they however thought they might be able to do it with another member of the circle, and we were informed that Mr. Guppy himself was to be the person; so his hands were tied behind him, and firmly secured to his chair, but as soon as we were in darkness, we heard him expostulating very strongly as to their proceedings, for they were unbuttoning his waistcoat, and emptying his pockets. After earnest pleadings on his part for a light, he at length obtained the desired permission, when we found that his coat and waistcoat were not quite taken off, but only turned back upon his arms: his watch had been carried to one gentleman, his note-book and cravat to another, and his spectacles to me. He was now very anxious to be loosened, but the knots had been too firmly tied for those who had done to *un*do them, so we suggested asking the spirits to free him, to which they agreed, and when the light was extinguished, did so in a few moments. We again lighted the candle, and Mr. Guppy placing his coat on the table, requested them to put it on some one else, and almost as soon as the light was put out, Miss Neyland exclaimed "Oh! they have dressed me in it;" which they absolutely had done, having put the coat on her, and then buttoned it.

The next time I saw Mrs. Guppy, she told me she had been experimenting with her Turkish bells, but had found it quite impossible to produce the effect of sound that I have striven to describe. It might perhaps be that her footing was on the ground, and thus the vibrating tones would be in a manner entangled with the furniture, instead of being in the untroubled space above our heads.

CHAPTER II.

ANOTHER course was commenced on the 14th of November of those pleasant Monday evenings in Harley Street, which seem to me to have had a value beyond later attempts elsewhere, from the fact that they were more generally popular, and the gatherings were from more universal quarters. The *larger* number of such efforts in the present day may, to a certain extent, account for that fact; some of the Spiritualists going one way and some another, whereas some have retired from any public demonstration of themselves at all. Is it that they have become lukewarm? or is it simply that they no longer have the energetic and enthusiastic Mr. Coleman to summon them together by beat of drum? It is true that many of the original frequenters of those meetings are gone, like himself, to the other side, but there still remain many of the dear old faces whom I would fain see sometimes at our own rooms in Great Russell Street. It may be that the weekly regularity of the meetings was one cause of the good attendance, by becoming a settled engagement, besides which the subscription to the course was at once paid, and it was a something outside of the usual round of life.

I am sorry to say that I kept no notes whatever of any of the details, but I remember that papers on the subject of Spiritualism were prepared and read by some of our friends, leading afterwards to discussion, and I believe it was during that series that we heard a very interesting one from the Rev. Dr. Davies, entitled "Am I a Spiritualist?" when the evidences he gave made it very easy to answer his question in the affirmative. I know, likewise, that Mrs. Hardinge again returned to England about that time, and she was always a host in herself when she formed one of the circle on the platform.

B

Am I a Spiritualist? What a difficult point to decide, even among many who nominally belong to our ranks, of whom it might be well if some would restrict themselves to the term that has taken such a hold upon a large proportion of our neighbours on the other side of the Channel, and call themselves Spiri*tists*, thus limiting themselves to the acknowledgment of intercourse with the dwellers in the beyond, whether through the means of physical or mental mediumship, without seeking to rise above the level of earth's puerilities; whereas, to be a Spiri*tualist*, appears to me to demand the addition of a religious basis, and on that ground most of the clergy *must* all unwittingly be allied to us, for their faith is founded entirely upon the Spirit intercourse of past ages, and if we can but clearly shew them that the past and the present are a portion of one unbroken chain, evidencing God's loving care in granting each revelation so as to meet the need of its own day, surely they will ultimately receive with joy the new truths that are coming now, although, like Saul of Tarsus, they may in the beginning have rejected them.

In the June of that year a lady (doubly connected with the family) came one Wednesday to see me, accompanied by Mr. L———, an artist friend, who had thought she spoke of impossible things when she had told him about my spirit drawings, but the sight of a few soon convinced him that they undoubtedly contained a something beyond his previous philosophy, and he was both charmed and interested with all I had to shew him, so that to such an appreciative observer, I had to vary my portfolios far beyond my usual wont, so as to give him a glimpse of their growth and changes. In the course of conversation he said, "Do you ever exchange sketches with other artists?" "Oh! never," was my rejoinder, and there the matter dropped, and for the time passed entirely out of my mind, and I scarcely know how long a period may have elapsed when the thought came to me in a sudden flash, and I enquired of my wise counsellors whether I ought to do such a thing. "Yes, in this one case," was the reply I received, but I was not yet to take any step in the matter, although they then selected the drawing, entitled "The Eye of The Lord," which was destined for the purpose. At length I was permitted to write to him, alluding to the question he had put to me, and saying that if he had intended it as an expression of his own wish, I should be happy to comply with it. I received an immediate reply from him, dated November 15, in which he said: "I should have been long before this, to renew my acquaintance with you and your wonderful spirit drawings, but that I have been out of town all the summer, and have since been fully occupied in working up my sketches for the winter exhibition. You seemed so unwilling to exchange one of your drawings for that of any other artist, that I had set aside all thought of it, but I shall indeed be delighted to make the exchange, and I shall also be very happy if you can come on Monday to see those I am going to send to the Gallery on that afternoon." I did myself the pleasure of going to see them, and on the following Thursday sent him my promised drawing, accompanied by the written interpretation, and his answer came with speed.

"*November 25th*, 1870.—MY DEAR MISS HOUGHTON,— I cannot tell you how much I value the wonderful and beautiful drawing you sent me yesterday: the subtlety and delicacy of both the colour and the design are to me quite a study: one is constantly seeing something new in its mysterious depths. The little book that you so kindly sent with it will require much thought before it can be understood aright. I am afraid I shall not be able in return to send you anything so original as to line and colour, but what I shall send you will be, I hope, characteristic of Yours very sincerely, L."

It is only now, while seeking out these dates, and finding harmonies all unsuspected in the past events, that I realize the above circumstances as in any way connected with the letter I received from Mrs. T. on the very evening that I had sent off the picture, which was eventually to lead to what has hitherto been the most important action in my life.

On the 22nd of November, to which she alludes, I had been to Cambridge Hall, to assist at a public "Welcome" to Mrs. Hardinge.

"*November* 24*th.*—MY DEAR MISS HOUGHTON,—I hope you reached home safely on Tuesday evening. It is a great comfort to know that you are never alone in a life that outwardly is so lonely. Last night (Wednesday), at about eleven, I had a distinct vision of you sitting at the table in your drawing-room, with a company of your spirit friends about you. One of them kissed you, and you felt the kiss, and you said, 'Yes, my dear, yes, my dear, but I am engaged now.' (You seemed to be writing.) Another passed his hand over your hair and forehead, and looked at you so lovingly; and then you raised your head, having felt the pressure and in a moment your face looked white and shining, like those of the spirits, and the change in you frightened me so much that I roused myself, and almost immediately the clock struck half-past eleven. Those little babies were on each side of you, pulling your dress and wishing to be noticed, but I do not think you saw them. I have thought of you all the morning with some solicitude, notwithstanding the care I am sure your spirit friends will take of you in any further development of your mediumistic powers, or in any events that may arise. Believe me, very truly yours, M. E. T."

At the time thus mentioned, I was engaged, as Mrs. T. correctly states, with papers and writing. Preston had stood talking until nearly eleven, on her way up to bed, and even while she had been with me, I had very strongly felt once or twice the signal of my two dear Baby sisters, which they afterwards repeated, and upon my questioning them, I learned that one object of their being with me was as a preparation for my séance on the 2nd of December, but they feared they might not, their own two little selves, be able to give any manifestation, although they are always anxious to try. Other spirits also gave me their signs, partly for the same purpose, but they all accepted my apology for giving them but a divided attention, as I had various letters to write, and other things to do. I think it must have been St. John whose touch changed the expression of my countenance, for I felt his signal more strongly than usual (it is the sensation of a tender hand on my brow and head), and I had a great feeling of happiness, and as if I scarcely knew how to be sufficiently thankful to God for all His mercies, I seemed as if my soul wanted to burst forth into songs of praise.

The above is my entry made at the time, but my occupation was not only letter-writing, one being to Mr. L——, but likewise copying the interpretation in the small book, to send to him the next day with the picture, and the unseen ones knew all that was to eventuate from that circumstance, although *I* did not.

I had invited Mr. and Mrs. Everitt to be present at my forthcoming séance, but at the same time I had asked Mrs. Everitt to come on some intervening Wednesday to see my drawings and become harmonized into my room, as that was a necessary condition before I could be allowed to invite any fresh guest into my circle, but *she* would then have to do double duty, she and her husband being so essentially *one* that her coming would be all-sufficient. This is a rule that the regulators of my séances have made from the very beginning, and there have been other small details upon which they have permitted no infringement; for the sittings in this house have been exceptional,—not at all intended as evidences for the sceptical, but for the purpose of reaching the highest phenomena they could, which can never be attained amidst conflicting atmospheres: therefore under no circumstances could a complete sceptic or a so-called enquirer have been admitted, although the favour has often been solicited, and might perhaps have been difficult to refuse, but that it is not *I* who have had to give the answer, I have been simply the mouthpiece, and my nay has had to be nay, for the *yea* is instantaneous, if it is to be granted at all, thus I am always saved from any feeling of doubt as to such matters, which of course must be under their jurisdiction; I have sometimes even had to refuse dear friends, but I have known there could be no appeal against the decision.

I had the pleasure on the last Wednesday in November of a visit from Mrs. Everitt, accompanied by Miss Nisbet, which I think we all enjoyed.

The séance was held on the 2nd of December, dear Papa's birthday and also Charlie's, and the circle consisted of Mrs. Ramsay, Mrs. T., Mrs. Guppy, Mr. and Mrs. Everitt, Mrs. Pearson, Miss Neyland and myself. Before the light was extinguished, the table was quite lifted from the ground, and gently floated backwards and forwards as if in greeting, but was quietly lowered as we commenced The Lord's Prayer, to which they, as usual, responded at the conclusion. Miss Neyland saw Mamma, Clarence, and Charlie near me, and when I asked if she saw who had touched my hand, she answered, "The young girl," meaning Môtee, who had been patting the ring. She also saw General Ramsay by the side of Mrs. Ramsay, and other spirit friends whom she described, near the different guests.

By the alphabet, I was desired to wish for anything I liked, so I enquired whether they could bring me Charlie's turquoise pin, sunk in the *Carnatic*, but as that was out of their power, I asked for something from the sea. In a short time Mrs. Guppy said she had been touched by a wet hand, requesting me to feel the back of her hand, which was quite wet, we next heard the fall of something small upon the table, and then a shell (five inches by four) was placed in my hand, and we were permitted to light the candle to examine it. To my surprise it was quite wet, and on tasting, I discovered that it was with *sea*-water. The shell is one of those with brilliant mother-of-pearl tints, and has been polished by the friction of the waves on the sea-shore, also rather cracked and battered by the same process, and I have been told that it is of a kind that is found on the borders of the Red Sea. What we had heard drop was another small shell of a different sort, and Miss Neyland had seen Charlie bring them both to me.

At intervals during the evening we all saw spirit lights, like small stars.

We heard the spirits busily occupied with the pencils and sheets of paper, and there were presently unmistakable sounds that they were drawing. By raps they then spelt out, "We will finish afterwards," and they allowed us to have a light to see what had been done. On the lower part of the sheet of paper is a slight sketch of me, with my hands upraised in prayer (the same attitude in which they had represented me in a direct drawing they had executed for me about two years and a half ago), two winged spirits, in profile, are floating above me, one of whom has both hands pointing upwards, but the other is bending towards me with the two hands just over my head, and there is a light fluffiness of some kind that I cannot at all make out, the sketch being so very faint and slight. While we were all eagerly looking at the drawing, Mrs. T. told me that in the second figure she recognised the face of the spirit whom she had seen with me, in the vision she had had ten days before, and whose touch had so transfigured me that it had startled her. There was some red colour used in the drawing, besides the lead pencil, which said colour the invisible artists must have themselves provided, as there was nothing of the kind on the table.

When we had put out the light, they recommenced work, and we sang the Evening Hymn, for which I had had previous directions. When next we were allowed to look at the drawing, a third figure in full-face, and also winged, had been added above the other two, and the drawing was altogether more worked upon. I asked if they would, in the course of the evening, give some interpretation of its meaning, to which they at once consented. There were now sounds as if pieces of paper were being gently torn, and then came the message, "Put the drawing away." They had torn a triangular piece from each of its four corners, which pieces (not quite equal in size) they had distributed severally to Mrs. Ramsay, Mrs. T., Mrs. Guppy and myself, who were seated together, signifying thereby that we each possessed a portion of the direct-drawing mediumship.

We next heard some writing being done, and it proved to be a message from Papa to Mrs. Ramsay, but it was written in separate letters *downwards*, forming two columns: "My dear Madam, I love you. God bless you." Another hand was now busy, and it was curious in the darkness to note the difference of sound, characteristic of the various productions; those we now heard were evidently long, bold strokes; and the result was a very rough outline of a rock, a vessel, and waves:—a companion sketch was then done of a rock and some waves, and below *them* the word "Charley!" By raps we were then told to "Go, refresh." So we adjourned to the next room for the purpose, but before we returned here, Mr. Everitt suggested that for Mrs. Everitt's manifestations it might be necessary to make some re-arrangement of the sitters, which was done according to the directions he received after we were again seated.

We were then told by the alphabet, "Read Ezekiel, 8th chapter, 3rd verse:" "And he put forth the form of an hand, and took me by a lock of mine head; and the Spirit lifted me up between the earth and the heaven, and brought me *in the visions of God* to Jerusalem, to the door of the inner gate that looketh towards the north." We were then directed to Ezekiel, 11th chapter, 1st verse: "Moreover the Spirit lifted me up, and brought me unto the east gate of The Lord's house, which looketh eastward: and behold at the door of the gate five-and-twenty men; among whom I saw Jaazaniah the son of Azur, and Pelatiah the son of Benaiah, princes of the people." And finally to Acts, 2nd chapter, first four verses: "And when the day of Pentecost was fully come, they were all with one accord in one place. And suddenly there came a sound from heaven as of a rushing mighty wind, and it filled the house where they were sitting. And there appeared unto them cloven tongues like as of fire, and it sat upon each of them. And they were all filled with the Holy Ghost, and began to speak with other tongues, as the Spirit gave them utterance."

The verses from Ezekiel gave the promised interpretation of the drawing, which is yet more significant from Mrs. T.'s previous vision, and my corroboration of it, which prove that the spirit who with his tender hand is leading me upwards to the New Jerusalem is St. John, who in the Apocalypse was permitted to describe it.

We received an injunction to "Pray," and in answer to our enquiries Mr. Everitt was selected to offer up a petition for us, which he did with much fervour.

We then sang another hymn. Delicious wafts of perfume were shed upon us. The tubes were lifted about, and efforts were made to speak, but the whispers were too faint for us to distinguish words. Mrs. Ramsay felt her spirit friends busy among the things in her pocket, some of which were taken out, and her spectacles were removed from the case, but with great care, so as not to disturb the triangular piece of paper, which she had laid there. After a time, the spectacles were restored to their place; but the manifestation had reference to a similar occurrence, when General Ramsay (who now did it) had, shortly after his entrance into the spirit world, treated in a somewhat similar manner the spectacles of Mrs. Ramsay's cousin, Colonel Burlton, who within the last two or three weeks has likewise passed away. Mrs. Ramsay's handkerchief, knotted up, was brought back to her, and Mrs. Guppy exclaimed that they had brought her something which, although not alive, felt almost like a little mouse, it was so soft and tender, but Mrs. Ramsay thought it was her glove, which had been taken from her, and when we had the light we found it was so, and that they had so knotted and twisted it that they had formed it into the likeness of a little black rabbit, the ears being made of the finger-tips, with the two buttons for eyes, and there was a glimpse below of two tiny feet. Mrs. Guppy regretted that she should have to give it up, for she says the spirits never bring anything for *her;* but

Mrs. Ramsay told her that of course she *must* keep it, as it had been given to her. Mrs. Ramsay's handkerchief had been tied so as to form a well-proportioned figure of the Cross.

Directions were then given that Mrs. Guppy and Miss Neyland should leave the circle, and take seats on opposite sides of the fire-place; and the *moment* they were seated, the light was extinguished by the spirits. We enquired if they were comfortable, but no answer whatever was returned, for in that same instant they had both become entranced. In a short time, without our having heard any sound of footsteps, I felt Mrs. Guppy place her arm round me, and, influenced by my Charlie, utter the words: " Dearest Auntie, I am here; I am not drowned." After a little more conversation, she was in the same way led to Mrs. Ramsay, under the General's influence; then to Mrs. Pearson by her mother, also to Mr. Everitt. Then to Mrs. T., who had a communication from a relative lately deceased, and for whom a message had been given her through herself by his son's spirit, which message he had never received, as it had been returned to her through the post-office from America; but he said he could now read the message where it had been given, and he thanked her for her anxiety to have helped him in his need, although he had not himself understood it. Mrs. Everitt was told by one of her spirit friends that she had not followed some directions that had been given her, but that she ought always to heed the advice from the unseen world. She could not at first remember what was alluded to, but afterwards she did, and acknowledged that it would have been wiser to have followed it. Mrs. Guppy then returned to her place, and Miss Neyland was heard speaking to some spirits whom she saw (observing that there were seven of them), but she did not say much, and we did not like to question her, as her trance seemed so deep. I now felt something being passed over my head into my hands, and I immediately discovered that it was Papa's picture, which he had brought to me from its place on the wall, as if to intimate that he wished to return thanks *in person* for our having kept his birthday.

Just then Mrs. Guppy awoke, and was surprised to learn that Miss Neyland was entranced, and still more so that it had been the case with herself. "But where are my boots?" she exclaimed, and then it appeared that they had vanished from off her feet, which accounted for the noiselessness of her movements.

Mrs. Everitt was now in a trance, and John Watt, who is the controlling spirit of her circle, made his voice heard through one of the tubes, which he carried to the ceiling, saying that "he could not stay long, having had much difficulty in entering, because the power here was so great; but he hoped to come again on some future occasion, with the same circle, when he might be able to hold a longer conversation, and he would wish then to bring a friend with him, through whose agency we might have a completely new manifestation." I therefore at once invited Mr. and Mrs. Everitt to join my circle on New Year's Eve, when I purpose holding a séance to commemorate the completion of eleven years of my mediumship, and John Watt, after a few courteous words to each, took his leave. We lighted the candle, and shortly afterwards one of Mrs. Guppy's boots fell with much clatter, apparently from the ceiling, in the corner of the room near the door, at the farthest possible distance from us, and while we were still talking about it, the other fell down just behind her.

Miss Neyland gradually roused, but Mrs. Everitt still continued entranced, and commenced mesmerising Mrs. Tebb, who had been suffering so severely from toothache that she had feared it would be impossible for her to come. She then came towards Mrs. Ramsay, but in passing gave me a warm shake of the hand, so I imagined she was probably under the influence of one of my own friends. She mesmerised Mrs. Ramsay's foot, which was in great pain, for some time, and Mrs. Ramsay, who experienced decided relief, asked if she knew who was controlling her, when Mr. Everitt suggested that she should be asked to remember on her restoration to her normal state, who it was that had been influencing her. She then returned to the table, where she appeared to be seeking paper and pencil, which I gave her, when she wrote, " Warm water bath every four hours, with gentle rubbing.—MESMER."

When she came to herself, Mr. Everitt asked whom she had seen influencing her, and she said it was the same doctor she had seen several times before; rather a fair man, of middle height. He had never hitherto given his name, which she thus learned through his signature, and he is indeed an old friend of mine, having been so strongly linked to me by my having twice drawn his spirit-flower.

The account of that séance seems to terminate in a very unfinished way, but I did not wish to make it too long, as I wrote it out for publication in the first number of the *Christian Spiritualist*, a new monthly periodical that was to make its start in 1871, the editor of which was the Rev. F. R. Young, who had solicited contributions from me whenever I could send anything of interest, and I was quite willing to accede to his request, being exceedingly rejoiced at the issue of a paper belonging to our cause that should stand on a completely religious basis.

At the meeting in Harley Street on November 28th, Mrs. Guppy, who was seated by my side, told me that she now frequently hears spiritual music, which is audible to others as well as to herself, and that while she had been dressing to come out, both she and Miss Neyland had heard quite a melody played.

There was a slight pause soon after Mr. Dove had commenced reading his paper, occasioned by Mr. Coleman leaving his place on the platform to escort Mrs. Hardinge and her party into the room, and just at that moment there was a sound, exactly between Mrs. Guppy and myself, as if a full, sweet-toned bell had been struck. I mentally asked our spirit friends if they would repeat it, which they said they would, but *not* while Mr. Dove was reading: by and bye he stopped, to move across the platform for the purpose of explaining a diagram he had there, and immediately the same sweet sound was heard, only there were two successive strokes instead of one; and when Mr. Dove had quite finished, we heard it *thrice*.

I now received permission from my friends to invite Mr. L. to come and be present some day while I was engaged on my artistic work. He was highly delighted with the privilege to be accorded to him, and *we* appointed the 13th of December, when I had an opportunity of shewing him three distinct stages of work, each of which seemed to fill him with more and more astonishment. I had two drawings in progress, and began upon the one that was nearly finished, so he watched with deep interest the fine lines that went on so smoothly and so unerringly under my hand, never failing to reach exactly their purposed destination, notwithstanding that I was fully engaged in conversation with him all the time; and there would be sudden changes of detail, and methods of manipulation, which clearly did not require my mind to be concentrated upon them, which must have been the case had *self* been the operator, even supposing the possibility of my powers being equal to such perfect work. I next took out the one that was perhaps about half through, when he marvelled indeed at the wondrous effects of colour that were produced, and learned to realize the immensity of labour bestowed upon each drawing, acknowledging that it would baffle any merely human artist to produce such harmonies, for they could only be achieved by work upon work, seemingly much of it to be obliterated, but nevertheless leaving its record and its subtle tints to penetrate through the after designs. It certainly was refreshing to my ears to hear his rapturous exclamations of delight as some new beauty was suddenly revealed from, as it were, the undercurrent of the earlier labour; and his intense sympathy prevented his being in any way a hindrance, as some on-lookers are. I was going to do Mrs. Guppy's Monogram, as a gift of love to her, which drawing was to be commenced on that day, and it was expressly that he might see it begun that I had been allowed to invite him, for an artist well knows that quiet study is usually needed as a preliminary adjunct of a new picture, but I got out the fresh block, telling him that of course I knew the letters were to be E. G., but that as to form or colour I was absolutely ignorant. Only a momentary consultation on that latter point was requisite with my invisible helpers, so momentary indeed that to him it was imperceptible, and the work was at once started, again and again to call forth ejaculations of wonder and delight, and although so much time had been bestowed upon the two previous specimens, this one had already become quite a pretty picture before he went away.

In the course of our talk he said,—what all artists have invariably said,—" Why do you not exhibit?" So I told him my main reason—that the religious symbolism would be out of place in a heterogeneous collection, and that my Royal Monograms had not been admitted by the Academy.— " Oh!" said he, " that is not what I mean :—why not have an Exhibition of your own?"—*Of my own ! ! !* what a bewildering thought :—of course it was quite *impossible*, even if such an idea could enter my brain :—I, in my lonely life, a weak woman, with none to help me in an undertaking of such magnitude :—the very notion of such a thing seemed an utter incongruity, and I could only point out to him that I should not even have an idea how to take the very first step towards such an attempt, or as to what *ought* to be the first step. Oh! as to the business management, he would only be too happy to put me in the way of it if I could entertain the idea ; and as I had given him a ticket of admission to Harley Street for the following Monday, I might then talk with him on the subject, and his farewell words were, " Think of it."

I *did* think of it! for, much to my surprise, when I appealed to my counsellors, the instantaneous response was that *it was to be*: and surely I had food for thought that evening. I considered every item that would enter into such an undertaking, and I do not believe that any single requisite was omitted in my cogitations as to what it would entail. I could of course make no estimate as to probable expense, but that must be left to the future; *it was to be*. He greeted me eagerly on the Monday night, questioning me as to my decision, which he was delighted to hear was in accordance with his suggestion, and he promised at once to speak to a gentleman whose professional services might perhaps be retained; so the mighty effort was thus put in train ! It is only now, while writing the history of the kindling of that small spark, that it strikes me as an evidence to outsiders as to the reality of the help granted by unseen intelligences, for if my artistic work had emanated simply from my *own* brain, that must assuredly have been quite incapacitated by the agitation into which my mind would naturally have been thrown by the first broaching of so momentous a subject, and I must e'en have folded my hands for awhile, so as to collect my thoughts before resuming my brush.

CHAPTER III.

I HAD heard of a séance at which Mrs. Guppy had been present, where ice had been brought by the spirits, and while making all my furniture arrangements on the morning of the 31st of December, for our evening celebration of the completion of my eleventh year of mediumship, I implored the invisibles not to bring any here, for I dreaded lest everything should be reduced to a state of wet untidiness, and my usual provision consisted of a plentiful supply of sheets of paper, a tray of pencils, eight tubes, the porcelain slate, a box of vestas, a candle, and any other odds and ends that might be suggested at the time. Our circle was but a small one, composed of Mrs. Ramsay, Mrs. T., Mrs. Guppy, Mrs. Pearson, Miss Neyland and myself.

The weather was intensely cold, so I had kept up good fires all day in both rooms, and did not take off the one in this room in which we were to sit until after we had had tea and coffee and had thoroughly warmed ourselves, and we also had hot-water bottles for our feet, so as to avoid the possibility of our getting chilled.

Shortly after we had said The Lord's Prayer, we saw some glimmering lights, and then a lovely sparkling one, which rose up spirally until it was just above the level of our heads, where it gradually faded away. We then heard the spirits making a great commotion among the things on the table, and throwing the tubes, sheets of paper, &c., on the ground, but carefully placing the drawing-block on my lap. Sprays of holly were brought to some of the circle, and then there was an exclamation that there was something cold and wet, and I must own to having made an ejaculation of dismay, for I was convinced that it was the ice that I had foreboded, and I implored leave to light the candle, which was immediately granted, when we found a quantity of snow-covered ice on the table; so I rang for a large dish in which to put it, and while we were removing it, we were all struck with the care the spirits had taken in first clearing the table of all that was upon it, so that nothing should be damaged by the moisture, and we speedily wiped away all vestiges of it from the table itself. When we were again settled, this message was spelt, "The water was from the river Jordan."

Miss Neyland presently said she saw Mamma, Papa, my brother Clarence, and Charlie, but she was surprised to notice that Charlie no longer had the water dripping from him, as he always had had when she had seen him before, which corroborated an impression I had received on the 29th after reading the first number of the *Christian Spiritualist*, containing the account of our last séance on Charlie's birthday; which was that Charlie would not again bring with him any symbolism of the wreck, for reference had been made to it in the *first* number of *each* of the four new Spiritualist periodicals, viz., the *Spiritualist*, the *Medium*, the *Spiritual News*, and the *Christian Spiritualist*, and strange to say, on the very day of the séance, in the January number of the *Spiritual Magazine*, under the title of "Representation of a wreck at sea," appeared that portion of the account I had written for the *Spiritual News* of the séance held at Mrs. Guppy's, so it seemed that the event was meant to be brought in every way prominently before the public eye, and that it might then rest. Miss Neyland also saw Môtee and General Ramsay, accompanied by many Indians. She also described Mrs. Pearson's sister to her, and on being asked for the name, she saw a C and then Mole.

Mrs. T. now became somewhat distressed, and seemed compelled to mention that she saw the figure of a man behind Mrs. Guppy, weeping very much; his face was partly hidden by a cloak, but he looked old although his hair was black. She was unwilling to say more, but the words appeared to be forced from her that "his trouble was about Mrs. Guppy's little boy, who was threatened with an attack of the throat, when an immediate remedy must be applied, which was to be a cold compress of some of the ice water that had been brought from the Jordan, and that the spirits would aid in drawing immediate attention to the attack." Of course poor Mrs. Guppy was much troubled, and told us that although so healthy a child, he had once had a seizure that had seemed to stop his breathing, when she instantly sat to the table to consult the spirits, who ordered mustard poultices on throat and chest, which speedily relieved him. That must have been croup, which was what I had feared from Mrs. T.'s account. By the alphabet Mrs. Guppy was then desired to leave the room, and by questioning we found that she was to absent herself for five minutes, so as to get over the shock that it had been to her nerves. We then heard more distinctly a sound that had been going on for some little time, as of a person passing with heavy tread round the room, and when Mrs. Guppy came back, Mrs. T. said the sounds were exactly similar to those she had heard in her childhood ("Yes," from the invisibles); and she gave the history she had narrated to me in one of our tête-à-tête séances, of the footsteps that had been continually heard going round the home of her childhood, an isolated house, every means having been ineffectually taken to find out the cause. The ground might perhaps be covered with deep snow when the foot-falls would be heard, and two of the inmates would go forth to investigate, one turning towards the right, and one to the left, no sign being visible on the fleecy whiteness; and they would meet midway in the round of the house, without having encountered any mortal form, while the sound came just as steadily to the ears of those within the dwelling: or in a clear summer night the footsteps would be heard, but still the bright moon-beams would reveal no human appearance. It was finally supposed to indicate the presence of the unquiet spirit of a young man who had quarrelled with his father, and left his home when about one and twenty years of age, and who had never returned: she gave some further particulars, but even when she had ceased, the tramp—tramp—tramp—still continued that we had heard throughout her narrative.

We were then told to break up the séance; and on our return from supper, Queen Elizabeth announced her presence, and had some conversation with Mrs. Ramsay. It was curious to note the imperious and decisive manner in which the responsive raps were given, one of the tubes being used for the purpose, and once, when a communication was being spelt out, as I continued to repeat the alphabet, not being quite sure that the message was concluded, the tube was applied to my lips so as to stop my speech, and not in the gentlest of manners, but still not roughly enough to hurt. It suddenly occurred to Mrs. Ramsay that she must have come for some special purpose, and enquired if her visit referred to something she had found that morning. "Yes." [Can you tell me to whom it belonged?] "Sarah Marlborough." Mrs. Ramsay then told us that it was a valuable antique fan, which she had discovered in one of her receptacles for by-gone treasures. It was very carefully done up, but there was no clue by which they could ascertain the original possessor, but it seemed of about the period referred to, and it doubtless had belonged to the famous Duchess.

I forgot to mention that in the earlier part of the evening, just after Mrs. Guppy's return to the room, we were sprinkled with a very delicious almond perfume. Fragments of orange peel were now distributed among us, and then pieces of orange, divided without having been cut, and Môtee rapped the message, "For my darling Mamma," and upon Mrs. Ramsay enquiring the meaning, she answered "Cough," so Mrs. Ramsay promised to take oranges for her cough, which was very troublesome, but Môtee also ordered her a compress of the Jordan water ice, and before they left, I had it put into four wide-necked bottles, for them to take home with them.

All this time, we still heard the tramp, tramp, of the footsteps, which sounded sadly solemn. We were then told to "Read a chapter :—8th of Romans : "—which we did. We were next directed to St. John, 14th chapter, part of last verse; "But that the world may know that I love the Father, and as the Father gave me commandment, even so I do." We were desired still to retain the light, and Mrs. T. passed under influence, so I took the porcelain slate, and wrote down what she said, but as it was afterwards partially effaced, I can only remember that it referred to the spirit she had been telling us about, "who had committed suicide, but not in the manner supposed, for he had cut his throat, but that his *walking* would cease from that night." At the very instant that I put out the candle, the slate was taken from before me, and we heard sounds of its being written upon in the air, at about the height of our heads. It was put back upon the table, and when we had struck a light, we found written upon it:

elbuort llahs I
you no more:

which meant "I shall trouble you no more;" the first words of the sentence having been spelt backwards. He had likewise rubbed out a considerable portion of the trance communication, I suppose to symbolise that his sin of self-destruction was thus obliterated; but in it I know that we had been given to understand that he had had to *walk* (probably at especial times and seasons) for nearly the number of years to which his life ought naturally to have extended, but that he had gained help in that respect by having been admitted to our séance, and I have no doubt that our conversation about him some time before might have contributed the needful elements for his coming.

Suddenly we heard the box of vesta matches fall to the ground, and I put out my hand to feel for the little table, but it had vanished from my side. By groping on the floor I found the box of matches, and obtained leave to light one, when we discovered that the small table had been placed face downwards upon the larger one, and the candle on the under side of the small table, but we were allowed to replace them as before. I then fetched some small pieces of card that I had been desired to prepare, and as soon as the light was extinguished we heard the spirits at work with the pencils, and the symbolical Eye was drawn upon the block and two of the cards, after which "Good-night" was spelt and our séance was brought to a close.

On the previous Monday week, in Harley Street, Mrs. T. had put me in a kind of maze, by a query as to what I might do if I had four or five little golden pieces to spend upon some indulgence, such as a something in the shape of lace or other embellishment. At first I thought she was jesting, but she told me to consider of it seriously, and on my way home it flashed upon me that I might possibly thus obtain an inlaid cabinet, that I had seen a couple of years before in a shop near me, and had set my heart upon as a future possession, to hold my books upon Spiritualism and various articles that had to be banished from this room, being no place wherein to bestow them: so I wrote the next morning to tell her of what had seemed to me a vain longing, which had been lately roused into fresh vigour, for the cabinet, which had retired to the back of the shop, had been brought forward again only a few days previously. She begged me at once to make the purchase, and hoped I might have it in time for the 31st; but I was to say nothing about it until *after* the conclusion of the séance. I puzzled my brains most ineffectually as to who could be the liberal donor, but my pretty walnut-wood treasure-case graced the room at the appointed time, and when the séance was over, I got up to shew it to my assembled friends, and to expatiate upon its beauty and its usefulness, and also the enigma that it was to me; when Mrs. Ramsay gave me a little purse-bag containing a cheque, and in tender loving terms told me that it was the joint gift of some who were united with me in the bonds of spiritual friendship, as a memorial of pleasant evenings spent here together in communion with the unseen world : mentioning at the same time who had been the contributors. I cannot here say how much I was touched, and how grateful I am to them for all their loving kindness. The gift has indeed been a most valuable one to me, and has become a complete store-house of spiritual curiosities.

I copy the following letter from the *Spiritual Magazine:*—
"20 *Rochester Road, January* 17, 1871.—MY DEAR FRIEND, —You have asked me to give you some account of the snow manifestation which I witnessed, through the mediumship of Mrs. Guppy on New Year's Eve.

"We met at Miss Houghton's, 20 Delamere Crescent, for the séance at seven, and Mrs. Guppy, Miss Neyland, and myself arrived punctually at that time. We were in the cloak-room together, and afterwards went up to the drawing-rooms, in which there were good fires. After the arrival of the other guests, refreshments were passed, and the circle was formed, as nearly as I can now recollect, at about a quarter to eight. Just previous to this time, the fire had been removed from the front drawing-room in which we were to sit, and the doors communicating with the back room, where a good fire remained, were closed. Three stone bottles containing hot water were so arranged as to keep our feet warm; and a number of paper tubes, drawing-paper, &c., were placed upon the table. The lights were now extinguished, and Miss Houghton opened the séance with The Lord's Prayer. Very soon there were movements of the table, and communications were spelt out by raps in the usual way. We were still engaged in conversation with our invisible friends, when a sudden and violent motion among the tubes startled us, and a quantity of snow and ice came down upon the table. We had the light at once, and found that although such a large quantity had fallen, there was none upon the carpet, or in any other part of the room. The lumps of ice were irregular in size, but the smallest must have weighed more than half a pound, and they were literally buried in snow. I noticed that the snow had the peculiarities of *newly-fallen snow*, and for a moment distinct feathery flakes could be seen, but the warmth of the room soon changed this appearance.

"I have given you the circumstances attending this

wonderful manifestation; and have, in conclusion, to remind you that Mrs. Guppy had been in warm rooms about an hour before the snow was produced. I remain, dear sir, very truly yours, MARY E. T."

In the editor's note, alluding also to another report there given of a somewhat similar event in Mrs. Guppy's own house, he says: "We especially invite attention to these manifestations, as we think they effectually preclude all possibility of imposture : our readers can judge for themselves as to the possibility of concealing snow and ice in comfortable well-warmed rooms, and under the circumstances here described. Nor do we see how they can be satisfactorily accounted for on any principles of purely physical science. If any scientist can inform us as to the physical laws which are adequate to these productions, we shall be glad to be enlightened on the point."

I went to a séance at Mrs. Guppy's on the 8th of January, of which I have kept no details, but she then told me of dear little Tommy's threatened attack of croup, which had taken place as prophesied, only a night or two after she had been with us. It had been exceedingly sudden and severe; and she thought it must certainly have proved fatal if she had not had the remedy within immediate reach, which restored him when it had seemed as if all power of breathing had entirely left him. She had borne up wonderfully while her attention was engrossed with his needs, but was completely prostrated when the deepest anxiety was over and she found that her child's life was spared to her, and she was herself really ill during all the ensuing day. She told me she was going to have a séance to celebrate her birthday, January 22nd, when she proposed having rather a large gathering, for she had many petitioners among those who attended the Harley Street reunions.

I think there must have been about three dozen. Mrs. Chevalier called here, so as to accompany me, and pleaded for permission to be allowed to sit next to me in the séance, which was granted to her by the invisible ones, and in the course of the evening, several of the manifestations (among them a direct drawing) were for her. There were two other sketches done, one being that of a dove. Also a stray pigeon of Miss Neyland's was brought back to her, and Mr. Guppy jokingly said it would be a very desirable thing if we could all be converted into doves. As we sat in the darkness, we had a feeling as if something very light indeed were falling upon us, coming down gently, gently, just like noiseless snow; and we all began wondering what it could be, for it was so tender that it almost seemed to elude our grasp; but at last we clearly made out that it was small downy feathers, and the weightless shower continued for some space of time, when "Light" was spelt, and we found ourselves all deeply sprinkled with down, which was also upon the table,—on the floor,—where I think it lay about a couple of inches,—*under* the table, and even in some degree under the chairs on which we were sitting!! It appeared as if the shower had come as equally, and had permeated every crevice as subtly as snow itself would have done. At first it created much laughter and amusement, but fancy the state of men's woollen coats, to which the small particles so clingingly adhered:—then the hair! the velvet dresses! oh! dear, it *was* a fluffy manifestation, and one not easily to be forgotten. The servant was summoned to do her utmost to rid the floor of some portion of it, for every movement raised fresh clouds, and a voyage of discovery was meanwhile made to the upper regions to ascertain if possible from whence the plumy downfall had come, and there we found the *empty case* of what had that morning been a feather-bed!

The *guests* were somewhat smothered, but the labour afterwards entailed upon the hosts and their assistants in clearing the house was something tremendous, and it was long before all vestiges of the birthday fête were absolutely removed. There was a great comparing of notes the next evening in Harley Street as to the state of our hair and attire, and we laughed over the many lamentations we had each excited on our return to our own homes, for that had been a snow-storm that would not melt away of its own accord.

I had had some little correspondence with my artist friend, Mr. L., who was making all kinds of enquiries on my behalf, and on the 27th he came for a long talk on the subject of the Exhibition, when he told me that he had had one or two interviews with Mr. McNair, the secretary of the society of artists who hold the Dudley Gallery, Egyptian Hall, Piccadilly, and that he seemed willing to undertake the management, and would fully understand all the business details that would be necessary, but that of course I must myself see him on the matter, so that he might be quite clear as to all that was wished and intended. There would, however, be no necessity for me to make any preliminary appointment, as I should be sure to find him at his post during the hours that the gallery would be open. I also consulted with Mr. L. as to what plan would be the best and cheapest for having the pictures framed, for, however economically it might be managed that would be sure to be a heavy item, and the amount of expense must necessarily in some degree influence the *number* of pictures to be shewn. He thought it possible that I might somewhere be able to *hire* frames, and he would make enquiries about it; but he afterwards found that it could not be done. He said he thought the grand difficulty would be to obtain a suitable gallery. I wished to have it in a good place, and at the best possible season, as I felt that perfection in *all* points must be aimed at in everything that was to be done for Spiritualism. He glanced through my portfolios with fresh delight, and warmly anticipated the pleasure of looking long and often upon them when on public view.

Mrs. T. came to me on Friday, February 3rd. I mesmerised her, and she passed into trance, but as she continued silent, I enquired whether she saw anything, and she slowly answered, "February 22nd, 1871. . . . It is written on everything I can see: there is a mark after the 22 like a very old-fashioned d, just over it. Mrs Houghton is here, she points to that mark." [May I ask if she can give us any explanation of it?] "I can't get any meaning, but the numbers have multiplied: they hang on a tree, written on strips of something like parchment as long as this (extending her hands about nine inches), February 22d, 1871." [I suppose we shall learn in time what it means.] "Yes. . . . They will leave the tree in that corner (pointing to the portfolio stand); it is like a fir tree, and it has an especial significance connected with the drawings. The tree will remain there during the séance." (The séance here alluded to is one that I propose holding on the 14th instant.)

After a short pause, she suddenly awoke with a start, and said, "I was just watching some oranges grow on a tree, and in great numbers, but they seemed to change; they were first green and then yellow, and I think I got frightened, they grew so fast."

After a little conversation I again mesmerised her, and she once more became completely entranced, but seemed unable to speak, and pointed to her throat, which I mesmerised for some time, when with difficulty she said, "It is like—it is like my breath going,—it is like a prayer said over and over—'O Lord! let me depart in peace if my work here is done. Thy Will, not mine be done, O Lord; let me depart in peace if my work is finished. Thy Will, not mine—not mine, O Lord! be done—Oh! Oh! The Lord loveth whom He chasteneth' (gasps as if for breath); there's such a silence now." [Who is it, dear?] "It is poor—I am trying to see;—it is a bed, and it is poor Mr. Spear,—and there are so many spirits. His wife can't have it, and she is begging his life all the time :—she *can't* say, Thy Will be done, and until she says it, he can't go. She is praying for help to nurse him back into life, praying, oh! so earnestly; she says, 'All my friends, everywhere, think of me, and help me to beg for this one life.'— There's such a silence :—the bed is so low, she throws herself on it with her arms up."

Her voice and manner of speaking now changed, and she said, "His work is not done yet, but that dear good woman must learn this lesson, to submit to the Will of The Lord: she will have to learn that lesson through suffering." Mrs. T. now opened her eyes, and said, "Mrs. Houghton has been talking to me, dear Mrs. Houghton; she is sitting close to me, and has something like a knitting needle in her hand: she is still talking, but I can't hear, I only hear the sound as of a voice. . . I have a feeling as though I had seen poor Mr. Spear die, and then come to life again: he will still carry on his work: . . there is some one repeating constantly, 'Thy Will be done on earth as it is in heaven.'"

We talked over together what had passed,—and wondered. . . We had known some little time before that Mr. Spear was far from well, and we decided that I should send a copy of the communication to Mrs. Spear, and when, in final course, her answer came to me, she said it was much as the circumstances had really taken place . . . Mr. Spear had used to tell us that a monition had been given him, many years previously, of the probable period of his death, although he did not reveal the date to us, but I have since learned that the illness in question took place at that specified term, and he considers that these later years have been as a granted boon.

In the course of the following week I paid my visit to Mr. McNair, and had a very practical talk with him, convincing him that although a Spiritualist and a woman, my head was clear and rapid as to business details, and that I had no difficulty in speedily deciding as to what I should, or should not like. He had already been in quest of galleries to let, and told me of two or three, giving me some particulars of each, but the most suitable as to size and situation appeared to be one in Old Bond Street, which however needed some considerable repairs, and he would see whether all could be got ready in time for the private view to take place, as I wished, on Saturday the 20th of May. He had made a rough estimate as to the probable expenses of such an Exhibition, to be open from three to four months, so as to include the whole of the London season, and said that they would amount to about £300. Then there would be the hope of a fair amount of receipts for entrances, and also the probable sale of some of the pictures. Now that was exactly the amount remaining of my Aunt Helen's money, so I knew that I should not be undertaking what I had not the means to meet, and could therefore do it with a safe conscience, although I must confess that I had not contemplated that the outlay would be so heavy, besides which I knew there would be many other items not included in his calculations, such as the frames, the conveyance to and fro, my own necessary personal expenditure, &c., &c., &c. However I authorised him to proceed with all speed, and to make the best negotiations he could for the said gallery, while I would go on with my share of the preparations. I had asked advice from one or two artist friends on the subject of the frames, and from all I heard, it seemed as if I could not do better than go to Mr. Spencer in the Harrow Road, who had hitherto supplied me with what I needed in that line, and upon whom I could depend for upright dealing, so I had talked the matter well over with him, and I was expecting his statement as to the lowest terms on which he could undertake to let to me have the slight gilt frames on which I had decided, and I should then be able to determine finally upon the number of pictures. His note came to me that same evening, agreeing for *so much* for each frame (according to the two different sizes), with the *best* glass, as that is an important consideration with respect to the exquisite colouring of the spiritual work; and that he would take them back at half price when the Exhibition was over. His terms were so fair and equitable that I made up my mind to exhibit the entire contents of my portfolios, and also to borrow back from several quarters some of those that had gone forth professionally into the world, and thus the grand undertaking seemed really to be taking shape.

CHAPTER IV.

On the 14th of February, the circle for our séance was composed of Mrs. Ramsay, Miss S., Mrs. T., Mrs. Pearson, Mr. L., Mrs. Guppy, Miss Neyland and myself. Shortly after we had said The Lord's Prayer, the alphabet was asked for, and Mamma gave me the following message, "My dear daughter, you must wear a coat of many colours." I said I had no objection, but that she must help me to get it, to which she gave me an affirmative answer, but Mrs. Guppy said she did not see how she could do so, and I explained that I had only meant that Mamma should, when I was buying a dress, let me know which she might look upon as fulfilling the suggestion, and we were still discussing the subject, when we felt a mass of something soft on the table, and then "Light" was spelt, and to our surprise we found a quantity of pieces of woollen materials of three or four inches in width, some square, and some about double the length, but they were of every shade and hue; red, yellow, blue, green, violet, orange, and if they can be made into a coat, it will certainly be one of many colours. They weigh a pound and a half

I was told to "Read Matthew, 11th chapter," and afterwards "Matthew, 2nd chapter, 11th verse." We then heard the pencil being used for direct drawing, and we subsequently found that the spirits had done three separate symbols of the Eye of The Lord on the drawing block.

We were then told to break up for a time, to take supper in the adjoining room: it was earlier than usual with us, but both Mrs. Guppy and Miss Neyland were poorly, and I suppose they were rather exhausted. On our return our spirit friends began to be busy with the tubes, and presently we heard a voice say, "Dear Georgiana." "Who is it?" I enquired, to which the reply was, "Your Mamma:—you will wear the coat?" to which I agreed. Miss Neyland saw Mamma standing by me while she was speaking. I then felt the tube give the signal of my youngest brother, who had never hitherto manifested himself at our séances; I mentioned the sign to Mrs. Pearson, who at once knew who it must be, and asked him to go to her, as he had always been fond of her, and she immediately felt him in like manner tap her under the chin with the tube, which referred to a well-known habit of his boyhood. I mentioned that I had felt his signal very frequently during the last week or two, and that he had told me it was in preparation for the séance. Miss Neyland said she saw a young man standing by me, but she could not see him very clearly. I asked her to describe the hair, which she said was light brown and curly, and that was exactly the description of Sidney's, he then said through the tube, "I am Sidney." She also saw Môtee and General Ramsay. By the alphabet we were then told to "Sing," but there was the difficulty of everybody having colds, and also what was to be sung, and they spelt out, "Wait for the waggon,"—and Mrs. T. exclaimed, "Oh! it is an Indian, and he wants to dance, he is standing with one foot raised, ready to start, and looks very eager." So a verse of the required song was got through, although rather bunglingly, but our Indian friend was contented with our good will to oblige him, and Mrs. T. said he had his squaw with him, and was come for healing purposes. She saw him operating upon Mrs. Guppy, and then place a feather in her hair, which Mrs. Guppy felt him doing, but then she said, "Oh! now it is gone;" for he had taken the feather out again, and then in an audible voice he said, "I can't spare it." He then told us he was the Indian who influenced Mrs. Lacy, and with whom, some five years ago when she was in England, I had had much friendly communication, and I remembered that he had then wished I was his medium squaw. "So I do now," was his prompt rejoinder. I then enquired about Mrs. Lacy, and he answered, "She is not very well." They asked him for some feathers, which he declined giving, and Mrs. Ramsay suggested that he should give us some beads, and we soon heard a scattering sound as of beads; but he had broken the thread of one row of Miss Neyland's coral necklace, and when she took it off, to prevent a further mishap, he took the whole necklace over to Mrs. Ramsay; and when we expostulated with him, he asked for the alphabet, and rapped out, "Thou shalt not wish for another man's goods;" but Mrs. Ramsay explained to him that she had only wanted something that was no longer of use to any one. The spilt beads were collected and restored to Miss Neyland, whose necklace can easily be re-threaded.—Mrs. Guppy was then told to go away to the sofa, so that she might lie down. I asked Miss Neyland if she saw any one near Mr. L., and she replied that there was an elderly gentleman standing by him with grey hair, not much of it, and Mrs. T. said, "Oh! it is Mr. Spear, and he is looking so earnest and so white." Miss Neyland said there was a lady with him, a good deal younger than he, with brown hair, but she only saw her very indistinctly. We thought that was probably Mrs. Spear, and we told of the vision Mrs. T. had had . . . I had better also mention here, with reference to seeing the spirit forms of living persons, that such experience is becoming rather frequent, and that Mrs. T. has several times both seen and spoken with Mr. Spear; and that Mrs. Spear has three or four times told me during her visits to England, that she had been quite conscious of being in my drawing-room, when, if I had had the gift of "discerning spirits" I should doubtless have seen her.

By the alphabet was then spelt, "No more darkness." I gave paper and pencil to Mrs. Ramsay, and then mesmerised her for some time, and when she began to draw, I was influenced to gō to Mrs. T., likewise giving her a pencil and paper, but before mesmerising her, I was thus spoken through. "And He shall give His angels charge over thee, to bear thee in their hands." Mrs. Ramsay was drawing with great rapidity, sometimes on her own sheet of paper, sometimes on the porcelain slate, and likewise on Mrs. T.'s piece of paper. Mrs. T. passed under influence, and

I asked her what she saw, to which she answered, pointing to a kind of palm tree that Mrs. Ramsay was doing on the slate, "I see that all covered with two's." Presently in a jerky sort of way, she wrote "February" on the paper before her, on which Mrs. Ramsay had also been drawing, and then on the slate, close to the tree, "22;" when it struck me that the whole manifestation referred to the vision she had had on the previous Friday week, when she had seen a tree covered with strips, on which were written "February 22d, 1871," and she was given to understand that that date was connected with something relating to my drawings.

The tree drawn by Mrs. Ramsay had the representation of a good many round fruits on it, which were probably meant to refer to the tree seen in the latter part of Mrs. T.'s vision, which was covered with oranges ripening rapidly.

I gave paper and pencil to Mr. L., and after mesmerising him for some little time, his hand was moved to make a kind of wavering line downwards. Our spirit friends then wished us "Good-night," and we brought the séance to a close.

At the time, I paid small heed to the fact that it was on the 20*th* (my important number) that I received Mr. McNair's estimate as to the probable cost of the Exhibition, giving me the different details bringing it to the amount he had mentioned to me, and according to previous appointment I paid my second visit to him on the following day, when he told me had made the best terms he could with Mr. Gullick; and that the rent of the New British Gallery was to be £100 for four months from the date of the opening, but that if I should decide upon closing it at the expiration of three months, he would make a reduction of £10. There would be much to be done in the way of necessary repairs, of which I should have to pay half (not included in the estimate), but Mr. McNair would do his best to keep them as low as he could, and would also strive hard that the opening should be on the day I wished. Of course we had a great deal to talk over, for it is only when entering upon a new undertaking that one realizes the many different agencies that must be put in motion to achieve the result, but I at length left him, with a promise to write that evening a formal letter, authorising him to call the next day upon the landlord and conclude the arrangement, and I had also plenty to consider as to the various preparations I should myself have to make, which would keep me very fully employed; but there was no fear of my being a laggard in anything that should fall to my share.

Of course we looked forward to something happening on the 22nd of February, and as it fell on Wednesday, I thought it might probably be connected with some visitor who might come on that my reception-day, but it passed off without any event of consequence. I went to the Gower Street Rooms in the evening, and on my return home found a note from Mrs. T., mentioning that I had been much in her thoughts all day, when all at once the elucidation flashed into my mind. It was the *taking of the Gallery* that was the event! a momentous one indeed, as connected with my drawings! Thus the Tree was planted, by the first positive step being taken, and it was done at the appointed season. I wrote to tell Mrs. T. that it was made clear to me, and this was her tender answer—" MY DEAR FRIEND, I have just received your note, and feel quite amazed at the coincidence. It was very singular that Mrs. Ramsay should have been influenced to draw the same golden-fruited tree at your séance on the 14th instant. Please God it may be for your good physically as well as spiritually, and may your whole future life be filled and rounded with every imaginable blessing. With kindest love, very truly yours,

MARY E. T."

She came to me again to-day, the 24th, and while talking, I said there was something more that yet remained to be unravelled, for that I thought there must be some significance in Mrs. Ramsay's having drawn a Palm, whereas the tree Mrs. T. saw in her vision was a Fir, but nothing on the subject came to us during our séance, which referred entirely to the coat of many colours; but this evening, in writing to a friend who had been present at the séance, I spoke of the fulfilled prophecy of "Mrs. T.'s *date*-tree," simply meaning, tree covered with the said date February 22nd, 1871, and the very expression taught me all it implied, for the *Palm* is the *Date*-tree, and thus the whole was made clear, and is another example of the humour often so delicately veiled in the spiritual enigmas.

I have done a tracing of Mrs. Ramsay's tree, before effacing it from the porcelain slate, so as to gather up every thread of this curious prophecy, and my heart rises in fullest thanksgiving to the bountiful Lord for His ceaseless mercies.

On the night of the 14th, we shewed the wonderful heap of coloured pieces to Preston when she came for good-night into the drawing-room in her way up to bed, and I asked if she thought she could construct a coat out of them, and she was very willing to set her ingenuity to work: she remembered a sleeveless upper garment of Javanese cut that my sister-in-law used to wear, and she suggested that the shape of that might be suitable if we could have the pattern; so I wrote to Isabel to make the request, and she sent me a charming little model thereof, telling me that its Eastern name was a Kabaya.

On Friday the 24th, when I had mesmerised Mrs. T., she passed under influence, and said: "Somebody is saying, 'Where's the coat? where's the coat?' and I asked, [Can you tell me anything about the coat?] "It is being put into my mind to say that it is intended as a symbol." [May I ask of what?] "There is a garment, a spiritual garment, in course of preparation, and all your life is being used, as needed, to form this garment, and it will be completed when your earthly life is finished." [How then is this one the symbol of it?] "The spiritual garment is of many colours, which correspond to deeds, good deeds. This was sent to remind you whenever you see it, and for that purpose only, of the beautiful garment now being prepared for you." [Then it did not in any way carry out the thought of Joseph's coat of many colours?] "Only a chosen few can ever wear the garment you will wear, only the best beloved (tenderly caressing my hand with hers): good deeds, and ill deeds as well, form substantial and,—in the sense that spirits understand,—*material* substances, which can be fashioned by loving hands to promote the comfort of the spirit. The spiritual garment will be lined with crimson, to denote the warm human love which you shed around you, and which will return *to* you. In the first garment you will wear after leaving this life, there are little stars, like silver stars, on the front; they are much brighter over this upper part, and they decrease in brightness as they go down towards the feet: there is one very bright star on the left side just over the heart. This garment is worn over a white lawn robe, and there is something like a golden ball at the foot of it: the arms are white, and the coat is on the front and on the back. They are shewing me the lining again, to impress upon me that the colour is deepened with every deed, active deed, and especially if good to others; and those who can read will see in a moment all your life when they look at this garment. From the shoulders to the neck and part of the back, is filial love (she moved her hand along each portion of her own body as she mentioned them: then down the *right*, from the neck to the waist), here is love for the Deity and for all the manifestations of God: (in the same manner down the *left*), *this* is *the* love and this beautiful star (over the heart) will be placed on your brow by *his* hand when he first meets you. From this part (round the waist) both front and back, are your loves for friends and for all the world fully typified.

"Some other coats are thrust forward for me to see, one of them is very, *very* brilliant in colour and in decoration, and a spirit's hand was put at the back so that I could see right through it, then the hand touched the flimsy looking substance, and it fell to pieces, and there were serpents crawling. Out of the dust it has made, there has come one great green slimy creature (she seemed much disgusted); and they say that those other garments, although so bright, are as frail as the one they shewed me, and have no substance (she still looked as if she were witnessing something unpleasant). There will be those who will dispute your right to wear this robe, and I hear them say 'Give it to me,—give it to me,'—so many voices—'give it to me, *I* should have that . . . (listening, and gradually smiling again), but when they see you, and feel the power that will come from this garment as you approach it, they will become silent and abashed. (She again moved her hands to the different parts.) The back is finished: this side (the right) is finished to the waist: this (the left) is finished half across the breast: this part (from the waist downwards) has much to be done to it: here and there it is complete, and then there are spaces: when it is *quite* complete, your work here will be finished. Do you need a sign of time?" [I do not *need* a sign; if one is vouchsafed, it will be because it would be *best*, I am content any way.] "It *is* well . . . When you, with your bodily hands and senses are able to touch, to see, to examine this robe, it shall be a sign to you that the end draws near," [Thank you, dear friend.] "for which you need make no preparation beyond your daily living and life."

Here she suddenly awoke, with the last words ringing in her ears. I then read the whole of it to her, as she had been totally unconscious all the time.

Before she went away, she reverted to the subject of the crimson lining, and said she should like to get it for me, so that the coat should as nearly as possible carry out the idea of the one she had seen in the vision: she accordingly got some beautiful crimson merino, having been aided by the voices as to her choice while making the purchase. The description she had given of the signification of the different parts enabled me to decide upon the position of some of the colours, leaving the rest of the arrangement to Preston, who fashioned the garment according to the small model, and the many coloured pieces with their crimson lining form a very striking and original looking coat, which

I have since worn at some of my home séances, over a white muslin body, thus carrying out the idea of the lawn robe.

I dare say the question may arise in some minds as to where these many tinted scraps may have come from ; but although there was no kind of clue, for I examined them all myself very thoroughly, they were clearly patterns of winter dress materials, such as we are all quite familiar with. The winter was over, the samples from henceforth useless, and had probably been cast aside to some place to which the invisibles had access through the presence of some medium, and could thus save them from being wasted.

A lady who had heard of the manifestation wrote thus to my cousin, from Hastings : " Do you know I fell upon rather a curious thing yesterday. In one of the little magazine books which adorn the side-table of our sitting-room, I came upon an article containing some extracts from a work by the Countess de Wilton, 'The Art of Needlework.' Among the extracts was one touching upon the custom in the East of dressing a beloved or favourite child in a coat of many colours tastefully sewed together. The account ends thus. 'It may not perhaps be absurd to refer to even so ancient an origin as Joseph's coat of many colours, the superstition now prevalent in some countries, which teaches that a child clothed in a garment of many colours is safe from the blasting of malicious tongues, or the machinations of evil spirits.'"

I had now to commence my Catalogue, and to shape the method in which it was to be made out, which required deep consideration and earnest prayer for instruction as to what would be most seemly, for in that especially I needed divine guidance, and, I am thankful to say, received it fully in every detail. The chief object aimed at in this Exhibition, was not so much to display the wondrous powers of the unseen intelligences, as to manifest unflinchingly to the world that true Spiritualism is inextricably bound up with the religion of the Sacred Scriptures. It would be in some degree necessary to add to the mere catalogue of the titles of the works, enough of interpretation to prove that the glorious tints and beautiful lines contained an inner meaning as well as an external semblance, and also that the minds of the visitors should be gradually led up to the higher teachings by fragmentary glimpses of the light that had been given to myself, for which purpose the significations of the Spirit Flowers and Fruits were written in the fewest possible words, while the interpretation of the Spheres was published as I originally received it. The Sacred Symbolism would have been far too elaborate to be condensed in any way, therefore I was only permitted to give an extract from the very first interpretation, and for each of the others a text had to be selected; and a clergyman will best understand the amount of time that such a work would require, and the entire absorption needed to carry it out. I had to place the drawing in front of me, and then to seek the special meaning that had been therein conveyed (which would probably be contained in its own interpretation), and by degrees I learned that each picture represented as it were a sermon on such or such a point, and with the aid of the concordance I found every text bearing upon it (perhaps under several headings), and then the selection would have to be made. There was yet another thing that I had contemplated as a possible hindrance. Six of those symbolical drawings had never even received their titles, and Mamma had often urged me to try for them, but the attempts had always been unsuccessful. Now, however, they were given to me quite easily, the texts being selected on the same occasion; and thus my work was gradually proceeded with, but I sat at it closely indeed, and burned more than midnight oil, for during the preparation of the catalogue it was often two or three o'clock in the morning ere I retired to rest. The interpretations of the Spiritual Crown and its representative Monogram were in a manner compilations; portions being gleaned from those of the different individuals, so as to be the concentration of the new thoughts that had been inflowed to me little by little during their progress. In due course Mr. McNair sent me a draft copy of the agreement for the Gallery for my inspection and approval, and on the 8th of March he brought the deed for my signature.

When the Rev. Mr. B., who had "held the key," first came to see me, a couple of years before, he had been so much struck with the Royal Monograms, that he had pleaded hard that I would have photographs of them taken for him (of course at his own expense), which I agreed to have done, although I was rather doubtful of a successful issue, because of the photographic difficulties as to certain colours; but I was much charmed to find that they came out very satisfactorily. They were reduced to about half the size of the originals, but they gave me the happy thought that I need never henceforth be utterly separated from the remembrance of any of my beloved pictures, however far away might be their destination, and I availed myself of the loan now granted of those that had left me, to have them photographed in the carte-de-visite size; and I made up my mind that for the future I would have that process gone through before sending away any that I might especially value to new owners, and for my present undertaking, I had a diamond shaped frame fitted in with sixteen of these little reminders; which had taught me a fresh lesson as to the perfection of my pictures, for I found that their perspective was so *true* (I do not mean as to rule and compasses) that when these photographs are looked at through a large magnifying glass,—or a good graphoscope would doubtless be better, but I do not possess one,—they have the effect of having been taken from a substantial object, instead of from a flat surface.

I went on the 16th of March to one of Mrs. Everitt's interesting séances, which are always imbued with religious thought; they usually commence with prayer, then the reading of a portion of Scripture indicated to them by raps, and hymn singing: in the course of which would appear little sparkling lights flitting hither and thither, and sometimes, if it were solicited, the responses to questions would be given by their movements according to the same code of signals as the raps. But the direct writing was at that time the main feature of her mediumship: sheets of note paper and pencils were on the table, and when there was an intimation that the manifestation was about to commence Mr. Everitt would begin, steadily counting the *seconds*, and simultaneously with his "One," the rapid movements of the pencil would be heard, and at the expiration of perhaps eight or ten counts, the pencil would fall on the table, *dropped* from the fingers of the invisible writer, when Mr. Everitt at once lighted the candle to examine the result, and to read to us the closely filled page of small but legible writing, when it might be found that upwards of eight hundred words had been written in eight seconds! generally containing some instructive message. On the evening of my first visit there, Mr. and Mrs. Everitt received directions to hold a series of séances, as the spirits wished to give some evidences (I think) as to the early Christian times, for which they were to have a special circle, and the meetings were to be held about once a week. They did not at that time decide who were to be invited as members of that circle, the list was to be given to them when alone, but I was not surprised to receive a note from Mrs. Everitt saying that she had been desired to request me to join them, and I agreed to do so as far as my present very busy time would admit. At each séance the appointment would usually be made as to when the next was to be held, and there was one circumstance that struck me very much, which was, that without my having said any word as to any engagements I might have, they always appeared to be known to those invisibles, for the evening that would be fixed upon was one that would not in any way interfere with them. I attended altogether five séances, and on the last occasion, May 11th, the message was given that the sittings were to be suspended for a time (I think through the agency of the spirit voice); when I said that although I was of course just then dreadfully busy, as soon as my Gallery was really open I thought my time would be in some degree more free, but I was told that I could not yet realise whether I should be much or little occupied. I have often referred in conversation to an instance then given me of the knowledge of small details possessed by my unseen advisers. The Everitts lived in Penton Street, Pentonville, and I generally went there by the Paddington omnibus that passes the end of the street, but as it was usually late when I came home at night, the question would arise as to whether the speedier method would be to return the same way, or to walk to King's Cross, and travel by metropolitan railway, therefore as I walked down the street, I would ask, "Shall I turn towards the left, to meet the omnibus, or towards the right to go to the station?" One night, to my surprise, I receivd *No* in answer to both queries, which left me slightly in a puzzle, but as I reached the end of Penton Street, the omnibus attained the same point at the very instant, so that I at once got into it, without having turned either to the right or the left. I may add that similar proofs come to me almost daily, although they are seldom such as I can remember in order to narrate them to others; but they are indeed such as to economise many a moment of my very fully occupied time, so that none may be wasted in idle speculation as to what shall be done next.

My catalogue had the unusual addition of a preface, for the purpose of explaining to visitors what really was meant by spirit-drawings, giving a slight idea of the steps by which I had travelled, and throwing what light I could to aid others in following the same path. On the 28th of March I took the finished manuscript to Mr. McNair, when we had a consultation as to the fashion of the various details. He suggested tinted paper, but creamy books are a trial to the eyesight; a delicate pink flashed at that moment into my mind, as a type of the Love exemplified in all the teaching, and the cover was to be brown, to exemplify that it was given through an earthen vessel. I told him that I wished a proportion to be covered in cloth, because it was not intended as only an ephemeral production, but one that I trusted might still go on doing a work when the Exhibition had become a thing of the past. He undertook all the arrangements as to type, planning internal varieties, &c., &c., so that my mind might be at ease about it until the proof should come to me for correction. Of course I told him any ideas on the subject that I had myself formed, but his taste was so good that I felt I might safely trust to it without any anxiety as to whether the result would be satisfactory, and I must here add a few words of intense gratitude to Him Whose aid is ever being lavished upon me, for having placed me in the hands of so upright and honourable a man, and one so competent in every respect to help me through my undertaking. We decided that there should be season tickets, at half a guinea for one person, and a guinea for subscriber and friend, and I firmly believed that by that means I should receive the warm co-operation of all Spiritualists, who could thus aid me in the great effort for the Cause that I was boldly entering upon single-handed. As I shall not revert to this subject, I may here mention that no such sympathy was forthcoming, for only four double tickets and three single ones were ever purchased, but the seven names are duly registered in the "Abstract of receipts and expenditure" connected with the Exhibition; for all my accounts have been rigidly and accurately kept, and the two facing pages in one of my little books tell the whole tale at a glance.

From the Dudley Gallery Mr. McNair accompanied me that same afternoon to Old Bond Street, to inspect what was to be the temporary home of my pictures, and very desolate it was then looking, with bare walls and busy workmen, but I gained at any rate some notion of its capabilities.

CHAPTER V.

ON the 21st of March I had a séance in remembrance of Mrs. Guppy's first visit here and our first séance in 1867. Our circle was but small, consisting of Mrs. T., Mrs. Guppy, Miss Leith, Miss Alice Leith, Miss Neyland and myself. When we had said The Lord's Prayer, the spirits gently lifted up the table three times in response. They then, by the alphabet, desired me to "Read Revelation, 20th chapter," and when I had done so, and extinguished the light, the message was spelt, "I will bring you a coat never touched by man :—kneel." We enquired if all were to kneel, but it was only I. Of course I immediately complied, and in a few moments I felt something being gently drawn down over my head, until it rested about my shoulders and waist: I then felt quantities of flowers being showered upon me, and Mrs. Guppy saw them descending as if from the ceiling. "Light" was then spelt, and Mrs. Guppy lighted the candle, so that I should not disturb anything, and they were all allowed to come and look. The coat was a white garment of Eastern make, most deliciously perfumed, the flowers lying upon it in masses as well as on me and the floor round about. A message was then rapped out while I was still kneeling, "Read Luke, 15th chapter, 22nd verse," which Miss Neyland then read, "But the father said to his servants, Bring forth the best robe, and put it on him." The material of which it is made is something like barège, only clearer and stiffer, with a few silk stripes bordering the very narrow breadths. It is very curiously made, being as it were without shaping or slopes, and at the bottom of the sleeves is a sort of edging done with the same silk that it is sewed with. We then collected the flowers, and the spirits said they were to be placed in water. There were tulips, ferns, hyacinths, daffodils, narcissuses, cyclamens, and wallflowers. When we were again settled, and the light put out, I said, " May I ask who was the *I* who brought the coat?" to which the answer was, "I am Gabriel."

Pencils and paper were then taken by the spirits to the two Miss Leiths, and we heard them using them, but it only seemed for the purpose of development, for there was no apparent design in what they did. I also heard the invisibles themselves at work, and we were told to sing the Doxology, during which time the paper on which the direct drawing had been done was brought to me, and then a second in the same way, after which a light was requested. The first was a slight sketch of The Eye, with the words, " God works all : "—the other was also The Eye, with a link above and below, and the words, " God's Love."

We all saw lights, one of which was visible at several different times ; it was about the size of a florin, and seemed ever in motion *within* itself, not flickering upwards like a flame, but as if into the centre, so that in that centre was the fullest light, although even that was delicate, and I think if our powers of spiritual vision had been developed, we should have seen the light rainbow-hued—at times it fluttered close to our eyes, at others to a distance ; then vanishing to re-appear shortly, and was very charming.

We were told to place our handkerchiefs on the table, and they were soon brought back to us, knotted in different forms and deliciously scented ; mine was as a cross, and Mrs. T.'s like a little animal, with two black seeds for eyes. Miss Neyland saw Mamma, and afterwards she saw her holding one of my dear little baby sisters by the hand, and described her just as so many other mediums have done. I also felt Môtee's hand stroking mine and tenderly patting the pearl ring.

Mrs. Guppy felt herself being mesmerised, and Mrs. T. said that something like a prophecy seemed to come to her about that influence, which referred to a year hence. I was then desired to light the candle, but it had all passed from her mind, and I was impressed to mesmerise her, and when entranced she said to Mrs. Guppy: "You are to be more free to work for *us* within a year. There is a will stronger than yours which is to be subdued, and you will be able to devote yourself more to *our* work. The Lord gave, and The Lord taketh away—you will be made to say, Blessed be the name of the Lord." She spoke a few words to another member of the circle; and afterwards, just as she awoke, she said, "Whom He loveth He chasteneth;" and when I asked for whom the last sentence had been intended, she placed her fingers just above my heart, and said she had read it there in letters of light. The séance was shortly afterwards concluded with a few words of blessing.

Mrs. Ramsay was to have been with us, but when she did not make her appearance, I thought she might probably not have returned home from Bath, where she had been spending a week, so we did not wait long for her as she is always punctual; and when we took our places at the table, Mrs. Tebb suggested that it would be well to place the seat there that she would have occupied, and she has since mentioned that several times in the course of the evening she had an impression that some one was sitting in it. I afterwards had a letter from her eldest daughter Mrs. Young, to say that she had that very afternoon received a telegram from Lucknow, communicating the sad intelligence of the death of her beloved and only son Jim on the 12th instant. I have since been told by the spirits that the message Mrs. T. saw in letters of light, "Whom He loveth He chasteneth," was intended for Mrs. Ramsay, who would have sat between Mrs. T. and myself had she been present, and when we had drawn closer to one another towards the latter part of the séance, I had exactly taken Mrs. Ramsay's place.

The prophecy to Mrs. Guppy was fulfilled by her grandfather's death, I think shortly before the expiration of the twelvemonth.

. . . .

Although I may now, at a distance of ten years, look

calmly back at that season of actively preparatory work, it was a time of considerable excitement, and the question of the dress I was to wear on the day of the Private View, was by no means an unimportant one. I had set my mind on one especial fancy, which originated in the drawing done for me by Emanuel Marshall. The seven spirits who are there depicted with me, all have starry robes, and I had wondered that such was not the case in the commissions he executed for other people, until he did the one for Mr. John Bennett, when again the stars were sprinkled on the flowing garments of the four spirits hovering around him, and that gave me the explanation; for those who were again distinguished in that manner were Archangels, the same as my friends. So I must needs set my heart upon a starry brocade, to be dove-coloured with sheeny tints: and about the middle of March came a letter from a loving friend, advising me not long to delay my search for what I wanted, lest there should be difficulty in meeting with it, and enclosing a liberal assistance towards the purchase, so that I might have no scruples as to price. When the time came that I could spare a day to visit Oxford Street and Regent Street, vain was my quest; the pattern of stars was out of vogue, and only some dreary, faded looking silks were in the deeper recesses of some of the shops; but I did see a dress that I might compound with, if by all my seeking I should fail to find the exact article, and to that I had finally to return. The shot, sheeny colouring was perfection, and the brocaded pattern was like dove's eyes besprinkled all over it, so that it produced very much the kind of effect that I had imagined to myself

The printer made quick work, and on the evening of the 8th of April Mr. McNair sent me the proof, with which I was highly delighted, and sat closely at it so as to return it with all speed. On the eighteenth I went to him to decide many small matters, such as the cards of invitation for the Private View, also the tickets; the grand bill that was to embellish the outside, his suggested advertisements, and so on; but most important of all, the covers for the catalogues.

I then broached to him (what I had *not been allowed* to mention earlier), my desire to have two or three specimen catalogues by the next day but one, my birthday, the 20th. He thought it would be utterly impossible, but he would try. I pointed out to him that that was the date affixed to the preface. Oh! yes, he had seen that and had been very near correcting it in the proof, even after I had sent it back to him, for he thought I must mean *May* 20th, but then he took into consideration how accurate I usually was, and decided against meddling with it; so he said he would try if possible to fulfil my date by sending some to me on the appointed day. The reason I had not been permitted to express my wish to him in an earlier stage, was to give me an additional proof as to the watchful care surrounding me, and to shew me that all events would work into exactly the right moment without the intervention of my own ordering. If I *had* spoken, even ever so slight a word, it would have seemed as if *I* had given the impetus, whereas it was made evident to me that my wishes had been tenderly forestalled, for it was now too late for the expression of them to have availed aught unless the catalogues had been ready for their covers.

I will now recur to my written records. . . Before giving the account of my birthday séance, I ought to mention that I had felt peculiarly joyous all day; it seemed to me that everything was going so propitiously for me; my dear friend had come on the previous evening, to stay with me, notwithstanding the many uneasy doubts I had felt lest at the last moment something untoward might occur to prevent her from making her hoped-for appearance. Another fear, too, was dispelled in the afternoon, for Mr. McNair was successful in sending me four copies of my catalogue, which looked even prettier than I had anticipated.

Soon after we had dined, Mrs. Ramsay called to see me, as she would be prevented by the expected arrival of a friend from Scotland, from joining our séance in the evening, which was a great disappointment both to her and to me. She expressed warm and loving wishes for my happiness for many future years, and she pressed a little packet of gold pieces into my hand, begging me to select a birthday gift for myself, to aid in my equipment for the momentous Private View day of my Exhibition. I shewed her the silk dress, that I had purchased a fortnight before, and she was much pleased with it. My catalogue was the next subject of observation, with which she was so much delighted that she wanted to have one at once, and in giving me the shilling for it, congratulated herself on being the very *first* person to make a payment relating to my great enterprise, tenderly hoping that it might bring me luck, adding that if I could have all the success she wished me in the undertaking, it would indeed "fulfil my desire."

There was yet another thing to see :—the coat of many colours,—that by dint of close work, Preston had finished by the previous day, in readiness for me to wear on that evening. Mrs. Ramsay was much struck with it, admiring the tasteful arrangement of the pieces, and the capital contrivance of the whole. She then helped me to put it on, so as to judge of the effect, with which she was charmed.

When my séance guests had arrived, the catalogue was naturally one of the first subjects of discussion, and the moment Mrs. Guppy saw the notice about season tickets on the fly-leaf, she exclaimed, "Oh! I hope no one has yet taken a guinea ticket, so that *I* may be the first." She *was* the first, and I must here express my gratitude to the loving Father who granted to me in two separate ways to reap the first proceeds of my contemplated enterprise on my birthday.

Having touched upon the subject of birthday gifts, I may say that others came to me on this occasion, for the purpose of contributing to my costume for the eventful 20th of May.

Our circle consisted of Miss S., Mrs. T., Miss Florence T., Mrs. Guppy, Mrs. P., Miss Neyland and myself, but before we sat down, they helped me to don the many coloured garment.

As I said The Lord's Prayer, we heard, after each petition,

three sharp little raps, almost as if made with a finger-nail, and at the close, the table was tipped three times for the Amen. By the alphabet I was then told to "Bring bread and wine, to perform the Sacrament. You are one of the priests ordained to the Holy Communion. Put on the White Dress."

I rang for a slice of bread (without crust) and a knife, and fetched the decanter of Canary wine and a glass from the adjoining room, and Miss S. assisted me to remove the coat of many colours and to put on the white garment brought to me by Gabriel at our last séance.

I then stood in my place at the table, and having poured some wine into the glass, and cut two strips of the bread, waited to be impressed as to my further proceedings. While thus in expectancy, I felt my spiritual crown on my head, as I had done on Mamma's birthday séance in 1867, while she still formed one of our earthly circle, on which occasion Mrs. Guppy (then Miss Nicholl) saw it; but she made no observation this time, so she could not have seen it, and I did not mention the circumstance, as it was impossible at the moment, and it might afterwards have been out of place. Upon further consideration it has struck me that the reason of Mrs. Guppy's not having seen it now, was that the candle was lighted, and on the other occasion we were in darkness.

I was then moved to dip one of the strips of bread into the wine, holding it with all the fingers of the right hand bent over it until it should be thoroughly moistened, then afterwards turning the other end, so as to soak the whole. I then broke off a piece of about the size we use in the Sacrament of the Church of England, and gave it to Miss S., with the words, "In the Name and in remembrance of Him Who lived and died for us." Those words were for all, for the remaining pieces were given in silence; the first strip being apportioned to four persons, and the second, having been steeped in the wine in the same manner, being divided among the other three, my portion being double the size. I was the last to partake of the bread, but I took the first sip of the wine, and gave it in rotation to each of the others, desiring Mrs. Guppy to finish it. I then extinguished the light, and the further message was rapped out, "Read a chapter;" and upon my enquiring which it was to be, was told, "Open, and read." So I lighted the candle, and got the Bible, when the pages were turned by me, until my hand was guided to the 3rd chapter of Hebrews, which I read. I then had to remove the white garment, ánd resume the coat.

We were no sooner again in darkness than we at once saw the pretty light I described on the last occasion, and it flitted about charmingly from one to the other. Mrs. T. distinguished a face as if lighted up by it. At one time it came so close to me that I exclaimed, "Oh! *do* kiss me," and I felt the touch of lips while the bright light was resting on my own, and when thinking of this circumstance after I went to bed, my spirit friends revealed to me that the light proceeds from the Divine Breath by Which man was quickened and "became a living soul," which expands in us as we become purified, until our whole body shall be full of light.

We then heard the invisibles very busy with the tubes, which, as well as the sheets of paper and card, they placed in the hands and laps of the party, and then we smelled the fragrant perfume of wallflowers and other spring blossoms, and when at length we were told to have a light, we found the table was quite heaped up with flowers in delicious profusion; and Mrs. Guppy, taking up one of the cowslips, called my attention to the fact that on squeezing the end of the stalk, juice flowed instantly, which is a proof that they were but just plucked, for that even in ten minutes after flowers are gathered, a kind of healing or drying process takes place where the stem has been broken off, so that it will not bleed. To us, who have seen such innumerable evidences of the wonders of Spirit power, no such proof of the genuineness of the manifestation was needed, but a statement of that fact may bring conviction to some vacillating minds.

We had the flowers put in water, after the guests had selected what they wished to take home with them, and Ann then thoroughly dried the table, the wet condition of which explained to us why the tubes and papers had been removed by the spirits, it having been to preserve them from being moistened by the rain-besprinkled flowers.

As soon as we were again settled, and the light extinguished, we heard a voice, but could not exactly catch the words, and upon asking what was said, heard in clear accents, "Don't be frightened," and after a moment's pause; "I wish you very many happy returns of the day." I recognised the voice at once, although I had not heard it for a year and eight months, when the speaker was with me in mortal form, but I asked who spoke. "Oh! you know." [But I want you to tell me.] "Give one guess." [Well then, it is Charlie.] "Of course it is, darling Auntie, and they are all here." He conversed with me for some time, and as far as I recollect I will record the whole, but I wish first to describe the character of the voice, for although I have for more than three years heard the spirit voices in many circles, never have they sounded to me so exactly like that of the human being in quiet talk: they are either boisterous, or laboured, or jerky, but it was as if Charlie in the flesh were one of the circle; it was the buoyant voice of young manhood, with exactly his exultant tones when telling me about his successful examination before leaving England.

[I am so glad to hear you speak to me, Charlie dear.] "I wish you could hear me always, and that you could *see* me." [Do you see me?] "Oh! yes, quite well. How do you do, Miss S.?" [Very well, thank you.] "I am glad of that: and you, Mrs. T.?" [Quite well, thank you.] "That's right. And I am glad to see you, Mrs. Guppy." While he was talking, I was being patted with a tube by another spirit, and a voice then whispered through the tube, "God bless your soul:" and I said: [Who is this, Charlie?] "Don't: Grandma, I'm jealous. Grandma is getting so close to you that she is in my way. Why is not

Mrs. Ramsay here?" [Because a friend was coming to her from Scotland this very evening.] "Oh! that is a pity. I am so happy, Auntie darling." [So am I, Charlie dear.] "Oh! yes, I know you are: I have been with you all day, and I have seen you frisking about. Grandma let me wish you many happy returns of the day for all of them." [Do you want to make a *speech*, Charlie? do you remember Christmas Day?] "Now *don't*, Auntie." ... In their juvenile days, Charlie was always intending to return thanks on Christmas Day, for his father, absent in India, and invariably broke down, with a flood of tears. [What about my Exhibition?] "I hope it will be a great success in every way." [How do you like the Catalogue?] "It is exquisite." [You see there is that about you, in the Flower of Consolation?] "Oh! yes, I saw it all. I looked it through while Mrs. Ramsay was looking at it, and, Auntie, your dress is a beauty, you must *always* wear it." [Oh! no, Charlie, I must have a variety.] "No, you must always wear that one." [No, Charlie, there is Grandmamma's brocade, I must wear *that* sometimes.] "No, it is old-fashioned." [Never mind, I must wear it sometimes.] "No, you must wear the new one, or else I won't go with you." [Ah! then some of the others will.] "Well, then, Auntie darling, you'll wear it sometimes." [Yes, I will.] I heard another voice whispering, and Charlie exclaimed, "I'll say it, Grandma" (then to me), "You must kiss Miss S. for the dress." Which I gladly did, and then he said, "I like that coat." [How does it look to you?] "Beautiful." [What am I to tell Preston?] "Tell her that she has made it so very cleverly that it ought to be sent to an exhibition, and it would be sure to win a prize." [But, Charlie, you should talk to the others, not all to me.] "Oh! they won't mind, because it is your birthday: I must talk to you." [Do you go to Arthur, and make him know you are there?] "I try to do so, and I think he does sometimes just a little." Some perfume was being sprinkled about, and he said, "There, is not that sweet?" I was afraid of my coat, which received a good deal, but

Charlie said, "Don't be afraid, it won't hurt it" (and it did not). . . .

A spirit spoke occasionally, in low tones, and when I afterwards enquired the name, he answered, "John Bunyan." I said I was very glad of his company, and enquired what had induced him to favour us with it, when he replied that it was because we were a good and religious-minded circle : he had also another reason that I knew, but he could not say more, as his voice was gone. And the tube then fell. Charlie, too, said that he must leave, and wished us all good-night, but I did not hear the tube fall, and it did not seem to me as if he had used one at all.

I now felt a spirit tenderly stroke my arm, and gradually move the hand down until her fingers touched my pearl ring. Upon my asking Miss Neyland if she saw any spirit, she said, "Mrs. Ramsay's young daughter is just come in, and I think she was touching your ring, I know she touched your hand." While she was still speaking, the hand was placed on my shoulder, and Miss Neyland said, "Now she has moved the hand, and is resting it on your shoulder, the one nearest to me." Môtee then took hold of my chin, and I suddenly lowered my head, so that I kissed the dear little hand; every circumstance of which Miss Neyland detailed.

"Good-night" was then rapped out, and this most deeply interesting séance was concluded in the usual way.

Miss S. afterwards mentioned to me that in a book she was then reading, allusion was made to its being a custom in the Greek Church to take the sacrament mingled together ; and on her return home, she sent me the extract.

From Ritchie's 'Religious Life in London,' 1870. "Then the priest comes from the altar, and stands on the steps. It may be to swing the censer, or to bring out the Gospels bound in silver, which almost all present come forward to kiss : or it may be in the course of the service some one wishes to communicate. Then while the clerks are reading, the doors of the altar are opened, and the priest appears with a cup in his hand, which the communicant comes forward to receive. (The cup, it must be observed, contains bread and wine.) Again the priest comes forward with his crucifix, to which they all bow."

I do not remember whose suggestion it was that I ought to endeavour to have the subject of my Exhibition brought before the notice of the Queen, but it was at once acceded to by my Spiritual directors, to my great satisfaction, as, with reference to her I must own that I am passionately loyal. On consulting Mr. McNair as to the possibility, I found it would be necessary to have a special catalogue which he thought must be printed on satin, but he was to ascertain the particulars, and let me know. On April 24th he sent me the estimate for, "Six copies printed on pink satin, bound in white calf and gold £21—or, Six copies on extra fine pink paper, bound in white calf and gold £11. . . . I have got the estimate for six copies, for in the event of the Queen or the Emperor (of the French) honouring us with a visit, one would have to be presented to them. I have made enquiries, and find it is not absolutely necessary to have satin, I should therefore recommend the other style. I have no doubt I shall be able to get the catalogue laid before Her Majesty, if you decide to go to the expense. No time must be lost."

Of course the more moderate plan was decided upon, and I ventured to hope that perhaps the Queen might come. The catalogue was duly forwarded to her, looking very lovely, but I have never heard any word as to whether it reached her own hands. Two of the others were conveyed to the Crown Princess of Germany, and the Emperor Louis Napoleon, but I am equally ignorant as to the result. When all was over, I gave one to Mrs. Ramsay and one to my sister, retaining the third for myself.

While upon this thought, I may mention that I was permitted to follow out *every* suggestion that in a worldly point of view would be likely to lead to the *pecuniary* success of my venture; so that in the aftertime no one would be able to say, "Oh! if you had done so-and-so, that would have made your Exhibition more generally known, and thus would have drawn crowds to see it." All *was* done in such respects. In the first instance, I had the following leaflets printed, which I sent in packages of half-a-dozen to all those friends (both personal and Spiritualist) who I thought would interest themselves in their distribution. Mr. Young likewise enclosed them in all his private letters as well as those connected with the *Christian Spiritualist*.

"New British Gallery, 39 Old Bond Street.
Exhibition of Spirit Drawings.

" Miss Houghton has taken the above Gallery for the purpose of exhibiting the collection of Drawings in Water Colours that have been executed through her mediumship during the last ten years, to offer to others, as well as to Spiritualists, an opportunity of seeing the representations of some of those flowers that may meet their eyes when they enter upon a future existence, and likewise to give some insight into spiritual symbolism in an artistic point of view.

" To those who do not understand the subject, it may be needful to explain that in the execution of the Drawings, she has been entirely guided by invisible spirits, who could thus delineate what was beyond the human imagination.

Open daily from 10 a.m., till 6 p.m."

There were placards on the walls, and at a later date, at some of the railway stations. After the opening, placards were carried about, and the men had likewise the pink leaflets to distribute, *with discretion:* advertisements in the *Times*, and other daily papers : in fact, I do not think that any single point was neglected. My effort was made without stint, so that no outside reproach could come upon me on that score. The result was in God's Hands, and I never received the shadow of a promise as to mundane success ; but I have had many evidences that it did a good work in the true sense.

In the meanwhile I was having anxieties as to my frames, 155 of which take time to put together ; I had duly taken that point into consideration, by settling all about them with Mr. Spencer at an early date, but *then* it was his very busiest season, being preparatory to the opening of the various spring exhibitions, and he concluded that there would be ample time when he had got through those others, but he did not calculate upon delay in his glass supply, which became a hindrance, but eventually it was all finished *to the moment.* Oh! that framing business! it was veritable labour, done almost without allowing myself breathing time. The servants assisted me in giving the final polish to the glasses, but no hand but mine was permitted to touch the pictures, each of which I put in myself, hammering in every nail with my own hands, and my poor fingers and nails suffered sadly in having to retain the small brads in steady position during the hammering process; which has formerly seemed to me easy enough while putting in two or three drawings, but becomes blisteringly serious when they mount up to upwards of a hundred and a half. Each picture, as finished so far, I handed to Ann and Preston, who pasted at the back the strips of brown paper that I had cut in readiness. Mr. McNair suited me exactly in being a neatly methodical man. I told him I would myself put the numbers on the pictures, and they would thus be a guide as to their chronological order in the gallery; so he provided me with the numbers in consecutive arrangement, tied up in their little packages of ten, and ready gummed at the back; so the sticking in the corner was duly done. There was still another point: a great many of my pictures were not to be parted with, having purely family and personal associations; some also of those to be exhibited were lent back to me for the time. Although the word "Sold" might be appropriate enough to these latter ones, it would not be so to the others, so I wanted a something else, with which he provided me in the shape of crimson stars, which figured lavishly on the collection, and I must own gave many visitors the idea that my *professional* success must have been very great.

Early in the morning of Wednesday the 17th, the van

made its appearance, with Mr. Spencer *in propria persona* to pack them all in safety, and I watched my treasures being stowed away into its depths, with a happy confidence that they were fulfilling their destiny—but—how empty the room felt, with nothing in the portfolios; a fact that I had failed to realize until they were positively gone! I gave them a fair start, allowing for van progress in contradistinction to that of omnibus, and followed in due course, with the full intention of performing the part of hanging committee. What was my dismay to find the workmen still in full possession, the white-washing not concluded, and no symptom of draperies, while the pictures were standing against one another for mutual support in the centre of the room. Mr. McNair came in very shortly after me, and assured me that however unpropitious might be the present aspect of things, all really would be accomplished by the needful time; but he nipped in the bud my notion of my being present during the arrangements, courteously declining any portion of my company until twelve o'clock on Friday, which was the hour specified in the invitation to the members of the Press.—I mentally queried, and was told that I might place implicit confidence in there being a satisfactory result, and so home I came, and doubtless that small season of repose was advantageous to me before the fresh plunge into active life.

His planning was admirable, but he told me that he had had them up and down several times before he could entirely satisfy himself, but there came ample evidence to me that he had not been completely *left to himself* in the adjustment, for there were several points that were very curious. The first pencil sketches were hung on the centre of the left-hand wall, and were carried on in about two rows all round, just at a favourable level for examination. A screen stood at the head of the stairs, shutting away the view of the street; and the last picture upon that screen was the *last* that was done while Mamma was with me. The later ones were then continued into and round that corner until they reached the pencil ones, and thus the first and the last were brought as it were into juxtaposition, with the non-coloured ones between, so that the enormous growth of the power during the ten years became self-evident, although the change from one to the other in gradual progression was scarcely perceptible. There were other peculiarities of arrangement that were very striking to myself, some of the details of which have nearly slipped from my memory during these ten years, while some were purely personal.

CHAPTER VI.

No one can figure to themselves my delight when, at the appointed time, I beheld the lovely array of the whole of those works that had grown under my own hand, with daily new revelations of unknown beauties and unsuspected truths. They came to me in a manner with fresh life and even greater strength than in their progress, for in reality I had never allowed myself the luxury of calm inspection : at the moment one drawing was completed I would straightway begin another. Even when I took them out to shew to visitors, I stood only at the side, and not where I could study them to the best advantage, while now I could indulge myself to my heart's content,—*and I did.* Moreover, I discovered forms, and designs, and distances, that had been utterly undreamed of, and I realised yet more fully the Love that had bestowed such a gift upon me.

It was a very pleasant day with the literary confraternity, answering all the graciously expressed wonderments, and doing my best to indoctrinate them with some notion of what Spiritualism means. I knew nothing of who was who, although I learned somewhat of them in the course of conversation, and there were also two or three visitors who did not come in a professional capacity, and the six hours passed away very rapidly, Mr. McNair congratulating me at the expiration of the time upon all having gone off so well; he and I having had various little bits of chat in the course of the day.

With reference to the prices to be set upon the pictures, I had written to Mr. L. to ask him if he would kindly have a consultation with me on the subject, as his knowledge on that point would be important, but, as his coming was delayed in consequence of his being much occupied, my unseen friends agreed to make a kind of provisional valuation, which I had accordingly written roughly out. Mr. L. was, however, able to come while my drawings were still in their portfolios, and would have gone very patiently into it with me; giving me his idea of perhaps the first half dozen, and in each instance he placed the amount *higher* than they had done, but with about the same *relative* differences as to the sum; so he finally gave it as his opinion that I had better adhere to the list they had helped me to make out, especially as he considered that it was a very moderate one, seeing that they were works of art without parallel in the world.

I must here touch upon the subject of the *guinea*, which I have been taught to look upon as a kind of sacred sum, being composed of a trinity of sevens, the same fact holding good with the half-guinea. It may be true that the coin itself is no longer to be met with, but the term in its amount still stands firm in this blessed land of ours to which it belongs, in all that is allied to spiritual sources, such as charitable donations, physicians' and artists' fees, and their correlatives, whereas the fee for law, which is of the earth earthy, is some aliquot part of only the Latin pound.

It strikes me that exception may be taken by some of my readers to the intense interblending of the heavenly and the mundane in these records, for many people seem to think that the one is for Sundays and the other for the *six* weekdays; but my feeling is to make one's whole life into Sunday, in so far as living close to God, so that the two phases of being must be inseparable :—the pound of flesh can exist only by the flow within it of the vital blood, and as long as it courses through my veins, may its every pulsation beat in harmony with the Will of my Heavenly Father.

The eventful Private View day arrived, and more than fulfilled my expectations. Many of my personal friends were there, and also many whom it was a great gratification to become acquainted with; among whom was Mr. de Bunsen with his wife and daughters, son of that Chevalier Bunsen whose name had been familiar to me from my girlhood upwards. They were very appreciative, both of the beauty of colour and work, and also of the inner meanings conveyed and interpreted: indeed I may say that was my almost universal experience. I had yet another happiness on that day, for Mr. Hardwick purchased one of my pictures, so that another red star was added to those that already graced the corners. It was one entitled The Ear of The Lord, and was the only one I had ever done representing that symbol, and was executed in exquisitely beautiful tracery on a substratum of variously harmonised tints. I retain its shadow in photographic form.

My own idea had been that I should probably attend that gallery once a week, and I had even told Mr. McNair that I would appoint one special day for the purpose, so that if any visitor should wish to learn more than could be gathered from the catalogue, or if any artist should be desirous of gleaning somewhat of the methods of manipulation and colouring, he could then arrange for them to meet me; but I was now informed by my teachers that I should have but the one day *at home*, my Wednesday according to custom, while the other five were to be spent in Bond Street, so as to give the fullest possible advantages to those who should go there, which proved that the spirit friends belonging to Mrs. Everitt's circle must have received an intimation to that effect from my own teachers.

On the Sunday morning Preston brought me up her paper, the *News of the World*, in great glee, as it contained the following notice.

"Exhibition of Spirit Drawings in Water Colours. An exhibition of a novel character is opened at the New British Gallery, 39 Old Bond Street, consisting of drawings by a lady, who states that her hand has been entirely guided by the spirits, no idea being formed in her own mind as to what was going to be produced. At the first glance the pictures seem only masses of lines and colours—extraordinary mazes, but without a defined plan; the brilliancy and harmony of the tints, however, engage attention, and the idea presents itself to the imagination of a canvas of Turner's, over which troops of fairies have been meandering, dropping jewels as they went. Miss Houghton, the lady executant, is a clever and tasteful artist; and furthermore, a sincere believer in what she says. We do not recognise in her extraordinary achievements more than what an accomplished and patient artist, with thoughts bent in a particular direction, could produce; but her conviction claims respect, and although we have met with nothing to induce us to believe in the spirit theory, we readily acknowledge the thorough conscientiousness of Miss Houghton's belief. Her inspiration is of a poetical character; indeed the lady and her drawings constitute a little poem, fanciful and beautiful, its aims and ends being to establish the holiness and beauty of pure religious principle, and the happiness which it creates in this life leading to the greater happiness hereafter. One of her ideas is that 'when a child is born, a flower springs up in the spirit realms, which grows day by day in conformity with the child's awakening powers, expressing them by colour and form until, by degrees, the character and life stand revealed in the floral emblem.' It is of these floral emblems the exhibition chiefly consists."

It was opened to the public on Monday the 22nd, when I had the pleasure of making the acquaintance (afterwards ripening into friendship) of Sir Charles Isham, an earnest Spiritualist, who frankly acknowledges his convictions to the world, and forwards the cause by every means in his power. On a later occasion he was accompanied by Lady Isham and their elder daughter.

In a long conversation with one of my visitors, Countess V., I learned that she has curious and interesting experiences, upon which my drawings seemed to throw some light; for she sees beautiful balls formed of brilliantly coloured fibres, which gradually open out, looking more and more attenuated, until within them is revealed a lovely face. It is generally in the early morning when first awakening that these visions are granted, and the fibre-like envelope had been a great mystery to her.

Oh! what a happy time that was! I never wearied of explaining and re-explaining all that I would fain impart to the whole world, sometimes to utter strangers, whose names perhaps I might never learn, sometimes to friends of many years ago, who had long seemed to have passed from my life, but whom I rejoiced once more to greet, for the red filaments from my fruit (to borrow a simile from my own work) cling with great tenacity wherever they may have rested, and I would gladly strengthen them whenever in my power. Mr. McNair used to wonder how I could bear up under the fatigue of so many hours of standing about daily (I used generally to be there from soon after ten in the morning, until half-past five), but I was the blessed recipient of such ceaseless care that my energies were never allowed to be called uselessly into play. My custom was to sit quietly with a book on the ottoman in the centre of the room, in bonnet and out-door costume, and when fresh visitors came in, I would *question* as to whether I should accost them in any way. The answer might possibly be, "No, sit still." There was nothing in my appearance or demeanour generally, to indicate that I was anything more than an ordinary visitor there, but I had my two magnifying glasses with me, and my excuse to speak to any one would be the offering of one of those to enhance the enjoyment of the spectator:—so sometimes I would receive the answer, "Hand the glass, and come away:"—whereas if it were any one with whom conversation might be a mutual benefit, the directions would be, "Offer the glass, and stand about," when the courtesy would lead to a few words, and so on till the tide of talk went on in full flow, when sometimes a small crowd would gather, one question or answer calling forth another, until my tiny congregation would almost unwillingly disperse carrying with them subject matter for thought for many days.

Mr. Burlton Bennett was a great frequenter of my gallery, and I owe him much gratitude for his earnest desire to extend a helping hand to me, for he was generally accompanied by a considerable party of friends. His admiration of the pictures was unbounded, and being a skilful artist himself, his opinion had much weight with those who might be doubtful of their own judgment, especially in regard to works that could not be criticised according to any of the known and accepted canons of art.

On the Saturday of that first week, a clergyman friend, Mr. Brereton, brought another to introduce to me, the Rev. Mr. Barrett, who paid me a long visit full of deep interest, for he was a mesmerist of many years' standing, and had performed some extraordinary cures. He afterwards proved a most steadfast friend.

Mr. McNair had provided a blank volume for the insertion of newspaper notices, fragments of which I shall extract by degrees, but one that appeared in the *Queen*, I will copy in its entirety. One old friend in speaking of it, said it was so good that she and her husband had thought I must have written it myself: I, however, had no knowledge even of the author, and remain to this day equally ignorant, but shall be happy to be made wiser if this should meet the writer's eye.

"*Spirit Drawings.*"

"Hamlet says, 'There are more things in heaven and earth, Horatio, than are dreamt of in our philosophy:' and truly, when in the latter part of the nineteenth century we have to consider a public exhibition containing pictures, possessed of some claims to artistic excellence, purporting to be the work of departed spirits, the saying of the melancholy Prince occurs to the mind with redoubled force.

"On Monday last, at 39 Old Bond Street, was opened an exhibition of spirit drawings in water colours, by Miss Houghton; and for the information of those of our readers who may not be acquainted with the *modus operandi* by which such works are produced, we may state that the pictures, although actually drawn by the hand of a living person, are stated to be so executed at the instigation, and while the individual is under the control, of one who has passed away from this earth; the person producing the picture being in fact a mere medium, or means of communicating to those alive the production of one no longer having an earthly existence.

"With the credence or disbelief to be accorded to so singular a theory we have little to do, but simply chronicle the fact, leaving it to our readers to please themselves in the view they may take of the subject. We may however remark, *en passant*, that what is termed spiritualism appears to have excited attention and aroused interest so generally, that learned and scientific men have taken up the matter, and it is probable the result of their labours and calm investigation will be the means of throwing light upon a subject at once remarkable and interesting, and of which, notwithstanding all that has been said and written up to the present time, but very little is really known.

"The works to which we are about to refer are from the brush of Miss Houghton, and that lady, with a courtesy and candour we should think habitual with her, emphatically assured us that, although these works are undoubtedly the production of her pencil, the directing influence producing them was altogether beyond her control, and she was in perfect ignorance whilst the drawings were in progress what was intended to be represented, or what the result would be.

"The subject which for want of a better title has been variously denominated 'Spirit-rapping,' 'Table-turning,' and 'Spiritualism' has been much ridiculed and roundly abused, probably for the reason that it is easier to ridicule a difficulty than to explain it, and also because satirical writing is a popular style with many persons. We disclaim any sympathy with the subject of Spiritualism; but surely the matter is worthy a calm, considerate, thoughtful investigation, for there is no merit in abusing those who, we may fairly believe from the object they appear to have in view, can only desire to elicit the truth.

"The water-colour drawings, numbering one hundred and fifty-five, are so extraordinary in character, and are so entirely opposed to one's ideas of *art*, ancient or modern, that criticism in the ordinary manner becomes difficult, not to say impossible.

"The assumption of Miss Houghton is that these works are the production of spirits of the deceased, and that they (the spirits) make use of her hand as a means of expressing themselves, the representations being those of fruit, flowers, &c., having an *actual existence* in the spirit world.

"This theory is perhaps repugnant to active, business, common-sense men of the world, but the ideas suggested are not uninteresting—at least, except to atheists or those who both theoretically and practically ignore the existence of a Deity or Supreme Being. Miss Houghton in the catalogue of her works informs us, although perhaps in a somewhat allegorical, mystical manner, that as soon as the breath of life enters the form of man his good and evil actions are recorded in the spirit world, and simultaneously with the birth of a child into the earth life a flower springs up in spirit realms, which grows day by day in conformity with the infant's awakening powers, until by degrees the colour and form stand revealed in the floral emblem and in the fruit thereof. And very beautiful are some of these delineations of fruit and flowers (for of such is the exhibition composed); open, we admit—but that is of little moment—to the bitter jest and sharp sarcasm which will assuredly be heaped upon them. Many of the drawings may look like singular and confused scrawls; but they are elegantly minute in their tracery, frequently beautiful in form, and in their bold and often violent contrasts of colour never *inharmonious*.

"We invite our readers to see the works for themselves; they must be prepared for a *singular novelty*, and one calling for calm thought and consideration."

I have just been reading through all those criticisms, which I never have done since my first perusal of them in the gallery itself, and I do find evidences of what are intended for sarcasm and jest, but I also realize that such characteristics are usually in perfect harmony with the whole diction of such articles, so that they are fitted to the place they hold. Frequent, too, are the objections to *named* colours being expressive of qualities, and no small amount of that class of wit is expended on the subject, so I will here quote a line or two from my book of interpretations that was *not* published in the catalogue.

" In thus giving the names as artistically known, we must be understood to mean that they are the nearest approximation to the tint expressive of the respective qualities, for some of the real hues are not to be met with in colours of earth."

I had of course been unable to do any drawing for some time before the opening of my Exhibition, being so fully engrossed in other ways, but on the following Wednesday I once more established myself at the easel, to the extreme delight of the Dove, who cooed and crooned to me in a perfect state of ecstasy, seeming to congratulate me and herself that I was again sitting still like a reasonable being: she never liked my leaving her, and my absences had latterly been both frequent and prolonged. I have never mentioned that on the very morning of my brother Clarence's death, she had laid an egg, the companion to it following on the evening of the next day. There were no more in that year; but others came later on, so that in the course of her little life she laid fifty-eight, all of which I sucked, preserving the shells, which I keep in a covered fancy glass that used to be the depository for cheese for Papa, who was the only eater thereof. That glass stands in the centre of the table, unless removed to make way for flowers, and often puzzles people as to its contents, which, by concave diminishment, look like small sugar-plums.

Having thus a drawing in progress at home, I sometimes invited any of the especially interested of my gallery visitors to come here on the Wednesday and see me at work, which was generally esteemed a great privilege.

Of course I was to have a séance for Whitsunday, which fell on May 28th, and when Mrs. T. came she was accompanied by Mr. Andrew Leighton of Liverpool, who was up in London for a few days, and wished to take his chance as to whether he might be admitted to the circle, and my spirit guides immediately granted his request, so that our party consisted of Mrs. Ramsay, Mrs. T., Mr. and Mrs. Everitt, Mr. Leighton, Mrs. Guppy, Mrs. P., Miss Neyland and myself, I having on the coat of many colours.

As soon as the light was extinguished, I felt Môtee's hand touching the ring, and Miss Neyland spoke of it at once, mentioning that Môtee was there, and what she was doing, and when I commenced The Lord's Prayer, she gently tapped upon it at each petition.

We all saw the lights, much the same as those I described on a previous occasion, and we soon heard our spirit friends busily engaged with the pencils; they did three small drawings, but without much defined form, presenting one of them to Mr. Leighton, for him to take away with him.

By the alphabet came the message, "Shall I bring you a spiritual inkstand?" The idea amused us, and of course I said I should be glad if they would. In a short time something was placed in my hand, and we were told to have a "light," when we found that it certainly was an inkstand, made of some light coloured wood, which Mrs. Guppy said she recognised, and that it was made from the wood of a tree that Napoleon Buonaparte had planted in Italy. I was then anxious to know whose it was, that I might restore it to its owner, and Mrs. Guppy said she would tell me if I would promise to keep it, but that I would not agree to, and it at length turned out that it was her own, but I believe had not been unpacked since her return from Italy. Mr. Leighton suggested that they ought to have said Spiritualist's inkstand.

We then smelled the perfume of an orange, and afterwards the orange itself was peeled by the invisibles and distributed among us, some having only the peel, but to me was brought half the orange, which I was allowed to share with Mrs. Ramsay and Mrs. Guppy. The message then given was "Elizabeth and Miss Neyland must sit on the sofa," and when they were there, Mrs. Guppy made some observation on the diminished power in the room in consequence of the absence of all my drawings, in which the spirits strongly acquiesced.

We were then told to "Sing," and in compliance with further directions we sang the first verse of the Evening Hymn, but they began carrying the sofa cushions, &c., about, to which I strenuously objected, as I never like rough physical manifestations; so they let us have a light, when we found one of the sofa pillows on the table, and the other on the floor, while in Mr. Leighton's hands was the china plate for cards, on his shoulders an antimacassar, and on the ground near him the album containing my family photographs, which had been placed in the card plate when taken off the table to make the preparation for my company. Mrs. Guppy asked whether Charlie would speak to us in the course of the evening, and received an affirmative answer, and we were then told to "Eat and return," which rather surprised us, as it was only nine o'clock, but we did as we were bid, expecting that probably some fresh arrangement might be made for Mrs. Everitt's manifestations, but when we came back the only direction we could obtain was a repetition of the suggestion that Elizabeth and Miss Neyland should sit on the sofa, and after some little time Charlie's voice was heard, but it seemed at a distance and was not nearly so clear as before, and when I wanted him to come closer to me, he said, "I can't, Auntie darling, because of the atmosphere." He again urged upon me that I should always wear my dove-coloured silk at the Exhibition, to which he had accompanied me every day, and he was glad that hitherto there had only been one day that I had not worn it. He expressed his pleasure at Mrs. Ramsay's presence, and conversed for a little while, but said he could not stay long: and after telling Mr. Leighton he was glad to see him here, said good-bye to all. Then "No more," was rapped out, but we thought that might refer only to Mrs. Guppy's portion of the séance, and as the response was a doubtful one, for a time we sat patiently listening for the raps from Mrs. Everitt's friends, but all the message we at length received was "No more to-night." When we had the light, I mesmerised Mrs. T., who passed into a sort of semi-trance, but there were only a few fragmentary words, and she said afterwards, that what she saw seemed to be taken away before she could gather the meaning from it.

Mr. Leighton feared that it might have been his unexpected presence that disturbed the influences, but I thought he would probably not have been admitted had that been the case, and I had previously almost feared that the séance would not be a very interesting one, because I had had scarcely any intimations from my unseen friends that they were gathering from me in preparation for the séance, all the thoughts of my own spirit circle seeming to have been concentrated on my Exhibition, which is to them one of the grandest events connected with the spiritual movement. I also believe that the absence of the pictures was very detrimental, and that the invisibles were not sorry that such a proof should be given of the value of the atmosphere appertaining to them.

It was a great disappointment to me that I could not hope for nice long visits to the gallery from Mrs. T., but she was going across the Atlantic in a very few days, to spend some time with her own relatives, so that this séance was our farewell, and on leaving me at night she expressed many tender wishes that my work might be blessed and blessing.

It is delightful to look back upon that time, and to recall the charming intercourse I had with so many intellectual people, some of whose names are well known in the literary world, although I may scarcely feel at liberty to mention them, for every one must take their own time for acknowledging their spiritual convictions. My sister Isabel used to enjoy spending hours with me in my calm retreat, quite out of the turmoil of the world and its ways. Two sisters from Reigate spent one long morning with me: they had relatives who were Spiritualists, but still had not gleaned very much from them on the subject, and only knew what they had learned from books, and we went into numberless questions. They were both struck with the beauty of the drawings, but the elder one had more faith in their spiritual origin; the younger sister seemed to think that it might be an outcome from my own passionate love for flowers and exquisite colouring, although her scepticism was very delicately veiled. Singular to relate, in the course of that same year, the gift of drawing spirit flowers came to herself, much to her own astonishment and gratification, and she must have looked back with dismay upon her original doubts: she has likewise developed drawing powers in various directions, with brilliantly gorgeous colouring. To her sister also had come mediumship of an elevated inspirational character.

Several of my visitors were much struck with the frame of photographs, and in such cases I was allowed to supply them with copies, which I had however to bring from home in readiness for a future visit to the gallery, or to forward by post, as I might not have any of them there.

One afternoon while Isabel was with me, two very charming young girls came in, one was in a riding habit, and it appeared that their Mamma had been in the morning, and had been so much struck that they had resolved to lose no time in sharing the same pleasure, over which they were indeed enthusiastic, flitting across from picture to picture as a fresh beauty caught their eye, and revelling in the various delicate details. An elderly coachman came up once or twice to remind them of the lapse of time, but they paid no heed to his suggestions as they seemed unable to tear themselves away, and each time when they were on the point of going some new attraction arrested their steps. I caught their Christian names, Izzy and Rosie, and a few days later made the acquaintance of their Lady-mother, who then had a married daughter with her, and I had the pleasure of several visits from her. She knew something of Spiritualism, and mentioned the name of some of my own friends with whom she was intimate. Isabel often used to revert afterwards to the freshness of enjoyment shewn by those two fair girls.

Mr. S., one of my visitors, told me on his first entrance that he must frankly inform me that he was yet on the debatable ground, not having made up his mind as to whether spiritual communion were a fact, or simply *self*-delusion, for he had seen enough of it to be quite sure that it was not wilful deception, and indeed I knew that some members of his own family were mediums, although it was my first introduction to himself. I said that I would not attempt anything in the shape of evidence, for that I had no doubt he would find it in that very room. He was an artist, and looked at the drawings with great interest. On reaching the one numbered in the catalogue as 29, he exclaimed, "*That* is a *proof!* Any one understanding anything whatever of the subject, knows that no artist ever springs *at once* from one method of working to another completely opposite. *That* drawing is by a different hand!" In which assertion he was perfectly right, for in all the previous drawings my hand had been guided by Henry Lenny, whereas for this one, which was the inside view of his own spirit flower, I had been promoted to the guidance of a spirit from beyond the spheres, namely, St. Joseph, the husband of the Virgin Mary, whose method of working was quite different from Lenny's, for the colours were laid on with much strength, instead of in a succession of most delicate washes. Mr S., pointing to another at some little distance, said, "*That*" (and again to a further one), "and *that*, are by this new hand; these bring a conviction that leaves no question." He thus recognised at once the same character of manipulation in the No. 37, "Mendelssohn's Flower," and No. 42, "The Holy Trinity," which were also by St. Joseph, bringing to him the certainty of the assistance of invisible spirits. He was intensely charmed with the whole exhibition, <u>studying each picture with additional delight</u> (carrying his chair with him from one to the next), and becoming so engrossed with the later ones that he could hardly tear himself away. He studies much from the old masters, and said that it is well known that one great point of their superiority to modern artists arises from the beauty and care of the underneath work : the men of the present age work much too rapidly; all is, as it were, on the surface. He could therefore appreciate the result in the later drawings executed through my mediumship, produced by the succession of work, which, although it may be trying to my patience, amply rewards me at length by the wonderful effects of inner beauties glimmering through, each of which beauties has rejoiced my eye as they were done, but I must confess that I often feel sadly grieved as I see it relentlessly covered, with only the smallest fragment left visible. But I have learned that only thus can perfection be attained in anything or any person: the hidden and inner must be true and complete, or the outer will be but as a whited sepulchre.

CHAPTER VII.

Cards of invitation had been sent out for May 19th to the editors of not only the regular daily and weekly newspapers, but also to those of a religious character of various denominations including also the Jewish papers; but I do not at all know whether notices of the Exhibition may have appeared in any of them, but it seems to me that as a return courtesy, they might as well have forwarded me a copy of such notice. One such instance (with a difference) amused me much. There was a complimentary article of about a couple of dozen lines in one paper, and the editor (and proprietor) brought in rather a considerable pile for me to distribute among friends, which I thought was intended as a kind of advertisement for his paper; but when they had all vanished (not by my giving, by the bye), he called in, with his small account for the same! When the editor (or his representative) of any paper came armed with that invitation card (irrespective of date), a season ticket for self and friend was given in exchange, and likewise a catalogue. All these scraps of information were novelties to me, and I dare say they will also be so to other people, and as I give my readers credit for liking to know *something* of everything, I pour them forth for public benefit. It was a very sightseeing season to me, for other exhibitors of pictures or curiosities came to see my gallery, and complimented me with admissions to theirs; and as mine would generally be a quiet time from about twelve or one o'clock till three, I could then go upon such dissipations. I saw the Double-headed Nightingale: the Queen of the Lilliputians, who was the most uninteresting little dwarf I ever saw, more like a lanky wooden doll than anything else, with a squeaky fretful voice. There was no appearance of plump humanity about her, like General Tom Thumb and his genial little quartette, consisting of himself, his wife, his sister-in-law, and Commodore Nutt; to say nothing of the dear little year-old baby Thumb, that had long ago toddled its small person to the front of the platform, to give me a solicited kiss, and whose death I was afterwards sorry to learn. I also saw Doré's Gallery, with which I was charmed; the French Gallery; Mr. Dobinson's Exhibition of the Old Masters, which was, like mine, under Mr. Mc'Nair's jurisdiction, &c., &c.

One of my visitors, after an intensely minute study of the pictures, told me that they had an especial interest for him, for that he was a microscopist, and that the effects produced exactly resembled the wonders revealed by the microscope, but invisible to the unaided eyesight. I *love* my pictures (although it is perhaps a work of supererogation to say so), and that season of public inspection brought much balm to my heart, inasmuch as by the aggregate of individual appreciations, they received their due praise in the multiplicity of points in which they excel. The scoffs of the ignorant were unimportant, they never gave me the shadow of a pang, unless perhaps for the unhappy perpetrators' sake. Taken in class division, the most sympathetic visitors were the clergy, of *every* denomination, and artists. The former were interested in the new truths revealed, for with them I generally had very long conversations, answering many questions of moment that might have harassed their souls, for my Bond Street room, like my own home, sustained much the character of a confessional, the avowals remaining equally a secret in my own bosom. One of my clerical friends, after having been with me for some hours, when I gave him my recollections of the interpretations of many of the symbolical drawings, told me that he carried away with him subjects for no end of sermons, and something to the same effect was often said. Some dignitaries of the Church visited the collection, and I am sure that in that respect my exhibition fulfilled a high purpose, notwithstanding the heavy pecuniary loss it entailed upon myself. When first the project began to take form, a friend living at a distance, who felt most anxious as to what I was undertaking, prayerfully sought to be directed to a text wherein she might find comfort. The one given to her was S. Mark xii. 42, 43, 44 : " And there came a certain poor widow, and she threw in two mites, which make a farthing. And He called unto Him His disciples, and saith unto them, Verily, I say unto you, That this poor widow hath cast more in, than all they which have cast into the treasury : for all they did cast in of their abundance ; but she of her want did cast in all that she had, *even* all her living."

The artists revelled in the glories of colour, the marvellous manipulation, the delicacies of delineation. At one time I was in conversation with a cluster of friends, when Mr. de Lisle (the sub-secretary) told me that a gentleman wished to have a few words with me, when I should be disengaged. He was an artist, and in the first instance he wanted to thank me for the boon to art in bringing these works to public view. "But," added he, "I *cannot* think how it has been possible to produce these opalescent tints." Of course I then talked, explained, and expatiated to my heart's content, and I warmly hope the information then conveyed, in going with him from one to another bearing that especial characteristic, may have enabled him to give a new charm to his own works. On another occasion there was a group of artists in warm discussion, and I ventured to draw near them, the subject matter being one particular type of work that is unusually striking, and I heard one of them say, in dictatorial tones, "*That* is done with a mechanical appliance." In my own private mind I wondered what *mechanical* appliance could perform anything like it, especially in its infinite varieties ; but I meekly differed with him, and suggested that it was not so. He adhered to his own opinion, to which I rejoined, "But it was *I* who did it, and therefore I must know, and I cannot understand what kind of instrument would serve the purpose." He had had his answer, but he walked off in dudgeon, and I believe that probably to this day, "he is of the same opinion still." That was the only fraction of discourtesy that came to me from *any* artist. One of those who had formed the group, and who is a landscape painter of eminence, was glad to get hold of the *mortal* exeçutant of these marvels, and questioned me about a multitude of details. I enquired if he had noticed a peculiar *sky* effect in one picture that he had passed, and which is in that single one *only* of all my collection. "Indeed he had, and had puzzled himself as to how it could possibly have been produced." So we went back together for him to have a fresh examination, while I explained clearly to him how it had been done, telling him the exact article that must be purchased for the purpose (which had surprised me when I had received directions to get one, which by the bye, is *not* a mechanical appliance, but a natural production); and I finished by recommending him to go home and try, to which his rejoinder was, "I most certainly shall." The method was so simple, yet so novel, and the result so true to nature as a cloud effect, although that was not its intention or signification in the drawing it embellishes.

One of my most delightful interviews was with Mr. William W. Story, sculptor and artist, whose "Roba di Roma" I am just now for the first time enjoying. He had not even heard of there being such an exhibition, but while walking along the opposite side of Bond Street, the large placard caught his eye, so in he came, and spent some hours with me, full of enthusiastic admiration for all the marvels that met his gaze on every side. He said that all artists well know (of course he meant those who are truly such) that the more entirely they yield themselves to intuition, subduing the self-hood, the more perfect becomes their work. Perhaps he did not mean that they in any way *realize* external aid, but indubitably they do receive it, for genius means affinity with the higher, whatever may be the dictionary definition, and the highest genius must be the most modest, knowing that their own unaided powers could never have soared to the heights that they are enabled to attain through the loving help of invisible agencies.

A large proportion of newspaper critics know nothing in

the world about *Art;* they can look at pictures, where they see that a horse is a horse, and they gather from the talk of the studios what is to be said of such or such a production, but my Exhibition baffled them utterly, therefore they sometimes took refuge in unseemly words about what they did not understand. It is not to be expected that I should perpetuate any of their follies, but I will now give other gleanings, in some instances only a few sentences, altogether without reference to the paper it is from, as my main object is to give some faint notion of the pictured results in the words of outside observers. . . . " Lines drawn with a marvellous combination of freedom and precision, and in a great variety of colours, depart from ever-shifting foci, either within or without the boundaries of the drawing, with every variety of curve ; they meet, and part, and intersect each other, incidentally yielding singular effects of linear perspective and colour blendings or contrasts." . . . "Everybody is talking about the Spiritual pictures in Old Bond Street. I went there yesterday, and a more surprising collection of 150 paintings I never saw . . . . beautiful workmanship, warmness, manual application — and the colouring is a new revelation. The groundwork is usually a mystified preparation—probably done on damp paper to make the colours blend and flow away" (No, he mistakes.) —"and on this groundwork are curves, spirals, floats of colour, curlicews, shell involutes, and ramifications that bewilder all attempts at explanation or resemblance, but clean, clear, and lavished in such profusion that curiosity is driven away from the cause of the observation to delight in the intricacy." . . . " The whole of these drawings, from their feeble beginnings to their finished accomplishments, are entirely new in their nature and variety, newness being shewn in many striking points. The most noticeable thing in these pictures is that they are translucent, that is, diaphanous, quite unlike anything that is seen in this world. But this must surely be the case in the spirit world, where there is not substance or matter, only spirit. Leaf is seen behind leaf, stem behind stem, flower behind flower.

... Nearly the whole of the pictures have four things in common—long sweeps, decided lines, beautiful forms, and never before thought of combinations. The impression created is that no idea existed in the mind of the drawer as to the tendency or effect of the lines of the pencil in producing the sketch. Yet every drawing shews all the effects which could only appear when the last shading of the picture should be put in by an intelligence embracing the *deepest* and *most exact* calculations." ... "The series forms an interesting study of the progress of mediumistic art. At first the performances were mere scrolls, which became more and more intricate; then another colour was introduced, then indications of design, and ultimately that harmonious and pleasing blending of colours drawn in richly varied lines over each other, producing an effect which it is impossible to describe. Some of the drawings may be likened to a mass of brilliantly coloured threads laid one over the other—not in confusion, not according to any rule, yet in the most pleasing manner possible. The beauty and richness of the colours at first fascinate the eye, and a closer inspection interests the mind by the wonderful indications of design which run through each drawing. The artist is enraptured by the delicate and skilful manipulation."

I had a visit from one of the Darwin school of evolution, and he propounded his theory with very great skill, proving how the utter nature may be changed into something else, and he explained to me how the pigeon's bill (and doubtless characteristics) had been transformed into the similitude of that of the hawk, by having been compelled, through successive generations, to subsist on raw flesh : although I must certainly object that even then, it was not *evolved* but *trained*. Our talk was pleasant, ranging over much variety of ground; but when he was gone, his theory bothered me, not for one moment as to the thought of accepting it, but as to how the specious arguments were to be met, and I appealed for counsel. " Receive your illustration from your own loved work. Look at the rainbow ! Where are the *links* in creation so close as the tints in its arching bow? Who may say where one shades off into another? yet the blue remains *blue ;* the red, *red ;* and the yellow, *yellow :* the several creations are distinct, however closely they may be allied, or however harmoniously they may be blended."

Colonel Guthrie, a dear old gentleman, came very frequently, sometimes with a large bevy of friends, for each of whom he would purchase catalogues, but he always liked a nice bit of talk, interspersed with anecdotes about the different people who had been. One lady had been much struck with the flower represented in William Borer's plant, saying that it resembled a fossilized Lily Enchrinite ; and when I told Colonel Guthrie about it, he at once agreed as to its likeness, and promised to bring me one of the fossils ; but on his next visit he expressed his great regret at having been unable to procure one, therefore in its stead he had brought me Dr. Buckland's Bridgewater Treatise, where the Lily is figured as one of the illustrations, and the resemblance is certainly wonderfully striking. He added greatly to the value of the book, by writing his name in it as the donor, in accordance with my request. I am very sorry that with the closing of the gallery ended my pleasant intercourse with him. At the time of the spirit photography, I thought how exceedingly interested he would be in all connected with it, so I asked Mr. McNair to try to discover his whereabouts for me, but all his efforts were unsuccessful, and he told me he feared he was dead. How much I regret having lost sight of him, but it never struck me to tell him that I should hope still to see him occasionally here, being always at home on the Wednesday afternoons, between one and five o'clock, but I trust that if he is still dwelling on this earth, and should, through any channel, hear of this mention of him, that he will thus give me the pleasure of renewing our friendship. That is a regret that I also feel with regard to several of my constant visitors there, and should this meet the eye of any of them, I beg now to tender the Wednesday invitation ; "better late than never." There was one lady, not a Spiritualist, who used to greet me with her cheery, "Here I am again;" bringing with her some fresh friend to enjoy the pictures with her, and I think that she too, liked the talks she had with me, for she said it was a great pleasure to meet with any one so thoroughly in earnest. There was another, who carried a magnifying glass, like my own large one; I believe she was an artist, and was generally accompanied by one or two companions, and I should feel very much gratified to see either of those two ladies here in my own home, and to shew them some of the fresh marvels that have come through photography.

Some gallery frequenters would perhaps say on their entrance, that they never cared for a catalogue, and would decline having one, but we kept one for the purpose of lending on the secretary's table, and he or I would offer the use of it, as being an assistance in the comprehension of something so novel. It has then been read through with much interest, generally followed by the purchase of one to take away.

It was while my time was so entirely engrossed that the marvellous circumstance occurred of Mrs. Guppy's being transported by the spirits from her home at Highbury to Mr. Williams's séance in Lamb's, Conduit Street; and I feel that I cannot omit the history of it, as published at the time, for I afterwards received the corroboration of every detail from Mr. and Mrs. Guppy and Miss Neyland. I may perhaps omit what seems superfluous, or make a few alterations according to what I heard from themselves: "On the evening of June 3rd, 1871, a séance was held in the rooms of Messrs. Herne and Williams. Before it commenced, the doors communicating with the passage outside were locked. The proceedings began, at the request of the mediums, with prayer. Then spirit lights, like small stars, were seen moving about, after which a conversation between the spirits John King and Katie King, was heard. John said, 'Katie, you can't do it.' Katie replied, 'I will, I tell you I will.' John said, 'Katie, you can't.' She answered, 'I will.' Within three minutes after Katie had said, 'I will,' a single heavy sound was heard for an instant on the centre of the table. Mr. Edwards (of Kilburn) put out his hand and said, 'There is a dress here.' A light was instantly struck, and Mrs. Guppy was found standing motionless on the centre of the table, trembling all over; she had a pen and an account book in her hands. Her right hand, with the pen in it, was over her eyes. She was spoken to by those present, but did not seem to hear; the light was then placed in the other room, and the door was closed for an instant; John King then said, 'She'll be all right presently.' After the lapse of about four minutes after her arrival, she moved for the first time, and began to cry. The time of her arrival was ten minutes past eight. Mrs. Edmiston (of Beckenham) and two of the gentlemen went at once to one of the doors, and found it still locked; the other door could not be opened during the séance, because the back of the chair of one of the sitters was against it. There was no cupboard, article of furniture or anything else where it was possible for anybody to conceal themselves, and if there had been, we the undersigned witnesses, are all certain that by no natural means could Mrs. Guppy have placed herself instantaneously on the centre of a table round which we were all sitting shoulder to shoulder.

"Mrs. Guppy said that the last thing she remembered before she found herself on the table, was that she was sitting at home at Highbury, talking to Miss Neyland, and entering some household accounts in her book. The ink in the pen was wet when she arrived in our midst; the last word of the writing in the book was incomplete, and was wet and smeared. She complained that she was not dressed in visiting costume, and had no shoes on, as she had been sitting at the fire without them. As she stated this to Mr. Morris (a merchant from Manchester), a pair of slippers dropped on the floor from above, one of them grazing Mr. Morris's head; this was after the séance, and in the light." . . . A document to the above effect was drawn up before the separation of the party, and they all signed it, to the number of eleven, including Mrs. Guppy, and it appeared in the *Echo;* and I will now extract from the fuller details published in the *Spiritualist.* "The séance was held in a small room, 12 ft. by 10 ft. 4 in., and it contained no furniture but the table and the chairs occupied by the sitters. The table was of oval form, the two diameters being 5 ft. and 4 ft. respectively. The sitters and table so nearly filled the room that there was no walking round three sides of the room without disturbing the rest of those present, and asking them to shift their seats. The fourth side of the room consisted of large folding doors, which were closed, and which communicated with the drawing-room. The opening of the small door of the séance room would have let in much light from the passage. There was no stool or anything in the room which would have afforded a footing to anybody trying to jump on the table. There were about two feet of space between the folding doors and the nearest sitter,—Mr. Herne; the other medium Mr. Williams sat opposite to him at the other end of the longest diameter of the oval table; he was thus 'sealed in' so to speak, at the further end of the room, by the table and the sitters. At the time of the solitary heavy 'thud' upon the table caused by the arrival of Mrs. Guppy, the members of the circle were sitting very quietly; Mr. Herne was talking, his hands being held by the sitters on each side. When a wax match was struck, Mrs. Guppy was seen standing like a dark statue on the centre of the table, trembling all over. The excitement, of course, was intense. As Mrs. Guppy continued to tremble in the same attitude, and not to hear the words spoken to her, the candle which had been lit was removed for an instant, and John King said, 'She'll be all right presently.' When she awoke she had tears in her eyes, and was greatly agitated. In the course of her statement about her removal from home, she said she was sitting by the fire with Miss Neyland, entering some things in her account book, and while writing a word she suddenly became insensible. When she awoke in a dark place, and heard voices round her, her first impression was that she was dead (and her instantaneous thought was, 'Oh! who will take care of Tommy?'*) Then it flashed upon her that she had been carried to a dark circle, and she was afraid that she might be among strangers; finally she recognised the voice of one of those present, and felt much relieved at once. She complained that she had no shoes or bonnet to go home in, and was not dressed for an evening visit; and it was then the slippers (which belonged to Mr. Herne) dropped on the head of one of the gentlemen to whom she was talking; a minute or two later, a bunch of keys dropped into her lap before the eyes of those around her; this was in the light. At the short dark sittings which followed (the account of which I have omitted), a bonnet was brought, and Mrs. Guppy recognised it as one she had given to Miss Neyland some time before: also Mrs. Guppy's boots and some articles of dress belonging to her were brought. . . .

"Mr. Ernest Edwards suggested that if Mrs. Guppy would grant permission, it would be as well for some of the witnesses to return home with her, to hear at once the statement of those at Mr. Guppy's house. Mrs. Guppy strongly approved of the suggestion, so four of the party accordingly went home with her in two cabs, which kept close to each other all the way, and all five persons entered Mr. Guppy's house together.

"Miss Neyland opened the door. She was followed by the whole party into the back parlour; no statement was made to her, but she was asked 'What had occurred?' She said that she had been downstairs with a newspaper on one side of the fire, while Mrs. Guppy sat at the other side entering household accounts in a book. The door of the room was shut. They were talking to each other, and on looking up from her paper after she had made some remark, she was startled at seeing that Mrs. Guppy was not there. There was a kind of haze about the ceiling as is sometimes the case after strong spiritual manifestations. She looked through the downstair rooms, and as she could not find

* Interpolated by me, G. H.

her, went and told Mr. Guppy, who was playing billiards with Mr. Hudson, a photographer who lives in the neighbourhood, and who has been helping Mr. Guppy in some amateur photography. Mr. Guppy said that 'No doubt the spirits had carried her off, but they would be sure to take care of her.' Miss Neyland then searched the rest of the house, and afterwards she, Mr. Guppy, and Mr. Hudson sat down to supper. Spirit raps then came upon the supper-table, and the spirits said that they had taken Mrs. Guppy to Mr. Herne's séance. Mr. Guppy asked whether Mrs. Guppy was quite safe? The spirits said 'Yes,' so shortly after supper he went to bed. . . .

"Miss Neyland was asked, 'What time it was when Mrs. Guppy was missed?' 'She did not know; it might have been about nine o'clock.' Mrs. Guppy here remarked that 'The clock downstairs was half an hour fast.' The whole party then went downstairs into the room from which Mrs. Guppy had been taken; her shoes were seen on the carpet in front of the fire, near her chair, and the clock in the room was half an hour fast.

"Mr. Guppy has since informed us that Mrs. Guppy came once or twice to him and Mr. Hudson in the course of the evening, suggesting that they should come and have supper; they replied that it was rather too early. He did not know what time it was when they last saw her.

"We regret to state that Mrs. Guppy was weak and unwell for several days after the occurrence of this manifestation of spirit power."

There were many dreary days during that summer (it was the year of the Franco-German war), and one morning it poured so heavily that I thought it would be almost useless to go to the gallery, but the advice I received was to go, and I did so. Within a few minutes after my arrival, a lady and gentleman made their appearance. They were Americans, and had only arrived in London a couple of days before, but they had resolved that *this* should be the object of their first sight-seeing, so they would not let the weather interfere with their plans, and we talked Spiritualism in full flood. Presently the husband said, looking after the lady as she crossed the room to examine a picture that had attracted her attention: "Ah! there goes the first medium in the world." "Oh! is it Kate Fox, then?" exclaimed I. "No, not Kate, but her sister Leah, Mrs. Underhill." Of course it proved a very interesting interview, which I should altogether have lost if I had been *left to myself*. A considerable number of Americans were among my visitors, and from some of them I heard that they had seen eulogistic notices of the exhibition in Californian and other papers, which had stirred up a curiosity and interest that were most fully gratified by what they saw, but I regret that the several publications never reached my hands.

A gentleman was one day coughing very severely, so I mentally enquired whether *we* should mesmerise him. The answer was in the affirmative, but that I was to wait a little while. He then sat down on the ottoman, when I quietly approached, and suggested that perhaps a few passes might do him good."—"Thank you. I have no doubt they will," was his answer. "I am a mesmerist myself, and know how effectual the remedy may prove." My few passes relieved him immediately, and led to considerable talk, in the course of which he learned who I was. I have often looked back to that incident as another proof of the restful security in which I dwell, for, except under advice, I could not have accosted an utter stranger with such an offer, but *they* knew that I might do it without appearing intrusive or receiving a scornful refusal. . . . I believe there were a good many military men who came more than once; for they are frequently skilful artists, and were therefore capable of appreciating such wonderful novelties in that line. Mr. Ward, a frame-maker, made a journey from Northampton for the express purpose of paying a visit to my gallery, and he, too, could estimate the charm of them from habitually living so much among works of art.

Mr. McNair arrived one morning rather late, having passed a night of anxiety and trouble, for his next-door neighbour, Mr. Corby, the printer of my catalogue, had been suddenly taken ill the evening before, when his alarmed wife and daughter sent in to request his aid, and he rushed off immediately for the medical man, and gave help in every way he could. I am not sure (at this distance of time), but I think his death took place before the morning, and Mr. McNair saw to everything for them, as they had no relatives within reach to do so. He had always been on most friendly terms, often spending quiet evenings with them.

One day a lady in deep weeds, came with her young daughter to the gallery, when they told me that they were Mrs. and Miss Corby, and that this was almost their first time of coming out at all, but they had felt that they would receive more comfort and consolation from me than from any one else in the world. They had studied the catalogue in its progress through the printing press, and had even from the first felt the grandeur of its revelations, but how much more did it speak to them when this sudden and heavy trial fell upon them! and what a blessing I felt it that I should thus have been the means to speak to their souls in readiness for the blow, and as it were, in the very moment beforehand. Of course it was a most touching interview, and remains a very sweet spot in the memory of that time.

I wrote as follows to the Editor of the *Medium*, September 4th.—" DEAR SIR,—I have received the following letter from a gentleman with whom I have not the pleasure of a personal acquaintance, but I willingly accede to the suggestion it contains, during the last two weeks of my exhibition (which will close September 22nd), and I therefore, with his permission, forward it for publication, and shall be obliged by your making at the same time the necessary alteration in the advertisement.

"I cannot but coincide in his observations as to the criticisms of the Press generally, which, with but a few exceptions, seem to have been written by those who only understand the management of the pen and not of the brush, whereas I had formerly really believed that the Art critics of the various papers must necessarily have a practical knowledge of the subject.—Believe me, yours, &c.

"GEORGIANA HOUGHTON."

"Will Miss Houghton allow a stranger and a Spiritualist to suggest a reduction in the charge for admission to her astonishing yet highly interesting exhibition,—say sixpence for the remainder of the season, if not too late? This might draw many and be serviceable to the cause. Being by profession an artist, can I venture to express my conviction that no artist (in the flesh), however eminent, can possibly compete (even materially) with the drawings in your wonderful and exquisite exhibition? As to the remarks of the Spiritual publications upon them, favourable they may be, yet they shew a want of knowledge of their characteristic manipulations, which are such as any mere human artist would in vain endeavour to accomplish.— Yours faithfully W. ELLIOTT.

"103 HAGGERSTON ROAD, *August* 30*th*, 1871."

I wrote thus to the Editor of the *Christian Spiritualist*, August 16th:—"DEAR SIR,—As my exhibition is on the eve of closing, I trust you will allow me in your paper to express my earnest hopes that the following idea given in the June number of the *Spiritual Magazine*, at the conclusion of the article on the subject, may lead to ultimate results:—

"'The Public Exhibition of Spirit Drawings is a bold experiment, we hope it may prove successful. Possibly it may prepare the way for one of a more extended kind, in which Spirit Drawings through many different mediums might be represented. These might be selected and arranged under the superintendence of a committee, chosen by the mediums themselves, and in whose judgment spiritualists generally would have confidence. We hope that those principally concerned will consider the suggestion.'

"A society might be formed, as among other artists, and I am sure the numerous varieties of style among drawing mediums would ensure a considerable amount of interest in such an exhibition, and if it could be held annually, there would be a great inducement for every medium to pursue the development of their separate phase of art, so that each year should evince a decided progress; and their spirit guides also would be anxious to do their utmost, and thus many new thoughts would find expression.

"I think the gallery I have had would be very suitable for the purpose, as it is well lighted, and the situation is good; perhaps too, the gentleman who has acted as my manager might undertake the secretaryship of the society, but all that would remain for after consideration.

"In my case it certainly has not been a financial success; indeed, I have been a considerable loser, but I do not think the result would be the same if it were taken up by a society of Spiritualists, for they would then each do their part by visiting the gallery themselves and inducing their friends to do so, whereas the larger proportion of my visitors have been those who know scarcely anything of the subject, but, generally speaking, they have been deeply interested in the spiritual teachings embodied in the catalogue, so that I have ample reason to believe that in the vital purpose of the exhibition, the success has been far beyond what I could have hoped. There have also been many who have been so much struck by the harmonies of colour and novelties of manipulation, that they have come again and again to study the drawings and learn some of the working details, the specialities of which have been best appreciated by artists, some of whom have resolved to try how far they could avail themselves of the new methods in their own work.

"We may also hope that each year will diminish the prejudice against Spiritualism, and now that I have ventured to break the ice, it would be a pity to allow the water to freeze over it again. Believe me, yours, &c.

"GEORGIANA HOUGHTON."

CHAPTER VIII.

EARLY in the last week I had another long visit from the Rev. Mr. Barrett, who had not been in London since just after the opening, and he went through the pictures again with redoubled pleasure, having as it were been digesting the thought of them through the intervening months. He was kindly anxious as to the pecuniary question, with reference to which my history was certainly a lamentable one, for I had not sold any picture since that single one on the day of the Private View. When in our round we had reached the Monograms, he astonished me exceedingly by saying that he would like me to do his: "Oh! but do you know it will be twenty guineas?" said I, for I half felt as if the proposition could not be a reality. "Indeed I do," was his reply, "and I also know that they have a value far beyond what any money can compensate for." Shortly after that, he took his leave, meaning to pay me another visit before the final closing, but he was then going somewhere into the country, to perform the marriage ceremony of a friend. He did come again on the very last day, Friday, September 22nd, when he gave me his address (of which I had known nothing), and agreed that on his next visit to London, he should come to my house to see his drawing commenced, writing to me beforehand, so that I might appoint the time. He would probably not come up for about another month, which would suit me very well, as I knew that I was to have a kind of season of rest before returning to my easel.

On that finishing day I had a great many visitors, nearly the last of whom was dear Mrs. Ramsay, who had called *here*, but finding I had not returned home, followed me to the gallery, for she wanted to consult me on a subject about which she was sympathetically anxious; namely, to take some step towards mitigating my very heavy loss, which, when all accounts were eventually balanced, amounted to £303. Her plan was to try what could be done by private subscription, but she would not enter upon such a step without my concurrence; saying it all to me with the most tender consideration so as not to wound my sensibilities. I could only with warm gratitude accept her kindly offices, but I told her that Mrs. Gregory had before suggested to me that I should make such an appeal to the Spiritualists, but I had told her that I *could not* do such a thing. It would however be very different if done *for me*, so I trusted that she would kindly explain the circumstances to Mrs. Gregory, which she undertook to do. I was most deeply touched by all her tender loving words, which seemed to add one more blessing to that dear gallery, and she then took her leave, promising to call upon me soon, when she should have formed a kind of plan.

Exactly at six o'clock, Mr. McNair and his assistants began the dismantling process of taking down the pictures, and removing the hinges by which they had been bound together, so that they should be ready for Mr. Spencer, who was to be there early the next morning to bring them all away. I watched their proceedings for a few short minutes with a regretful heart that such a season should ever have a close, and then I bade farewell to the gallery as *mine*.

Saturday morning came, and I went off to Mr. Spencer's in the Harrow Road, laden with my empty portfolios. He expected to reach home with the van at about eleven o'clock, and when I arrived, they were still unpacking, and carrying the pictures to an upstairs room, where we at once commenced operations, and, even as I had put every picture *in* to the frames, so now did I take them each *out*, not allowing any other hand to touch them. Mr. Spencer and his most trustworthy assistant drew out the nails, and removed the back-boards, then I took out the drawing, and deposited it in one of the portfolios. We went on steadily and methodically, but still it was a work of several hours, and I was desperately tired when it was all over, and I was at length packed into a cab with my treasures to bring them home just in time for my dinner, and, in classic phrase, I felt dead beat. But, after dinner, I had qualms of conscience, because of course my drawings had been put all irregularly into the portfolios just as they might chance to come, so I thought I would begin to do something towards an orderly arrangement, therefore in spite of previous fatigue I roused myself to work. With a silk handkerchief I carefully wiped each picture both front and back, so that no speck of dust should adhere to them, arranging them by degrees in their orderly sequence, and before I went to bed that night, I had the whole array of my drawings deposited according to their original system, and their portfolios in their old place, exactly as if they had never been disturbed! It was no light work to get through without the aid of any fingers but my own!

I seem now to have had rather a gay time, going out to dinners or to spend the day, in a manner quite unusual with me, but I suppose it was as a sort of interlude, before settling down into my customary habits of close work. Among other entries, I find that I called on Kate Fox, who had then just arrived in England, but she was unfortunately out. However, I had the pleasure, later on, of meeting her one evening at Mrs. T.'s, when she willingly let us have evidence of her power with reference to the raps, which came with wonderful strength and sound upon everything on which she laid her hand :—and she puzzled the sceptics by allowing them to stand on the other side of the closed door, to make themselves quite sure that she had no *mortal* confederate to bestow the blows.

I had been one day to see Mr. McNair, and brought away with me the two natty books in which all the entries had been made; and in the evening I was making out the abstract of results, the little parcel lying in my lap (for I had opened it, glanced through the books, and partly closed it again, not yet requiring them for my purpose), when a peculiar feeling that I have heard described, but have never experienced save on that one occasion, came over me. It was as if I were, just for a single instant, enveloped in a kind of haze or mist, and the thought flashed upon me, Something has happened! what can it be? I looked at once to the parcel in my lap, and one of the books was gone! I could scarcely believe the evidence of my own senses, and hunted over the floor and everywhere for the little volume, but all unavailingly. When seeking was proved to be in vain, I applied for information, and the explanation that came was most singular. One book, that which was left me, was the only one of real importance as to my accounts. The other was the one kept by the money-taker, and "they" tell me it had thus received the impress of *every* visitor to my gallery, and the book has been taken to my spirit home, as an evidence *against those who did not go*, and who, in a certain sense, *ought* to have done so. For instance, those who had visited me in my own home, and who have been known to say with reference to coming to my exhibition, "Oh! I have *seen* Miss Houghton's drawings," and it has not struck them that in return for my courtesy, they might have extended me a helping hand. During that time I did indeed realise the value of each separate shilling, especially when on some days so very few would come in. Once there was but one single shilling, and the *average of daily* expenses came to £4. I have to narrate these things because people are but too apt to forget that life is made up of small details, and while waiting to do *great* benefits to their friends, they overlook the tiny channel which they may help to fill.

On the 25th of October Mr. Barrett made his appearance soon after one o'clock, and we had a nice long afternoon together while the monogram grew; and he gave me many interesting details of his mesmeric experiences, the cures he had effected, and the revelations given through some of his clairvoyant patients; so the hours flew rapidly with us both. He had brought his cheque-book, and handed me the amount at once, lest, as he said, anything should happen to prevent a settlement. I was not to hurry myself over the drawing, especially if any other commission should fortunately come in, besides which, he hoped I would proceed with the symbolical one on which I had been at work on the home Wednesdays of my gallery time, and that I was going to endeavour to exhibit.

Mrs. Ramsay came to tell me that she had consulted with several friends, and they had drawn up the following paper. Her own real contribution was £10, but she thought it might seem like ostentation to head it with that sum, and might likewise deter others whose means were limited from giving the small amount that they might wish to do as a help for Spiritualism; so she then brought me £8, which she most kindly begged me to consider as a part of the sum in question, and subscribed her name for two guineas to the paper privately circulated.

"The friends of Miss Houghton having heard that she has been a great loser by the Exhibition of her 'Spirit Drawings' are very anxious to help her in paying for the Room in which the Pictures were exhibited. Miss Houghton hoped to pay the expenses of the Gallery, &c., with the Entrance-money—in this she has been disappointed—it is therefore earnestly requested that Spiritualists will kindly support the object for which this paper is circulated."

Dear, warm-hearted Mrs. Ramsay! her efforts were very successful, for the sum ultimately amounted to £50, including her own £10, and two £5 notes contributed by anxious friends, and I must here express my gratitude not only to her, but to all those whose names were inscribed on the list I received from her, which I of course copied into my own records.

I was indeed glad to see Mrs. T. on her return from the United States. Her first visit here was on the 29th of November, when she told me that on the previous evening she had been thinking much about me, and then she had heard the same message repeated to her over and over again. She enquired whether she was to mention it to me, and received an affirmative answer. It was, "Tell Miss

Houghton that she must not expect the fruit till the branches come:—the root is planted." The message referred to her vision of the *date*-tree on the 3rd of February.

I sent the following letter to the Editor of the *Spiritual Magazine* :—" DEAR SIR,—Will you allow me once more to revert to your suggestion for an extended Exhibition of Spirit Drawings, as I find there are many persons who look upon it as a very desirable step; and I have, therefore, endeavoured to gain all the information I could as to the method by which it may be accomplished.

"Mr. McNair, who has acted as manager and secretary for my exhibition, and has had much experience in similar arrangements, would be willing to undertake the working details, and he tells me that the usual plan is for a sum to be guaranteed sufficient to meet the working expenses, say by subscribers of £5 each; then there must be one gentleman who will undertake the duty of treasurer, and at least three or five who will finally form themselves into a hanging committee, and perhaps for that purpose some artists may kindly volunteer, who already have experience in that line. It will also be requisite to know if the pictures will be forthcoming, and whether the numerous artist mediums will kindly do their utmost to ensure a successful result, by contributing their works for the purpose. I shall be happy to send, perhaps, a dozen of mine, or more if they should be wished for, and I have also six or seven drawings by other mediums, which I shall have much pleasure in lending, and perhaps other Spiritualists may be able to do the same, even if not artists themselves.

"The more I have heard on the subject during the four months that my gallery has been open, the more convinced I am that a very interesting collection may be made, and I would still urge its being held annually, when we may hope that Spiritualists from all parts of the world will unite in contributing to it. Some persons may question the utility of spiritual art, or indeed art of any kind, whether poetry, painting or music, spiritual or unspiritual, but we need in this world something more than mere food and clothing;

and drawing is one method by which our invisible friends have illustrated many new thoughts. I remember that Mr. Varley, in the latter end of 1863, put some question with reference to comets (while he and I were sitting alone), and through my hand a drawing was executed, which I did not at all comprehend, but he said he did, and that it answered his question.

"May I ask such of your readers as are willing to co-operate in this undertaking to send a few lines to R. F. McNair, Esq., Egyptian Hall, Piccadilly, either as contributors of pictures, and how many, or as guarantors to the extent of £5 (which will not be required until 1872), and perhaps in the course of the next month some idea may be formed as to whether there is any probability of the plan being really brought to an issue, not forgetting the necessity for working volunteers as committee, &c.—Believe me, yours, &c. Georgiana Houghton."

My letter was written in October, and a month later, Mr. McNair sent the following to the Editor of the *Medium*:—
"Dear Sir,—Deeply interested as you are in Spiritualism, no doubt you will be anxious to know how the proposed exhibition of spirit-drawings is progressing. I regret to inform you that up to the present time I have only received the names of three guarantors of £5, and not a single offer of pictures or drawings; however, it may be from the failing that artists have of leaving everything to the eleventh hour. It may be wise in some instances to do so, but there is so very much preliminary work in getting up an exhibition, that it would be an act of kindness on the part of the proposed exhibitors to make known their intentions as early as possible. Thanking you for the very kind interest you evince in the project,—I am, dear Sir, yours truly,
"Robert F. McNair."

["We think the intelligence this letter contains is of a very hopeful kind, and no doubt sufficient discussion of the question will call forth the necessary amount of co-operation.—Ed. M."] Notwithstanding the hopeful view Mr. Burns took of the subject, it finally ended there; but I am still glad that I made all the enquiries on the subject that I did, for it may even be that years hence the project may again be mooted, and may meet with a more enthusiastic reception, and it may then be well to have some glimmering notions as to the needful steps to be taken.

On New Year's Day, 1872, I took my new drawing to the Dudley Gallery in the hope of its admission to that exhibition. It was a lovely symbolical Eye, but I had heeded the prejudices of my objectors, and had entitled it, "May It watch over you;" motto on an old seal. But alas! at the expiration of a week, I had to bring it away—and I was extremely amused to learn that one of the accusations against it was, that it had been executed by the planchette! It would indeed have been yet infinitely more marvellous if that amazing amount of exquisitely tinted and beautifully fine work could have been achieved by that little wooden instrument! surely whoever said it could never have seen a planchette, or they could not have uttered such an absurdity.

On Monday, January 15th, Mrs. T. came to see me, and in course of conversation mentioned that a day or two previously she had been saying something to her daughter about the American spirit photographs, wondering whether they would ever be produced in England. She was hardly aware of having lost consciousness, and not more than five minutes could have elapsed when the control passed off, and her daughter, who was much impressed, told her that she had been speaking about the photographs and had said that "they would come to Miss Houghton."

We sat talking, I holding her hands, in which almost from the first I felt little jerks, as if some influence were passing into her from me, but we were in such deep conversation that she did not perceive it for some time, but then she said, "What a strong power I feel coming from you, and it is now going through my hands and arms up to my head." I was then impressed to mesmerise her slightly, when she passed immediately under influence, and said:

H

"I see a sheaf of wheat very full of grain, it curls as it hangs down very much weighted. The kernels of wheat are all opening and shewing me what a large kernel of wheat is enclosed; they open like wings. The wheat is falling into a white vase; it seems to be thrown in, though I can't see what makes it go. They have filled the vase, and now they are scattering the rest, throwing it a long way on every side, or it seems to be blown as by wind; and now it is gone, and the kernels are all taken from the sheaf and it is fallen down. It stood before, like a person, and when first I saw it, it bowed and seemed to recognise people like a person." [Do they tell you anything about it?] "The seed that was scattered has taken root, and I see large fields about so high (from about nine to twelve inches), and when that wheat is fully matured, then the vase of wheat that is saved will be sown in distant places." [May you tell me what is meant by the wheat?] "It is the fruit of the work already accomplished by you. You have done what is typified by the scattering abroad of what remained after the measure was filled. Do not at present sow the same ground over, as what you have done has taken root, and will in due time yield abundantly. The best grains were selected for the vase, and those must be kept for special work. A soil is even now in preparation, and when conditions are just right you will be impressed to sow a little of this precious grain. The best grains were plucked from the sheaf first, and those lie at the bottom of the vase, which has an actual existence. . . . A change in the direction of your work is typified by the *laying aside* of the sheaf, which has done its work." [Was that the Gallery?] "And all that went before." [Is that as an answer to my question?] "The Gallery *and* all that went before. —Many individuals are willing to sow—few are content to wait for growth. In due time, according to your work and your faith, *you* shall reap." She then awoke with a slight start, and asked if she had been talking, so I read it over to her, but she only remembered having seen a sheaf of wheat, and some fields of poppies beyond it, and I often find that she has a glimmering recollection of the very commencement of her visions.

It was afterwards explained to me by my own instructors that while the grains of wheat typify the full rich Truths given by the spirit world, the poppy fields represent the large masses of gaudy weeds of which a considerable proportion of the spiritual manifestations and teachings consist, attracting the eyes and the senses without reaching or strengthening the inner life; but the wheat and the weeds both grow, and both do their work.

While copying this long-ago prophecy I am wonderfully struck by realizing how speedy was its fulfilment. At that time I of course thought that I should go on at least as steadily as ever with my artistic work, and yet, early in the March of that same year, an absolute "change in the direction of my work" took place; for the spirit photography arose, engrossing my time gradually more and more, so that the "sheaf" appeared to be utterly "laid aside." The history of that phase of my mediumship is given in a separate volume, so that I am only likely to allude to it now and then incidentally in this, but I may not omit all mention of it, or these Evenings at Home would fail to represent my full life since I began to receive in my innermost soul the certainty of God's daily and hourly supervision.

And about my Gallery! my beloved Exhibition! Heavy as was the loss, never for one moment have I experienced a shadow of regret for having undertaken it. I threw myself and my substance heart and soul into God's Treasury, and not one fraction would I wish to withdraw. People have sometimes said to me, "You did it at a wrong time; if you had waited a few years, the subject might have become more popular." . . . No, I did it at the *right* time, for then I *had* the money, which would have melted away in daily needs as the years sped on. What went into it was all and entirely *my own*. There could never since that very moment have been a possibility of my having the wherewithal to attempt so arduous an undertaking. Hard, and indeed I may say, sorely bitter, have since been my pecuniary trials, coming each year with gradually increasing pressure upon me, but still I have ever recognised that it has been God's Hand working His own purposes, and that if it should be His Will I should still be upheld through it all, whereas even if I had been let apparently to fall, I should never have doubted that it was for my ultimate best. Thanks be to His loving care, in my deepest straits, help has ever come, even if only sufficient to meet the day's absolute needs, but somehow the morrow's have afterwards been provided, and thus He has sustained His handmaiden, almost, as it has seemed, from hour to hour.

Before giving the account of my next séance, I must make an extract from the *Spiritualist* of March 15th. "The following strange story is taken from the *South London Courier* of March 2nd, 1872. It is printed in that journal in large type, and on the leading article page :— 'In the present day it is rare to hear of a *bona fide* ghost; but the following story is authenticated in a private circle of friends, to some relations of whom the ghost made his attentions particularly disagreeable. It is, of course, impossible to vouch for the exact truth of every detail of the ghostly story; but the facts are fully believed and certified by the circle above alluded to. The facts are as follows :—A few months ago a couple about to be married took a house in Berkeley Square, and upon concluding the transfer, &c., they were solemnly warned by the agent that a certain room in the house was haunted by a ghost. Of this they thought nothing, however, but, partly out of curiosity and partly out of necessity, the mother of the bride said she would have no fear to sleep in the haunted room, as she was at the house superintending the arrival of furniture, &c. The brave lady was not alone in the house at the time of her venture—there were two or three servants also sleeping there. At the usual time the lady retired. Nothing alarming was heard by the servants during the night; but the next morning, when they went to call up their mistress, they found her dead—in her bed—with open eyes wildly staring at the ceiling. A medical man, who was called in, could give no satisfactory cause of death, which seemed to have taken place through some violent shock to the brain and nerves. But the newly-married couple, much shocked as they were by the untimely death of their relative, were quite incredulous as to its having been caused by any supernatural agency, or that the supposed ghost had anything to do with it; nay, even the husband of the lady said that he would have no objection to sleep in the haunted room, and he at length prevailed upon his wife to consent to his making trial of the powers of the ghost. But the lady stipulated that she should sleep outside the room in the adjoining passage, and that she should have the protection of a fierce bull-dog and a pair of pistols, while two policemen were to be within call in another room. The gentleman retired to rest without any anxiety, the only precaution he took being the taking with him a pair of revolvers, in case of any emergency. He also agreed to ring a bell twice should the ghost appear, and he require the assistance of the police. About half-past twelve p.m. the anxious wife heard the bell ring, first rather rapidly, and then faintly and feebly. She flew into the haunted room and found her husband dead, with his eyes fixedly gazing at the ceiling. Such are the facts. We have not inserted a story merely to gratify our readers, but we have simply recounted the facts as they actually happened. We do not believe in ghosts, and we have no doubt that the whole mystery will ere long be cleared up; but until we hear the explanation, we cannot help thinking the story a very remarkable one.' We wrote to the editor of the *South London Courier*, Mr. J. E. Muddock, of 121 Fleet Street, and asked him for information which would enable us to enquire into and verify the strict accuracy of the narrative. Last Monday we received a reply, in which he stated :—' While not being able to give you names and particulars at present respecting the Berkeley Square ghost, I vouch for the accuracy of the facts as narrated, and you are at liberty to use my name, if you think proper.' In a subsequent letter, Mr. Muddock says:

—'I believe that in each case a coroner's inquest was held, and the verdict returned was *Died by the Visitation of God.*'"

I had a strong impression during the necessary furniture-movings in preparation for our séance on the 20th of April, that it would be the *last* held here of that character, or at least that a very long time might elapse ere I should have another, but I did not mention the feeling to the friend who was staying with me, for I scarcely liked putting it into words, and our chief conversation was on the subject of the spirit photography, which was beginning to engross me very completely. Our circle was composed of Mrs. Ramsay, Miss S., Mrs. T., Mrs. Guppy, Miss Leith, Miss Alice Leith, and myself.

After we had said The Lord's Prayer, we sat in quiet conversation, when Mrs T. said the very thing that had been running in my mind, and expressed the feeling that this was to be the last of *these* séances; and then I said how powerfully the same thought had been asserting itself all day. Mrs. Guppy exclaimed very much against the idea, unless indeed *she* were going to die, but she did not think that was likely. We could but leave the future to shew it forth in due course, knowing that it would be worked for the best. Mrs. T. saw and described Mrs. Ramsay's son, Jim, with his hand resting on his mother's shoulder, and on it was a ring, which she says will be photographed. The ring contained a deep blue stone, which sparkled as much as a diamond, and was a sapphire. On it were two letters which she had some difficulty in making out: they were J and I, and she added that the two letters united formed a third, and thus we understood that it made Jim all in one monogram ﬁ. Mrs. T. said that the stone signified *purity of life*, which knowledge would give comfort: she was in a kind of semi-trance at the time, but roused almost immediately.

I asked her how they were succeeding in their quest for a house (they were then living in the Rochester Road), and she said they had seen one in Oakley Square which had seemed in many respects suitable, but that she thought it was haunted, for both she and Mr. T. had heard rustling movements follow them as they looked through it. I observed that they seemed fated to dwell in haunted houses, for the one they had lived in before coming to the Rochester Road had been very terribly so. She thought it might lead to difficulties with the servants as had been the case at Dalston. Some one suggested that the children might be alarmed, but Mrs. T. said that they would have no fears, it was only about the servants that she had any misgivings. I said that perhaps the hauntings were harmless, and would not trouble any of them, to which we had assenting raps. The conversation then turned naturally to the fatal events in the haunted house in Berkeley Square, where two deaths followed one after the other.

It then became a question as to whether the persons had died of fright, but I said I believed they had been *murdered* by malignant spirits—" Yes " was rapped out, and we debated whether it would be possible to free the place from such influences, which I thought it would. Then I was asked if I would be willing to sleep in the room, but I said that in the abstract, I could not answer that question positively, but I could assert that I would do it willingly and fearlessly if I were told by my own guides to do so. To which some one added that the two persons of whom we had been speaking had trusted only to their *own* courage. There now came a request from our invisible friends for the alphabet. " Read a chapter." [Which?] "St Luke." I was then to say the numbers, and they rapped at *ten*. [The whole of it?] " No." The verses were to be from the 17th to the 24th, and while I was reading, the spirits assented strongly at different parts. "And the seventy returned again with joy, saying, Lord, even the devils are subject unto us through Thy name (raps). And He said unto them, I beheld Satan as lightning fall from heaven. Behold I give unto you power to tread on serpents and scorpions, and over all the power of the enemy (raps); and nothing shall by any means hurt you (very powerful raps). Notwithstanding in this rejoice not, that the spirits are subject unto you ; but rather rejoice, because your names are written in heaven (raps). In that hour Jesus rejoiced in spirit, and said, I thank Thee, O Father, Lord of heaven and earth, that Thou hast hid these things from the wise and prudent, and hast revealed them unto babes : even so, Father ; for so it seemed good in Thy sight. All things are delivered to me of my Father : and no man knoweth who the Son is but the Father; and who the Father is but the Son, and he to whom the Son will reveal Him (raps). And He turned Him unto His disciples, and said privately, Blessed are the eyes that see the things that ye see (strong raps) : for I tell you, that many prophets and kings have desired to see those things which ye see, and have not seen them (raps) ; and to hear those things which ye hear, and have not heard them " (raps).

We were all much struck with the marvellous adaptation of these verses to the various points of our discussion, and we are indeed thankful for the wondrous blessings vouchsafed to us.

After a time the alphabet was again asked for, and they spelt—" Miss,—walk." I named each person in rotation, and learnt that it was to be Miss Alice Leith : they then gave *four* raps to indicate the number of times she was to walk round the circle ; and when she had done it once, we were sprinkled with most delicious perfume, which seemed to fall more and more lavishly. Then flowers were showered upon us : —wallflowers and other scented blossoms, while to me were brought some everlasting flowers, which appeared like a reminder of my *first* birthday séance in this house, when my spirit friends crowned me with a wreath of everlasting flowers, and at a séance on Mamma's birthday of the same year, the same kind of flowers were given to me, with the message, " Faithful can only have everlastings."

Alice told us that she had been promised flower mediumship, if she would sit regularly every day, in the dark, for a month, which she has never yet been able to do, although she has tried several times, but some hindrance has always arisen before the completion of the stipulated time, so perhaps the walking round the circle may have been intended to assist in her development.

One of the tubes was taken up, and brought close to my cheek, so that I felt the breath of the spirit who spoke to me, saying that "orange blossom and acorn had been put into *her* hair: the first meant marriage, and the acorn prosperity." Alice then said that something had been put into her hair, and when we had the light, we found that it was a little bridal favour of orange blossom, oak leaves and an acorn. (On the 15th of May, Mrs. Leith and her daughters called, and Alice told me that she had received the interpretation of her bridal favour, for that she had been invited to be bridesmaid to Miss Chalmers, who was going to make a very wealthy marriage, thus fulfilling the symbol of the acorn as well as the orange blossom.)

We were then told to have supper, and that afterwards Mrs. T. would have a trance; so when we returned into this room, she and I seated ourselves at the little table as we do when we are alone, Mrs. Guppy being behind me, Mrs. Ramsay and Miss S. behind Mrs. T., and the two Miss Leiths at the larger table. I mesmerised her, and she soon passed under influence, and said: "He is shewing me a long road, and the stones along that road. One of the stones is broken. Each stone marks a year for each one."

There was a change of voice, and a prophecy was given as to a specified date; which prophecy gave me much anxiety. It was eventually fulfilled to the day and the very hour, although in quite a different manner to what I had understood, but the whole circumstances of that time have been most wonderful to look back upon. Turning to another, she said, . . . "Your stone is straight, apparently firm, but there is a defect near the top: with care the stone will last longer." . . .

Turning again to me, with a perception that I was troubled, she said: "Sometimes it is seen that a work begun, and well begun here, can be better finished or carried on by changing the conditions surrounding the human life. . . . There are few so faithful to their work, and so able to continue that work in this life as yourself, and it is permitted for you to know that you may expect a long life here. It will be a long life most usefully filled, but *as* the years pass on—as *many* years pass, and you come to this day (my birthday anniversary), there will come an hour when you will feel to say, 'I am lonely—those I most love wait for me—I am *willing* to work here, but, O Lord, if it be Thy Will, when my best work is finished, let me also depart, that I may be a little nearer those I most love.' In one sense you take up a Cross in living the long life before you, but as is the Cross behold the Crown!—The work you have at heart (the spirit-photographs) will be carried on, but not quite in the way you have thought. My ways are not your ways, saith the Lord, neither are My thoughts your thoughts:—man proposes, God disposes." I said, [I only wish to follow as I am taught.] "It is well, if you add also,—as you are *led*." [Oh! yes, that is what I mean.]

Taking the hand of Mrs. Ramsay, she continued: "There are those who watch and wait, and you feel sometimes so drawn to them that you say, 'If it be Thy Will, I am willing to go:'—you are drawn from *this* side too: when the grief is less bitter you say, 'I am willing to live or willing to die, The Lord strengthening me.' There are trials still to come, but as hitherto, you will be able to meet them. You are one called to die many times for those you love: be thankful for the strength given, and rejoice when *you* may take the Cross instead of those less able to bear it. You may send a message, a love thought, and it shall go far beyond that milestone where they wait, ready when you reach that place to lighten death for you.

"If it is desired, the hand of the medium may be taken, and something of the future may be, if best, revealed; but it is seldom wise to seek such knowledge: at long and very rare intervals it is sometimes permitted that a chosen few may look forward." I said that we did not wish to *seek* into anything, but were content to accept any revelation that might be voluntarily granted; to which she answered; "Not to seek, but patiently to do each duty as it comes, is true wisdom, that wisdom which is of The Lord."

Mrs. Guppy had felt ill, so she had quietly slipped away without disturbing the trance, she was therefore not present to hear the part addressed to her—or rather, of her: "Elizabeth, while seemingly more enwrapped in her daily life, will find the ties which hold her, and which in a measure confine her, being surely loosed; there has been a change within the year just passed, and in one that is to come, she may expect a similar change: she will be taken care of, and will pass safely through the trial: her stone is firm, and will scarcely be shaken.

"Each day, each hour, and each minute should be so lived as though that portion of time were the last for that life, and no *moment* in a true life should be wasted either in regrets or in anticipation of any possible future. There is plenty of time, for what is Eternity but Time lengthened? Think of Time as your most precious gift: *one moment* is worth all the jewels in the Queen's crown: think then of the value, if you can, of the days, weeks, and years, of a *long* and useful life: as those moments are spent, as those moments are *used*."—She was speaking very forcibly, and I think thus roused herself, for she suddenly awoke, and said, "I was seeing rows of pearls, and I thought they were being brought in."

Our marvellous séance was then brought to a close, and the forecasting of Mrs. T. and myself proved correct, for upwards of nine years have since elapsed, and I have never held another dark séance in this house, and indeed, all the thicknesses of curtains that I used for darkening the room, have latterly been applied to other purposes. The promise of the photographed monogram was also fulfilled.

CHAPTER IX.

I HAVE alluded in the preceding chapter to Mrs. T.'s Dalston experience in a haunted house, but of course, after all these years, she could only give me fragmentary reminiscences, but I told her yesterday evening that I was now going to give some details about it, and I then heard some particulars that were new to me.

The first occurrence took place one evening while she and Mr. T. were sitting in the garden, when there came a sound like the firing off of a pistol from one of the upper windows; when of course they both ran in great alarm into the house, to discover the perpetrator, thinking that thieves must have broken in, but all was quite quiet and undisturbed, and notwithstanding their rigorous search no one was to be found. . . . There would be noises as of scuffling and struggling, then a sound as of heavy footsteps of several persons coming down the stairs, as if dragging a something heavy down each stair, which she describes as resembling the thud of a thick roll of carpet. There was a flight of stairs above their bedroom as well as below, and down both flights the weight would be dragged. She has sometimes opened the bedroom door and looked out, but nothing was to be seen, and the sound was not stayed by her presence. . . . There would be like pistol-shots fired in their bedroom, when they *both* not only heard the detonation, but would see the flash. It would sometimes awaken them from their sleep, producing a quickening of the heart-beats with Mr. T., but she says she always awoke with a prayerful aspiration for the unhappy ones. There was one spirit whose clasp would come on her throat, even in the daytime, as if to throttle her, and—whatever she might be doing at the time—she would at once go to her room and kneel by the bedside in prayer that the perturbed soul might receive help, when the grasp would relax; and by degrees that manifestation entirely ceased. The struggling noises were the most heard in the children's room, and people have said,—Did she not fear to leave the children there lest harm should come to them,—and her answer would be that on the contrary she thought the atmosphere of those two innocent darlings would be likely to help and to soften the unhappy ones. On one occasion while they were all out of town, they engaged a man in whom they had confidence, to sleep in the house as a safeguard against burglars. He did it for two nights, but then declared that nothing should induce him to do so again; and the next night he slept under the verandah, so they had to come up to town and make fresh arrangements. Towards the latter part of their residence there they were almost undisturbed, and I believe that to have been the result of her prayerful intercessions. In the winter, and about Christmas time, the disturbances were generally louder and more frequent.

Just at this moment I seem to have the subject of hauntings brought strongly before me, for a day or two ago, Mr. Debenham kindly sent me the photograph mentioned in the following account, which I received about a year and a half ago from Sir Charles Isham.

Mr. Easton, the eminent miniature artist, when staying at Th—— Hall, July 1872, was disturbed next morning after arrival, by a woman in the room. He told her she had made a mistake, whereupon she soon left. On mentioning this, the owner, Mr. G., apologised for having inadvertently given him that room, as July was the month in which a similar figure had frequently been seen in the room, but that his apartment should be changed. Mr. Easton, with great credit to himself, begged to be allowed to remain, as not being a believer in ghosts, he wished to have an opportunity of observing a phenomenon of such transcendant interest. He was rewarded by the figure coming at three o'clock for seven nights, and remaining some twenty minutes, whilst he made a water-colour drawing, of about six or seven inches, for which he has been offered £50. Mr.

Easton tells me he could not copy it, but photographs are to be had of it at Debenham's, 158 Regent Street, price two shillings and sixpence. The figure appeared to have been having a desperate struggle: the room and foot of bed are correctly drawn. The mouth was not fixed.

Mr. G., the owner of the property, partly revealed a story of a member of the family, "The wicked Mrs. L———," who died in 1792, after confessing to the murder of the child heir, by which means she obtained the estate and ruined it. The room is now closed up, and the house is let. The form has been seen by about sixty persons, and as the servants would not enter the room, a person in the neighbourhood was engaged to make the bed.

In addition to the above narrative, I subjoin what was in Sir Charles's accompanying letter.

"Mr. Easton would not allow me to publish the account of the ghost, neither can I give the name of the place where it was seen. I enclose a slight statement which was submitted to him, and he pronounces it correct; except that I omitted to say that a lady who saw the picture, said it was the exact likeness of the picture of the person mentioned, in another house, which Mr. Easton had not seen."

The portrait is by no means prepossessing: the eyes are staring, and the mouth open; but all the more does it carry the tale of crime unrepented, even remorse being as yet unawakened, although eighty years had passed on since that sinful soul had quitted its tenement of flesh, and yet she is still bound to the scene of her iniquity, the possession of which was her temptation to commit it. Are there none of her own blood who may strive to arouse her soul to the knowledge of a Pitiful God to Whom such as even she may look for pardon and peace? But there are loving ones whom perhaps these words may touch, and to them the mission may be given to pour balm into her self-inflicted wounds.

The day before yesterday I received a letter from Miss Walker of Cleckheaton, containing another history of a haunted house that she had just heard from an old lady on a visit in the neighbourhood, who has scruples about her name being mentioned, so I will call her Mrs. A. "She lived within a few miles of Leeds, and frequently, before she had retired to rest, although she had herself fastened the gate, a horse would be heard coming at full speed right up to the house door; but nothing would be visible, and on examination, the gate was always found fast. . . . Noises were heard where there was nothing to account for them, and they generally seemed to proceed from a particular closet or cupboard. For a considerable time Mr. A. tried to persuade his wife that it was imagination, though he well knew that she was neither nervous nor superstitious, but he wished her not to mention the matter for fear of creating a rumour that the house was haunted. There was one night that she says she can never forget. On her bedroom door was a latch that was never left unfastened: the latch made a noise in being undone that was not to be mistaken for any other sound. They had retired for the night, when both husband and wife heard the latch undone, and a pair of not very light feet walk into the room and to the foot of the bed (hung with furniture-print, closely drawn), and Mrs. A. indistinctly saw what she thought was a man put the curtains *quite* back. Not having had a visit of that kind before, she thought only of robbers, and was quite sure that some one had got into the house. Mr. A. must have had some impression that the visitor was from the unseen source of the strange knocks, for he wished her to keep still, but she was sure thieves were in the house, and sprang out of bed, determined to save their belongings; but excepting the open door and the drawn-back curtain, all was exactly the same as they had left things on going to bed. 'Now,' said she to her husband, 'will you believe?' And he answered that he never would again doubt that the house was haunted. She said that during the last two years of her residing there, the sounds had ceased, and on my asking how she accounted for that, she told me that when she was quite a young woman, a gentleman had lived in that house who was in the habit of going to Leeds on horseback. One night the horse returned to the very spot where it was customary for his master to dismount, but no master was on his back. He had had too much to drink, and it was thought that he had fallen off his horse, for he was found in the road *dead.* Mrs. A. accounted for the cessation of the noises, by inferring that they had probably lasted until the period that *ought* to have been the term of his natural life."

It is the conclusion arrived at by Mrs. A., that has induced me to copy the narrative, for it was doubtless upon the calculation of dates that she founded her theory, which tallies with the information given to us in our séance of December 31st, 1870, where the suicide had been doomed to *walk* during the fulfilment of the number of years that he had cut off from the term apportioned to him:—and the lesson that this seems to teach is, that the drunkard had in like manner committed suicide by rendering himself incapable of taking care of his life! That fatal, fatal sin of drink! the curse of our fair land! Mighty efforts are being made to eradicate it; may we all work towards that end, each giving the little bit of help in the way of strengthening counsel that may come in our power. "A word spoken in due season, how good is it."

On the 1st of April, I once more took a pair of drawings to the Royal Academy, with the hope of their acceptance for exhibition. In addition to the "May It watch over you," I now had the lovely monogram in iridescent tints of Mr. Barrett, with full permission to mention his name in connexion with it. But disappointment again ensued, and although I know that such a result *must* be what was best for me, it has only been in the looking back to those days that the fact has been *shewn* to me, for the spirit photography gradually in various ways occupied the whole of my time; and had I obtained commissions for pictures, either the one phase or the other of my work, or perhaps both, might have suffered by the divided attention.

In one of the learned criticisms on my own Exhibition occurs the following paragraph, which rather amused me at the time, because the *non-mention* of a fact is certainly no proof of its *non*-existence, besides which *I have* heard of similar *personal* flowers having been drawn by mediums, as well as seen and described by clairvoyants, and it may be that if *all* literature had been *read*, it might have been met with, as in my succeeding quotation. "There is a possibility that Miss Houghton accepts literally, teachings intended to be symbolical. . . . In *all* (?) the English and American literature of Spiritualism there is no corroborative testimony as to the objective reality of flowers such as Miss Houghton believes her drawings to represent, but if the drawings and their explanations be regarded as symbolical . . . as others would doubtless define them to be, there is no doubt that the teachings are most of them very pure and good." Now, about a twelvemonth ago I was reading "Isis Unveiled," where Madame Blavatsky (vol. i. page 601) narrates a Chinese legend from Schott's "Essay on Buddhism in China and Upper Asia:" and in a foot-note refers to my Exhibition thus, "Colonel Yule makes a remark in relation to the above Chinese mysticism which for its noble fairness we quote most willingly :—'In 1871,' he says, 'I saw in Bond Street an exhibition of the (so-called) *spirit* drawings, *i.e.*, drawings executed by a *medium* under extraneous and invisible guidance. A number of these extraordinary productions (for extraordinary they were undoubtedly) professed to represent the "Spiritual Flowers" of such and such persons, and the explanation of these as presented in the catalogue was in substance exactly that given in the text. It is highly improbable that the artist had any cognizance of Schott's Essays, and the coincidence was certainly very striking.'" (The Book of Ser Marco Polo, vol. i. p. 444.)

In the course of the photographic work, I had some correspondence with an authoress of popular literature, and I must quote a fragment from one of her letters. "Thank you very much for so kindly sending me the catalogue, which I shall value much more than the one I have treasured ever since that memorable visit to Bond Street in 1871. I believe that was the first day I was impressed with the conviction that there was more in Spiritualism than the light foam which shewed the direction of the stream. The drawings filled me with a vague, mysterious feeling of wonderment that so many distinct drawings could have been produced without any apparent evidence of design, and which seemed something altogether beyond the conception of any mere mortal hand and brain. . . . I am very anxious to go to London for many reasons, and one of the most prominent, that I may become personally acquainted with you." Her visit to the gallery had been on a Wednesday.

When Mrs. T. came to see me on the 29th of November, immediately after her return from America, where she had been during almost the whole of my Exhibition, having started within a fortnight after the opening, she exclaimed, "Your home feels *just* the same; I feel no kind of change in it, and I had thought there would have been a great deal, as you have been all this time so prominently before the world, mixing so much with strangers, but it feels as if neither you nor your pictures had ever stirred from here."

I mention this now, because to-day (April 3rd, 1872), when I have been for a month all but a day engaged in this new phase of spirit-photography, and had on Thursday last received the wonderful manifestations of the Palm and the Cross (see "Chronicles," page 12), her exclamation soon after entering the room, was, "Oh! what a difference I feel in you: it is as if you were much fuller of life in some way." I said, "Well, you see, I have felt in a great state of excitement respecting this new work." She rejoined, "But I did not feel it in this way when I came to you on the very next day after the first photographs had been taken, when the excitement must have been newer. I now feel when I approach and when I touch you, as if you had gone off into a fresh life,—more forth into the world, and as though you could not in the future be to individuals as you have been hitherto, but as if you belonged to *all*——It is a curious feeling, as if you might be in a large spacious hall or something, and that your presence filled it." I here reminded her of Mr. Spear's prophecy of my being called to an *outside* work after the expiration of my twelve years of mediumship, but she had quite thought that had alluded to the Exhibition; but that had taken place in the *course* of the twelfth year, not after its termination.

There was a very pleasant gathering at the Cannon Street Hotel on the 29th of April for the presentation of a testimonial to Mr. and Mrs. Everitt for their exertions in the cause of Spiritualism, when I am happy to say we mustered in strong force; for indeed they are true and earnest workers in the highest sense, for not only are the phenomena manifested through Mrs. Everitt's mediumship both striking and various, but the religious tone pervading the whole renders them yet more valuable, and that is due to their own harmonious atmosphere which can thus be inter-penetrated by the higher influences. The tokens of remembrance and appreciation took form as a pianoforte and a sewing machine, which will do good service both for harmony and industry in the new suburban home to which they are about to remove, but I rejoice that the distance will not be such as to preclude them from occasionally receiving friends and enquirers as they have been in the habit of doing in the past, so that they may still be allowed the privilege of occasional admission to their interesting séances.

In the May number of the *Christian Spiritualist* was a letter from Mr. Whiting, from which I will extract a few paragraphs. . . . " Spiritualism has been tested in thousands of homes in the United Kingdom, and to earnest patient enquirers it has been clearly demonstrated to be the greatest truth of the 19th century. These investigators are of all classes of society and people holding extremely opposite views upon religious subjects; but a large number are known as CHRISTIAN *Spiritualists.* This is not surprising when we remember that the Bible is the Christian's book, and that it contains more wonderful spiritual phenomena than any other book. I think the time has arrived for *Christian* Spiritualists to come forward and maintain their right position, believing as they do that Spiritualism (as they know it) is a fact; and not opposed to other great truths they publicly acknowledge. I think it would be a very pleasant gathering if those holding the principles of the Christian Spiritualist were to meet in London, in the course of a short time, at a suitable time and place to be hereafter settled; we should then be able to talk over this interesting and comprehensive subject. . . . I shall be glad to receive communications from those who feel interested in the matter, so that something definite may be done for future arrangements.—I am yours, &c.

"H. G. WHITING.

"224 KENTISH TOWN ROAD."

Of course I wrote immediately to say that I quite concurred in his views, and should have much pleasure in attending any such meeting if his plan were carried out, and in reply, he said :—" MY DEAR MADAM,—I was quite sure I should have a letter from you, knowing the zeal you have in the cause of Christian Spiritualism. The sacrifice you have made in reference to your Exhibition I understand is great, but I have reason to know that you have scattered Truth. I have a friend at St. John's Wood College (Dr. R.), and he told me that you gave him some valuable ideas in reference to Spiritualism, and doubtless you have sown good seed. Pioneers are always sufferers in Earthly things, and they sink a capital of this World's goods, to realize both capital and interest in the next." I regret to say that his suggestion received scarcely any response, so that no such meeting ever took place, but perhaps the day may yet come for its fulfilment.

In the earlier sittings for my spirit photographs, I had been assisted by Mrs. Guppy's mediumship in addition to Mr. Hudson's department of it; but on the 9th of May, he and I were alone, and obtained success, so now it was to take with me a professional form, and on the 16th, dear Mrs. T. was to have a séance with me in that capacity, (when from her I received my first fee), and I find the following entry in my note book, and give it in full, although there have been a few previous words alluding to my sense of God's Care, but as that is ever rising in my soul, I cannot resist giving it the additional expression.

I scarcely slept at all on the Wednesday night before the eventful Thursday, being kept awake by my spirit friends, who told me they were preparing me for my next day's work: (was it like the vigil of the Knight of old before obtaining his spurs?) It was half-past three ere I closed my eyes, to open them again within an hour, and I was told that I should gradually have very much to do, but that an ample supply of strength would be granted to me. I now see the Wisdom that prevented my pictures from being hung, for if they had brought commissions to me, I should have lived in a constant state of anxiety, because this photography already keeps me so much from my easel, for in addition to the work itself, it entails such an enormous amount of writing; for instance, I was occupied until nearly five o'clock to-day in considering and inscribing the condensed explanations in very small writing on the backs of those photographs I had brought home with me yesterday, and in writing two letters with some additional details, to enclose four of them which had been previously ordered; besides which, I am very particular, and find many pin-holes, &c., in the photographs, which want touching up, even after Miss Hudson has done her part: I would fain make them as perfect as they can be.

On one of our tête-à-tête Friday séances here, after I had mesmerised Mrs. T. and she had passed under influence, she said, "I see a great many rays of yellow light, coming up from a central point, as they do in your drawings. Some of them go straight up, and some are curved, but they are all of a yellow colour.

"I am looking at some foliage,—beautiful shades of green —I think it must be a garden:—there are trees twined together—they are planted in two rows, so as to form a walk between them, and then they join above, over the walk.—I see a young man walking in this path—in an officer's dress. He has got on one of those large, curious cocked hats, fastened up at one side. I thought he had light hair, but I see it is sprinkled with grey; he is older than he looked at first: he has a large nose.—I see such a beautiful young girl:—she has come down some steps, and has given a flower to this gentleman, and he kisses it. From the flower go those lines, and they go over his face, and seem to brighten it; they are typical of her influence over him, which is most beautiful." [Can you learn his name?] "He points to his hand: I think he means that he will try to write his name." [Through you?] "Yes." I then placed paper and pencil before her; again mesmerising her for some little time, until she took up the pencil, and with considerable difficulty wrote eight letters, all united, of which we could not make out the meaning; but then joined to them, were the letters Môtee, which shewed me that I had not been mistaken in thinking that the vision was of General Ramsay and his daughter Môtee. In another hand was then written the word Charles, and finally some letters of which I have only just (on the following evening) elucidated the meaning, for they are A r e d l—which I find out is Pearl (the English for the Indian word Môtee), the letters having been scattered about, and the P placed upside-down, and curiously formed. Mrs. T., in her normal state, said, "She came down with her left side towards me, and gave the flower with her right hand; it was a rose. She wore blue, and her dress was not high in front, and with such lovely lace! it was so clear, and seemed almost like her flesh. Her face was quite radiant."

I shewed her the photographs, and she recógnised both the General and Môtee; but of the latter she said, "Here, in the photograph, she looks quite like an angel, but there is a timid shrinkingness about her. But as I *saw* her, every feature was so animated and radiant, and her whole figure seemed in buoyant motion. Her face in spirit life expressed such an assuredness of the blessed happiness around her that it was perfectly beaming."

I again mesmerised her, and then under influence, she

made a movement of the hand, as if desirous of writing, so I again gave her paper and pencil, and Môtee wrote the following, "I will try to do a direct drawing for Mamma, if your spirit artist will help." [Do you mean Sir Peter Lely?] "Yes." [Does he see you?] "I think so." [Do you see him?] "Yes."

A clergyman from Norwich came in before she had quite finished writing the above, which did not, however, disturb her, but she awoke when the message was concluded. He told me that his wife, who had been an invalid for about a year, had lately passed into spirit life. This, of course, changed the character of our séance, so that Môtee could not then make her attempt, and our sittings for direct work were shortly afterwards suspended, still I hope the day may yet come when Môtee may fulfil her desire.

May 19th. To-day, *Whitsunday*, my Dove has laid the first of her fourth pair of eggs for this year. I record it, because it is the fourth anniversary of her being in my possession. If she had been as regular to the day as for the other three pairs, she would have laid this one last Tuesday, but she seems to have *waited* until this day. She has been curious in her laying, for in the year 1870, when I was making all sorts of enquiries as to the customs about Easter Eggs, she laid one on Easter Sunday, quite out of all course of nature, for she had laid one on the evening of April 7th, and the second on the morning of April 9th (thirty-six hours between is her regular time), and then she laid *one* on Easter Sunday morning, April 17th (to which she laid *no* companion), when she would, naturally, be presumed to be sitting!! That has been the *only* instance of that kind of irregularity in her egg-laying. I am glad to find that I had recorded these peculiar eccentricities of hers, for although I had remembered them, I should not have felt quite certain of giving them with perfect exactitude.

Long ago, Mrs. Cooper kindly lent me Dr. Eadie's "Life of John Kitto, D.D., F.S.A.," from which I copied the following vision (page 74); not only from the marvel of its exact fulfilment, but because of the lesson inculcated towards the close, that prophecy is *not* identical with predestination, for that circumstances *may* arise to change the current of events. As we are warned in the past, so is the teaching even for the present time. 1 Cor. xiii. 8, 9: " But whether there be prophecies, they shall fail; whether there be tongues, they shall cease; whether there be knowledge, it shall vanish away. For we know in part, and we prophesy in part."

"John Kitto, born December 4th, 1804. The following entry is found in the workhouse minutes, Plymouth :—'July 17th, 1823. John Kitto discharged. . . . Taken out under the patronage of the literati of the town.' . . . The following *dream*, as he calls it, and which, though probably a waking reverie, is very remarkable as a true presentiment, a *correct* delineation of his subsequent career. It is dated three days prior to his discharge, and occurs in a letter to Mr. Tracy :—

"Methought (this is the established language of dreamers, I believe) I was exactly in the same situation in which I really was before I slept, and indulging in the same reflections, when there suddenly appeared before me a being of more than mortal beauty. He was taller than the sons of men, and his eyes beamed with celestial fire; a robe of azure hue, and far richer than the finest silk, enfolded his form, a starry zone of glittering gems encircled his waist, and in his hand he bore a rod of silver.

"He touched me with his rod, and gently bending over me, he said, 'Child of mortality, I am the Angel Zared, and am sent to teach thee wisdom. Every man on his outset in life proposes to himself something as the end and reward of his labours, his wishes, and his hopes; some are ambitious of honour, some of glory, and some of riches. Of what art thou ambitious, and what are the highest objects of thy earthly hopes?'

"I was astonished at the visit and the words of the angel, and replied not to his demand.

"'Thou canst not readily find, O child of earth, words to express the scenes which thy fancy has drawn. It matters not; I know thy wishes, and will give you the possession of the state that is the highest of which thou art ambitious.'

"He touched me with his rod, and my form expanded into manhood; again he touched, and then left me. On looking around me, I found myself seated in a room, two of the walls of which were entirely concealed by books, of which I felt myself conscious of being the owner. On the table lay letters addressed to me from distant parts of the Island, from the Continent, and from the New World: and conspicuously on the chimney-piece were several volumes, of which I was conscious that I was the author, and was also sensible that the house wherein I was, was mine, and all that was in it. I went forth into the street. Ridicule no longer pointed her finger at me; many whom I met appeared to know and esteem me, and I felt conscious that I possessed many sincere and disinterested friends. I met a blind fiddler, and placing my hand instinctively in my pocket, I found that it lacked not money. I returned, and exclaimed as I took Cæsar's Commentaries, in their original language, from the shelf, 'Now at last I am happy!' but before I had concluded the word, the Angel Zared again appeared before me, and touching me with his silver rod, restored me to the state in which he found me.

"I felt a momentary sensation of disappointment and regret at the transition, till the angel spoke to me, and said:—

"'Listen to my words, O child of mortality, while I withdraw, as far as I am permitted, the veil of thy future destiny. Thou hast been afflicted with misfortune, and taught in the school of adversity. Think not that He Who made thee and me also, regards with displeasure those whom He purifies by sorrows, or that those are His peculiar favourites who are permitted by Him to enjoy the good things of this world. Whenever thou findest thyself inclined to murmur at the dispensation of Providence, recollect that others, greater, better, and wiser than thou art, have suffered also—have suffered more than thou hast, or ever wilt suffer.

"'The time approaches when thou shalt attract the notice of thy superiors, who shall place within thy reach the means of acquiring that knowledge for which thou thirstest. They will transplant thee into a soil fit for thee, and if thou attendest well to the cultivation of thy intellectual and moral faculties, thou mayest perhaps become a permanent occupant of a station like that which I have permitted thee to enjoy for a moment. I say, *perhaps*, for only He knows, in Whose breast is hid the fate of worlds, whether thou art to live beyond the day on which I visit thee; but of this I am permitted to assure thee, that the period of thy sojourn on earth, will not be, at the furthest, very many years.*

"'Be not, O son of earth, dejected if thou again meetest with disappointments and misfortunes; neither suffer prosperity too highly to elate thee; and in every situation, and in every moment of thy life, remember that thou art mortal, and that there is a God and a hereafter. So live, that thou mayest not fear death, at whatever moment he may approach thee; and if thus thou livest, thou wilt have lived indeed.'— Zared perhaps would have spoken longer, but a book falling from the shelf upon my head, I awoke, and as honest John Bunyan says, behold it was a dream!"

"One might say to such a wondrous dreamer—

> "'Thy life lies spread before thee as a sheet
> Of music, written by some gifted hand,
> Unsounded yet: to longing, listening hearts
> Translate its small mysterious silent notes
> Into full thrilling chords of life and peace.'"

I ought, at the same time, to have made a few extracts as to John Kitto himself, but I had no thought of ever making use of the vision; but I know that he was either a mason or a bricklayer, and fell from a scaffolding, receiving an injury that rendered him stone-deaf. He must have had

* He died, November 25th, 1854, aged 50.

a predisposition for study, that may have been indulged in the hospital. But a boy of nineteen in that class of life, would not have been likely to have had such a "waking reverie;" still less would he have ventured to reveal it, so that I consider the remark absolutely puerile.

CHAPTER X.

MUCH as I have learned to value the *Spiritual Magazine* as a *répertoire* of every phase of phenomena connected with our grand subject, we had not taken it in from the beginning; for in fact it seemed that I was to learn about it only from the spirits themselves, instead of perhaps being biassed by teachings that would emanate from other sources: so that it was not until towards the latter end of 1865 that we ordered it from the stationer in our then neighbourhood; telling him that we would take it from the commencement of the year. When we had duly perused those numbers, Mamma suggested that we had better have the complete set from the beginning, and we had no misgiving as to there being any difficulty in obtaining them. But there were many numbers quite out of print—not in any regular order, but here and there odd ones, to the extent of a dozen and a half,—which I then made every effort to obtain from private sources; giving my list likewise to Mr. Burns, and saying that I would willingly pay double their price if he could get them for me in any way. I used to carry my list in my purse, so as to take advantage of every available opportunity, and thus, during the Harley Street evenings, I did my pleadings to Miss Deekens, who was able to supply me with some of the missing pamphlets, from those in their possession, for Mr. Coleman always had some extra numbers of those containing his own very interesting articles on American Spiritualism. Gradually, by hook or by crook, I had made them so far right that there remained but *two* wanting, and those I had long given up as utterly unobtainable, having also made up my mind some day to borrow them from my cousin Mrs. Pearson (who had taken them in from the very first), and absolutely to *copy* them, as neatly and orderly as I could, into the size to match the others; so that if a time should ever come when I could have them bound, there should be no deficiency in the real contents. I had had permission from my invisible friends to do so, but they always *postponed* the labour when I suggested commencing operations. On the 6th of June 1873, I spent a charming day at Betchworth, with Mr. and Mrs. Bennett, in the course of which I mentioned my difficulty as to the magazines, and Mr. Bennett made a note of the two that were missing, for he knew there were *some* among the books of his father (lately deceased), and perhaps he might there find my two defaulters. On the following Wednesday, he and his sister-in-law, Miss Hunt, did me the pleasure of coming to see me and my drawings; and he had not been long here when, from the recesses of that most useful bag of his, he drew forth the much longed-for magazines. I was busily engaged shewing the drawings, when a "word" came to me to say to Mr. Bennett, which was—"*I am not* to offer to pay you for these magazines, but am to beg your acceptance of a couple of photographs in exchange." "There, Annie," said he, turning laughingly to his sister, "it is quite clear that *some one* hears us wherever we may be." Then explanatorily to me, "I said at breakfast time this morning—If Miss Houghton offers to *pay* me for those small books, I won't take the money, but I should be very willing to accept a photograph if she will give me one." It amused us all very much; for the inbreathing had been so *positive* to me, and had come while I was thinking more about the drawings I was shewing to them than anything else; and it was a couple of photographs from those that he selected.

The evening before my Betchworth visit (which was on a Friday), as I parted with Mrs. Guppy I said, "What will have happened before we meet again?" "Oh!" she exclaimed, "that comes like a prophecy—I hope it will not be anything bad." To my surprise, a something *had* happened, that was bad enough, but might have been even worse; for the window curtain in her bedroom had caught fire, and almost everything in the room was destroyed.

Fortunately she was at home, and has much presence of mind, as well as real working capacity, so that she saved all that she could, and was a good general, in directing the labours of others; thus the fire was prevented from spreading beyond that room, although much damage was done by the water, and the place did indeed seem a wreck when I got there, the misfortune having only occurred on the previous evening. But she cautioned me against prophesying any more.

I sent the following to the *Christian Spiritualist.*

An extraordinary phenomenal séance took place this afternoon, August 14th, at Mrs. Guppy's, the circumstances of which I will narrate as briefly as I can. The room having been thoroughly darkened, we entered it about five o'clock, and having locked the door, all took our seats round the uncovered table, from which everything had been previously removed. There were present, the Countess Poulett, Mr. and Mrs. Guppy, Mrs. Fisher, Miss Mann, Mr. Traill Taylor, and myself. "Get Bible," was spelt out, which direction was obeyed, but we found that the appointed portion was not intended to be read yet, so it was placed on a side table. "Rub feet," was the next message, while at the same time the table was moved round by the spirits with a backwards and forwards sort of movement for the purpose of gaining physical power which would be increased by the action of our feet on the carpet. We soon felt something like a cloth being placed on the table, then there was a clatter as of plates, knives, spoons, &c., which seemed to come from a corner of the room as if invisible waiters were preparing to attend upon us; then we heard and felt that things were being placed upon the table, and each found a plate given to them. Then a knife was carefully placed under my right hand, and a plate of butter in the left, a clattering noise going on all the time. Suddenly Mr. Taylor exclaimed, "Oh! here is a hot kettle before me,"—when Mrs. Guppy instantly struck a light, fearing lest any one should be hurt, but she might have felt perfect confidence, as our circle was a completely harmonious one.

On the table were six cups and saucers, tea-spoons, a small plate, and a table napkin for each of us; a jug of milk, an empty jug, one of her flower jars filled with sugar, a plate full of black grapes, a loaf, two tea-cakes, a large tea-pot (a recent purchase of Mr. Guppy's) in which was a goodly supply of tea, as yet quite dry, and there really was the kettle of boiling water in front of Mr. Taylor, but the spirits had been so considerate as to put a cork into the spout, to avoid the possibility of an accident. Mrs. Guppy withdrew it, and made the tea with the contents. While it was brewing, we examined the various articles that had been brought; the plates, jugs, knives, &c., were Mrs. Guppy's own, but the cups and saucers were strangers, and Mr. Taylor thought they resembled his set (at Wood Green), but he could not be quite sure, as he is accustomed to use a large one; however, he studied them closely, so as to ascertain on his return home. We enjoyed our most excellent tea (to the extent of twelve cups), and learned on questioning the spirits that it was out of a packet that Mr. Taylor had presented to Mrs. Guppy the evening before. When we had finished our meal, we put all the things in the middle of the table, so as to remove the cloth sufficiently to place our hands again on the uncovered part, and extinguished the light. We then again heard a clatter with the cups and saucers, and after a minute or so had elapsed, we were told to strike a light, and found that *they* had vanished, Mrs. Guppy's *own* crockery being still left on the table, and were answered in the affirmative when we asked whether they had been taken back to the place from whence they had been brought. Mrs. Fisher felt busy fingers meddling with her comb, which was withdrawn from her head, then the brooch was taken out of her dress. Katie's voice was heard in gentle whisper, but we could only distinguish such words as yes and no, the power having been used for the other class of manifestation.

We were then directed to have a light, and Mrs. Guppy again gave me the Bible, when I was guided to turn over the pages to the required part (and at this moment in taking up my own Bible to seek for the passage, it opened at the very place), and my finger was pointed to Isaiah xxix. 9 to 18: "Stay yourselves, and wonder; cry ye out and cry; they are drunken, but not with wine; they stagger, but not with strong drink. For the Lord hath poured out upon you the spirit of deep sleep, and hath closed your eyes: the prophets and your rulers, the seers hath he covered. And the vision of all has become unto you as the words of a book that is sealed, which men deliver to one that is learned, saying, Read this, I pray thee: and he saith, I cannot; for it is sealed: and the book is delivered to him that is not learned, saying, Read this, I pray thee: and he saith, I am not learned. Wherefore the Lord said, Forasmuch as this people draw near me with their mouth, and with their lips do honour me, but have removed their heart far from me, and their fear toward me is taught by the precept of men: therefore, behold, I will proceed to do a marvellous work among this people, even a marvellous work and a wonder: for the wisdom of their wise men shall perish, and the understanding of their prudent men shall be hid." When I had finished reading, our spirit friends wished us "Good-bye."

Mrs. Fisher's comb had been placed in Mrs. Guppy's hair, but the brooch was nowhere to be seen, and she was troubled about it, having been her brother's gift, and the invisibles did not promise to return it. However, we all adjourned to the next room, where we were in full daylight, and suddenly something struck her cheek, and fell to the ground, which proved to be the missing brooch.

Mrs. Guppy afterwards gave me the small cork that had been so protectingly employed (having been taken by the spirits from an empty medicine bottle), for me to keep as a memorial of the séance, and I still preserve it among my various relics.

What was called the Annual National Conference of Spiritualists was held in Liverpool on the 5th, 6th, and 7th of August 1873, and their consultations eventuated in the formation of an association which has existed ever since, and which I trust may grow with ever-increasing strength. The name bestowed upon it was the British National Association of Spiritualists, about which there have been many carpings, but it is difficult in such matters to please everybody. Some think it is much too assumptive; but it does not mean one atom more than was hoped for it by its founders, some of whom were warmly earnest men, with their hearts set upon doing their very utmost for the cause they loved, and they hoped that the whole body of Spiritualists in England would join their ranks. Of course there were others with mixed motives, who thought they might obtain personal advantages and influence by belonging to it. Our energetic friends Mr. and Mrs. Everitt gave themselves into it with fervour, and their example would sway many, as they have a numerous circle of friends in different parts of the country, and Mr. Everitt was appointed President *pro tem.* London of course must be the seat of the Society, and it was another effort to form a kind of nucleus for the working out of Spiritualism in every form; such as the Spiritual Lyceum of Mr. Cooper, to which both books and spirit-drawings had been contributed; but that work died out for want of support; and when afterwards the Spiritual Atheneum in Sloane Street was started for the purpose of giving Mr. Home the secretaryship, Mr. Cooper forwarded to it the books that had been presented for public use, and I believe there was a very fair library, but what became of them when Mr. Home's misfortune overtook him, I know not, for that society collapsed; and when afterwards a new attempt in the same direction was made by Mr. and Mrs. Spear and their friends, in the endeavour to establish a kind of central focus in Bryanston Street, Mr. Cooper (the original trustee, as it were, of the books) authorised them to gather together that collection of literature, all vestiges of it seemed to have disappeared. These various undertakings had each struggled on for a short time, but they had been principally the work of *individuals*, whereas this new one became at once a considerable knot, and some influential people gradually joined this more inclusive body,

K

but for a time I declined doing so, although I had been solicited from several quarters; but it was because No, was the advice then given to me.

On the 16th of August I had a visit from Mrs. Ramsay, Mrs. Gregory, and Mr. Noyes, to ask me to go that evening to a séance at Mrs. Gregory's, as they were desirous of having a series of regular weekly sittings without the presence of any public medium, and they wanted me to form one of the circle, which I agreed to do. After they had left, I was told that there would not that evening be a manifestation of any kind, which proved correct; but it was a very pleasant, harmonious circle, and we had, at any rate, conversation in accordance with what we were seeking. On the following Saturday we had the most exquisite lights I have ever seen. They had the pure whiteness of alabaster, and looked almost as semi-transparently solid. We saw nine of them in the course of the evening of different sizes, more or less elongated, but I should think the largest was about nine inches in height, and from three to four inches in width, rounded off at the top and bottom, and giving one the idea of roundness in its substance. One or two were, I think, nearly circular, but I write only from memory, as my entry is simply, "Mrs. Gregory : séance, nine lights." But I believe we never saw those lights except on that one occasion.

On Sunday the 31st, I went to Mrs. T.'s in the afternoon, to accompany her in the evening to the Cavendish Rooms, where the Rev. F. W. Monck, a Baptist minister from the neighbourhood of Bristol, was to give some of his wonderful experiences, having been rapidly developed into very extraordinary mediumship; many circumstances of which I had read in the *Christian Spiritualist*. He has since become more generally known under the title of Dr., conferred upon him by some American college.

One evening in July I had a visit from Mr. W., an artist friend whose acquaintance I had made at the old home, being already intimate with his daughters, who, like myself, belonged to the choir of Kentish Town Church, and to its choral society. My drawings had at once brought conviction to him of the unseen agencies around, and he was truly grateful to me for the assurance thus gained; more especially as he afterwards became a victim to rather untoward influences, although at first he did not at all understand what had come upon him. He feared he was either going out of his mind, or that he was suffering from some severe calamity to his eyesight, which might become fatal to his professional career; for in the evening and at night he would see dancing lights, of all kinds of grotesque forms, which, like will-o'-the-wisps, would frisk along the staircase before him as he was going up to bed, and he would likewise see them flashing about him after he had put out the light and was in bed; sometimes there would seem like a reptile face within them. He had by that time made the acquaintance of some Spiritualists, and one of them recommended him to sketch these uncanny beings, and perhaps by that means he might be able to rid himself of them. He followed out the advice, and with the most complete success, for gradually the unpleasant ones left him, and he has sometimes seen very lovely spirits. He promised to bring his sketches with him the next time he should come here; but in the meanwhile he met me several times at Mr. Hudson's for photographic séances, so that it was not until the 10th of September that he fulfilled his promise, and they certainly are most curious and interesting. He then begged me to select two for my own acceptance, as a token of his gratitude for the new truths which I had been originally instrumental in bringing to his knowledge. He left the whole collection (nearly two dozen) with me that evening, and on his next visit, he warmly urged my acceptance of nine others, and heartily wished he could give them all to me, but the gentleman in whose charge they had previously been, had somehow understood that he had given half of them to him, and although he did not remember having done so, there was no remedy, although he would very much have preferred that I should have had them all. They are marvellously clever, simply as sketches, in addition to the peculiar interest attaching to them. Some of them are spirits in an unhappy state, others are the grotesque little monsters of which I have spoken, while others are pleasant looking spirits. Some time later I had a pair of the pictures photographed (to be professionally parted with), of the two different characteristics. They are chiefly in neutral tints with warm colouring here and there. He sees them in the dark, then strikes a light and sets to work upon what he has seen, working very rapidly. He feels very much exhausted when he has finished, and I have no doubt that he is spiritually aided in the artistic work. Sometimes he does several different sketches on the same sheet of paper in one night. On the upper part of one is a skull, by no means unpleasant looking (in fact I have taken quite a friendly feeling towards it while in front of me to describe); by the side of it is an outline face as if formed of blue flames. On the left is a fine looking upturned countenance, while below it is the small figure of a nun with a mallet in her hand as if breaking huge stones that lie at her feet; and by her side, just below the skull is a profile face with a villanously low forehead, in blue tints. . . Another contains a profile face, set in a medallion or frame;—two faces side by side, upside down, in which position he saw them; and above, is a hand and wrist, as if coming out of clouds. . . Another is an awful face with wide-open mouth, and through my hand was written that it was a drunkard. . . While one of those that went away had a ghastly expression, with the tongue thrust out from the mouth, and that, in like manner, was interpreted through me as a blasphemer. . . Another picture has pairs of eyes, and single eyes; with perhaps scraps of features attached to them. . . . Another has rather a fine face, but the expression of the eyes is unpleasant, while down in front flow seven golden orange-tinted round objects, which I think represent coin, so that he may probably have been a miser: a larger face seems to look askance at him, and above is a little horned and winged monster, red, yellow, and blue.

The last I will attempt to describe has, at the upper part, a face not unlike a toad, spreading out sideways with blue flames,—beneath, on the right, is another frog-looking face with sulphury-looking flames, which give the effect of a rather large body of those flames, and on the left is the semblance of a pin-hole eye within the hollow of bluish flames. There can be no question that some of these extraordinary beings are those known by the term "elementaries," and one great value of these sketches to me (which makes me still more regret not having the other half of them, as they each contain their separate lesson), is the indubitable evidence they give of the objective reality of those said elementaries, on the subject of which I have heard so many cavillings and scoffings. I am fully persuaded that the atmosphere is filled with myriads of beings invisible to us, that have a life *perfectly distinct* and *separate* from us in *every* respect, having *no* affinity nor any future point of union with us. We realise that the microscope has revealed a living insect world in the air and in the waters that our ancestors never dreamed of: the spirit world has likewise its varied creations that may never come within our ken, except to the eyes of the seer, that are also entirely unconnected with us in any way, unless we in a manner degrade our souls towards their level, which I believe to be the case with drunkards, when their eyes possibly *may* behold the reptiles they shrink from. I must here give an extract with regard to these *elementaries* (which *is* a name, and therefore I employ it whether or not it carries any sense), from "Ghost Land," against which I have heard harsh language fulminated : but in my opinion these very drawings bear strongly corroborative testimony to the truth of what is there stated ; and I must say that I have seldom read a book that has interested me so much as that has done, and I would fain in some way become acquainted with its author.

Extract from "Ghost Land," page 111 :—

"The more dim and shadowy the outer world grew to my sense of sight, the more real and horrible became the objects revealed to my interior senses. The air, the earth, the waters, appeared to be thick with grotesque and hideous semblances of half-man and half-beast. Creeping, crawling, flying and leaping things, of all shapes and sizes, held goblin carnival around me. The outer world was receding, and I passed into a veritable realm of demons. I scarcely dare even now recall the full horrors of this vision, nor should I have attributed to it any objective reality had I not witnessed the terror of the poor horses, and connected the whole scene with subsequent incidents. I was aroused from this palsy of horror by the voice of Professor von Marx, whose tones, though modulated almost to a whisper, so as to reach my ear alone, sounded like thunder, as he murmured, 'Louis, Louis! rouse yourself, or you will let the demons of hell get possession of you!' My strength and composure returned with the touch of my master's powerful hand. Even my poor horse owned the spell of his resistless influence; for I found it standing, with drooping head, and at my side, and though trembling violently, it was no longer restive or intractable. 'You have forgotten your Eastern training, methinks,' said the professor half reproachfully, as I looked at my poor steed. 'No training will avail here,' I replied in the same tone; 'through this accursed spot I will not attempt to lead this suffering creature.' There was no time for further discussion. In a single instant a thick, vaporous mist fell upon us, enveloping us in its damp, slimy folds as in a wet garment. It rolled, surged, and filled the atmosphere for a moment, just as I have seen the air grow instantaneously thick and almost impenetrable in the murky folds of a London fog; but before we could comment to each other on this remarkable phenomenon, the mists rose, curled, and separated into ten thousand fragments, and with slight, sharp, detonating sounds, exploded into the well-known appearances called will-o'-the-wisps, or as the country folk of England call them, 'jack-o'-lanterns.' Truth to tell, the appearance of these phosphorescent lights in a place where no marshy ground existed, and where, as our whole party affirmed, they had never been seen before, in no way tended to re-assure us. As for me, I saw around these glimmering lights, which danced, flitted, wheeled, or floated, by hundreds on every side of us, the opaque bodies and grotesque outlines of the elementaries, not as before in distinct resemblances of animals and men, but in a vague, undefined burr around each shimmering flame, which was situated, as my shuddering fancy suggested, just where the nervous centres of their strange life might be supposed to inhere. Sometimes fierce malignant eyes glared at me through the fast-deepening gloom, when the sudden start and unmistakable terror of my poor horse, which I continued to lead, proved either that he shared with me the goblin sight, or that my hand communicated a sense of repulsion to the sensitive animal. Soon after leaving the village, the phantom lights disappeared one by one, and we reached our home without further interruption."

I sent the following account to the *Christian Spiritualist* . . . I have again the pleasure of relating a few of the circumstances that took place at a séance of Mrs. Guppy's, which was held on the evening of September 4th. The circle consisted of Mrs. Ramsay, Mr. and Mrs. Guppy, Mr. Walker, Mrs. Fisher, Miss Mann and myself. The room was darkened, and the door locked, as on the former occasion.

After we had said The Lord's Prayer, the alphabet was requested, and we received the following message :—" Wish for two things, flowers, fruit, roots, or vegetables." Mrs. Guppy begged Mrs. Ramsay to make the decision, and she chose flowers and fruit. We were then told to "rub feet," and while we did so, we heard that something wooden was placed on the table with which a sort of knocking was made ; then we both smelt and felt flowers ; a clatter, too, as of plates, added to the noise, and one was placed in front of each of us. When this had gone on for some time, we were told by raps, " Call them down to look at the manifestations :" the *them* alluded to were two gentlemen, who were upstairs playing billiards, and we were now allowed to have a light, when a lovely sight greeted our eyes. On the centre of the table had been placed a smaller one (with the feet of which the hammering noise had been made), producing the effect of an épergne, for on it was a magnificent dish of pears, elegantly ornamented with a whole plant of nasturtion, the leaves and flowers drooping gracefully down, while on the lower table, round which we were seated, were four dishes of plums, of two different kinds, and a large glass dish filled with grapes; the fruit being half hidden from our view by the masses of beautiful flowers that were grouped over them. The gentlemen and little Tommy were much gratified by the summons to see the wonders. The green dishes and plates formed an entire dessert service, *not* belonging to Mrs. Guppy, nor to any of the party; the fruit consisted of a large supply purchased for Tommy's birthday party, to take place on the 6th; the glass dish also was Mrs. Guppy's property. Of course we all partook of the dessert thus provided for us, and when we were again reduced to our own circle, the door was closed, and the light put out. We made many conjectures as to the crockery, but obtained no information, and I laughingly suggested to the invisibles, whom we still heard busily occupied, that I hoped, if they took away the plates and dishes, they would leave us the fruit. Suddenly I felt my arm firmly grasped, so as to turn my hand palm upwards, and within it was placed a little bird. By and by "Light" was spelt, when lo! the fruit was *gone*, having been cleared from the dishes, &c., which remained there in their emptiness. The bird was a green canary, which became rather restless when it saw the light, so I wrapped it in my handkerchief, and Mrs. Guppy said she had a small cage in which I could bring it home, but it presently turned out that it was Mrs. Guppy's own bird, so, of course, I would not have it. She was then told to "walk round the garden," and was going through the other room to fulfil the injunction, when she made an exclamation that summoned us also into it, and there, in the middle of the room, under the full gaslight, was heaped on the ground all the fruit that had been carried away from us, making a goodly pile; and I took that opportunity of replacing the bird in its own cage on the mantel-piece. When she had returned from her threefold circuit of the garden, and we were again quietly established; by raps I was asked, " Why did you not keep the bird?" To which I answered that I only considered that such manifestations were intended as proofs of an outside power, and I certainly should not consider myself justified in carrying off Mrs. Guppy's goods and chattels; but she said she wished I had, for that as they are shortly going to Rome, she would be glad that the bird should be sure of a happy home. As she said that, I felt a small cage placed in front of me, and when we had the light, in it were both the birds, which I then accepted as her gift. There were a few other incidents, spirit lights being also seen, but they were not very vivid, the power having all been used for the physical manifestations, and they finished with the rapped-out message, " May God give you all good gifts."

The same party, with one or two additions, are invited to Mrs. Guppy's for the 16th of this month, and I hope to gratify your readers with an account of the séance in your next number.

At *this* distance of time I may frankly own that the gift of the birds was anything but a desirable one to me. I had my own little pet, the Dove, and my life is always too fully occupied for me to have much time to bestow the little attentions that birds and animals like to receive, so that I was not at all sorry afterwards to learn that Mr. Guppy would have preferred giving them into the charge of a young relative of his own; so that I gladly replaced them in their small cage, and took them back to Highbury a week or two later.

A circumstance highly important in the history of Spiritualism, is best narrated in the following letter which was published in the *Spiritual Magazine* for October :—" *Upper Norwood, September* 11*th*, 1873 :—MY DEAR MR. HOWITT,— You have been, I believe, already apprised by your daughter, Mrs. Watts, that I have succeeded (in response to my personal applications to a few of your friends) in obtaining the means of purchasing your portrait, which the late Mr. Thomas Heaphy, the artist, considered one of his best efforts; and that I am authorised to present it to Mrs. Howitt by the ladies and gentlemen whose names are appended to an address to yourself, which accompanies the picture. I content myself by saying that it affords me very sincere pleasure to hand these testimonials of respect and friendship to you and Mrs. Howitt, and with best wishes to you both, I am, my dear Mr. Howitt, very truly yours, BENJAMIN COLEMAN."

The address was written on parchment, beautifully illuminated and handsomely framed, and was thus worded: "To Mr. William Howitt—In testimony of our appreciation of your literary efforts for the best interests of humanity, and for your firm advocacy of a pure and elevating Spiritualism; we, a few of your many friends, have the pleasure of presenting to Mrs. Howitt your Portrait (painted by the late Mr. Thomas Heaphy), as a token of our personal regard for your private worth, and our acknowledgment of the great services you have rendered to all who have come within the sphere of your most useful labours." The list of signatures and the warm letters of thanks from both Mr. and Mrs. Howitt also appear in the magazine, but I feel that I must yet extract Mrs. Heaphy's letter, for I know how intensely grateful she is to The Loving Lord for the many true helps He has vouchsafed to her in her arduous task of providing for the maintenance and education of the younger members of her very numerous family thus left fatherless, with but scanty means, for artists generally find their profession most truly a hand-to-mouth one, and in his case the provision for the future was narrow indeed.

"DEAR MR. COLEMAN,—I know not how to thank you for the very kind interest you have taken in my affairs. The £50 you have been the means of getting me for the portrait of Mr. Howitt has done me the greatest service. It has enabled me to outfit and pay the passage of one of my boys (17 years of age) to Canada, where employment is offered him. My youngest girl of twelve will, I believe, be taken in at an excellent school at Tunbridge Wells, the Artists' Orphanage, which was mainly instituted originally, by the suggestion and energy of my late husband. I feel so gratified that it is to you I am so much indebted, for my husband entertained the highest opinion of you, and regarded you with feelings truly brotherly. I beg you to make known my thanks to all those ladies and gentlemen who have so kindly taken part in this transaction: and with best wishes and thanks to yourself,—Believe me ever, my dear Mr. Coleman, your obliged ELIZA HEAPHY."

CHAPTER XI.

At our fourth séance at Mrs. Makdougall Gregory's, Miss Ramsay was developed for music, and her brother Jim manifested his presence by the performance of the military roll call, which had been his signal to me by the movements of my pen, on the evening that I had heard of his unexpected decease in opening manhood, and he then gave me messages for his mother and sisters when I had just sent off a letter of sympathy to Mrs. Ramsay, but I was thus enabled to send her another which should contain more comfort than only my words could give. I think it was on this same evening at Mrs. Gregory's that Miss Ramsay received some degree of vision, and trance mediumship. In the course of our series, she had some very interesting visions, but I do not know whether any record was kept, although at the commencement Mr. Noyes had undertaken that department. On the following Saturday, Mr. Rouse was with us, and from him I received one or two striking descriptions of my personal friends whom he saw near me. One was especially graphic of Papa, when he spoke of his merry twinkling eyes, and I received at the same time the signal by which he intimates his presence to me, which was a yet further corroboration of Mr. Rouse's seership. He had one vision of a spirit I do not know, but I was told that she was one of my spiritual co-workers. "I see a gate, with its side-posts and cross-bars just like an earthly gate. By the side of it stands a female figure, wearing a dress high up to the throat, with plaits or folds to the waist: her hair is banded rather low at the side of the face, and then carried up behind the ears. The gate is wide open, and you are standing by it; beyond it is a large field, very large indeed." . . I did not think to ask him whether I was withinside the gate, but it seems to me to indicate that there is a very large field of labour open before me.

Dr. Monck formed one of our next week's circle, and the chief circumstance I recollect is that he was closely hemmed in to the corner of the room, as we sat round the table, whence he was suddenly lifted up and carried right over it into the centre of the room, and was afterwards floated about, while we heard his voice from different parts; and he wrote with a pencil on the ceiling, I think, twice. I have no memoranda about the other séances, but they were continued for fourteen weeks, with always some members of the original circle, and only occasional admixtures, so I think they demonstrated a good share of steadfastness in those who comprised it.

On the 17th of September, Mr. Enmore Jones initiated a series of Wednesday evening free meetings at Lawson's Rooms, Gower Street. I am happy to say that his desire is always to promote *Christian* Spiritualism as much as possible; he is a most energetic worker in the cause, and has been so for very many years. The first public meeting that I ever went to, bearing upon the subject was, I think, some time in 1860, when I accompanied my cousins to a lecture in a room that belonged I believe to the Whittington Club, Mr. Jones being the lecturer, when he shewed us some interesting magic-lantern slides, representing the aura seen by clairvoyants as issuing from magnets, shells, and other objects, giving at the same time very lucid explanations of what he was exhibiting. Mrs. Fussell and her daughter were among the small audience, and although I had not at that time the pleasure of knowing them, I remembered their faces when I was some time afterwards introduced to them by Mrs. Coleman, whose then residence was in Bayswater. Mr. Jones's free meetings were held on four consecutive Wednesdays, and on the fifth we concluded with a social tea assemblage, enlivened by speeches.

That was rather a busy season among the Spiritualists, for it was then that Mrs. Tappan made what I believe was her first visit to England, and I went on the 21st of September to hear her in St. George's Hall, Langham Place.

At Mrs. Gregory's on the 13th of October, I had the gratification of meeting M. Aksakof of St. Petersburg, with whom I had much interesting conversation, and there was the additional link between us of his having been a most intimate friend of the late Mr. Shaw (tutor to the Imperial family), my cousin-in-law. He then arranged to meet me on the following Thursday for a sitting with Mr. Hudson; and at a later date we were together at Mrs. Guppy's, when some of the circumstances that occurred are detailed in the latter part of the following narrative that I sent to the *Christian Spiritualist.*

I almost feared that I should be unable to fulfil my promise of giving an account this month of Mrs Guppy's next séance, as it had been unavoidably postponed, but was finally held on October 16th. The circle consisted of Mr. and Mrs. Guppy, Mrs. and Miss Ramsay, Mrs. Wiseman, with her daughter and son-in-law, Mrs. Fisher, Mr. Volckman, and myself. The room was darkened and the door locked.

We commenced as usual with The Lord's Prayer, and in a short time we heard five raps for the alphabet. As the number was rather large, so that we were crowded, Mrs. Fisher had at first seated herself at some little distance, and the message given was to desire her to stand behind us, and to place her hands, one on Mrs. Guppy's shoulder, and one on mine, and when that arrangement had been carried out, we received permission each to wish for something. A few wishes were definite, flowers of course being in the ascendant, but some were left to the choice of the spirits. Mr. Volckman asked for a sunflower, and Mrs. Fraser requested them to bring her a brooch which she had left with her wraps in the hall, from which we were divided by the locked door. Mrs. Guppy heard a voice whisper, "rub feet," and we accordingly rubbed our feet on the carpet, for the purpose of increasing by movement the outflow from ourselves. We heard sounds about the room, and presently found that something large was placed upon the table, while at the same time we perceived a strong odour of earth. "Get a light," was now spelt out, and, to our surprise, on the centre of the table stood a magnificent sunflower plant, towering far above us, which had been dug up by the invisibles, roots and all, from Mrs. Guppy's garden; but, alas! the quantity of mould that had been brought with it, was scattered both on the table and on the carpet, so it was deemed advisable to clear all that manifestation into a large cloth. The table was thoroughly wiped, and the gas again extinguished.

Once more we heard sounds as if our unseen friends were very busy: there was a clatter as of porcelain, and some of us felt the hands which were placing the cups and flowers in front of us. We saw glimmering lights, and then I felt my head tenderly caressed by the fingers of dear Môtee. I asked her to let me kiss her hand, as she has done twice at my own home séances, and after coaxing my cheek awhile, her fingers pressed my lips, and she indulged my request more than once. Mrs. Fisher was several times so forcibly pulled back by the spirits that she had to grasp our shoulders very tightly not to be withdrawn from the circle. She then exclaimed that they were doing something to her hair, and Mr. Fraser felt a small article strike his back and fall down behind him. We heard Katie's voice, and she made some amusing personal remarks about those present. When we were permitted to light the gas, we found that the table was covered with some of the china ornaments from different parts of the room, interspersed with a goodly supply of variously coloured dahlia flowers. On the floor behind him Mr. Fraser found the brooch that had been wished for by his wife, but it proved to be Mrs. Wiseman's instead of her own. Mrs. Fisher complained that her flower had not been brought to her, when we laughed at her for her ingratitude, for a white dahlia had been most tastefully inserted in her dark hair at the time she had felt it being manipulated. Katie then rapped out, "I cannot do any more," so we thanked her and her assistant band for the pleasure they had given us, and wished them good-night.

I may now add a few of the incidents that occurred at another séance at Mrs. Guppy's, on the 23rd of October, when the circle consisted of Mr. and Mrs. Guppy, Mr. Serjeant Cox, M. Alexandre Aksakof, Mr. and Miss Shorter, Mrs. Fisher, Mr. Volckman,˙ Miss Ingram and myself. Miss Shorter, at Mrs. Guppy's request, thoroughly examined the room, and the door was locked when we were all assembled.

After having said The Lord's Prayer, we were desired by raps to wish for something to be brought, but we were clearly not to wish *unreasonably*, for several suggestions of that class were negatived. Serjeant Cox wished for chrysanthemums, but dahlias were brought instead, and perhaps our invisible purveyors might not have known them by name. Then various fruits were asked for, also vegetables, so there was a curious medley of apples, plums, almonds, carrots, turnips, &c. Mrs. Guppy requested them to bring her a mussel out of her aquarium, and Serjeant Cox exclaimed that there was a live fish in front of him, which was flapping about very energetically: a light was immediately struck, and there indeed were three of Mrs. Guppy's gold fish, which she took away in great haste to replace in the water, as she feared for their little lives. While we were sitting in the light, waiting for her return, some observation was made as to the advantage of a knife and fork wherewith to eat our dessert, and as soon as the gas was extinguished, down they fell on the table.

When the little fish were brought, Serjeant Cox observed that eels would have been more serviceable, and presently he said, "Surely this is an eel," and at the same moment Mrs. Guppy shrieked most fearfully, desiring that a light should be struck at once, when there was seen one live eel round her neck, and another on the table between Serjeant Cox and myself, and likewise a live lobster in the middle of the table. Poor Mrs. Guppy was sadly terrified, and with much reason, although in the dark she did not know what the moving creature might be that was performing the part of necklace, for I am told that eels bite very hard, refusing to loose their hold. They and the lobster were taken downstairs and put into water, and then the spirits told us they could do no more, and wished us good-night.

Mrs. Guppy is not at all partial to eels, but as I *am*, I asked if I might have them, to which she gladly assented, insisting also that I should bring away the lobster, so they were all packed in paper and a basket for me to carry home, and I must beg to thank the spirits for three very nice dinners that I thoroughly enjoyed. The main body of the lobster was picked out of the shell without its being broken, so that I have it as a bright coloured souvenir of that wonderful séance. M. Aksakof, who came to see me a few days later, was glad to have one piece of claw, as it could travel without being broken.

It will have been seen by the above list of the members of the circle, that Miss Ingram was once more in England, after her long sojourn in America. To my great gratification she arrived about the end of September, and I am happy to say with considerably renovated health, and hitherto she has not again strayed away from England.

I had the pleasure of a visit from M. Aksakof on two consecutive Wednesdays, and he came once again for me to take him for a séance with that worthy veteran medium Mrs. Marshall, but I do not remember any of the particulars.

On the 15th of September Mrs. T. moved into her new house in the Albert Road, Regents Park, and I was most thankful to have her established within convenient reach, for there had been great tremours in my mind as to what might be the ultimate result of the various places under consideration. I wish I had written down all that she told me at different times after first making the change, for such experiences are very instructive, and to her it had occasioned extreme discomfort if not absolute suffering. The house had a feeling of spiritual emptiness, and as if there were a coldness in the atmosphere that prevented the unseen ones from approaching her, and that sensation continued until she had gradually permeated it with her own emanations, which of course was more speedily done in the sitting-rooms than the staircase, and for a long time she missed the accustomed companionship of the invisibles in her journeys up and down; I believe, too, that it was in some degree detrimental to her physical health, from the drain it made upon her system, and which she always feels to some extent when she leaves home: and I am instructed that it is, for special reasons appertaining to her own mediumship, so injurious to her *not* to be surrounded to at least a certain distance, by a fluidic compound of her outflow and the influences of her guardian circle, that when she goes into a new place they are compelled to *draw* rapidly from her, so as to mingle therewith their own sustaining element. She is thus *drained from* at first, so as to enable her at all to exist amid the fresh surroundings; for which reason it is that travelling about is essentially unsuitable for her, and that her own home is her fittest abiding place. I went to see her for the first time in her pretty new dwelling, on the 19th of October, while the cold chill was still upon it, and she then told me many of her sensations that have now slipped from my memory. Even on my following visit to her, that sense of spiritual isolation still continued. I have referred in the photographic chronicles to a communication I received when she came here on the 16th of December, but I am to recapitulate it here. She was far from well, and I therefore mesmerised her, simply, as I opined, for curative purposes, and afterwards did it a second time, when she passed into trance, and presently was thus spoken through very slowly :—" Just this thought, —be prepared for changes — chang*es*.—She has been brought here on purpose to tell you, so that you may be prepared." [I suppose it is better that I should not question in any way.] After a long silence, she added, " Be prepared to lose a valued friendship—but be not disturbed —it is best—but be prepared, lest it should come upon you like a thief in the night." She then awoke, and I told her a part of what had been said.

The solution came in a form that troubled me a good

deal at the time, for towards the end of January I received a letter from the Rev. F. R. Young, to say that after due deliberation he had decided upon giving up the *Christian Spiritualist* into the hands of Dr. Sexton ; and I felt that the after-tone of the periodical would not be likely to harmonize so well with my own feelings as it had done during the three years that he had conducted it ; I also thought that thenceforward I should probably not be a contributor to it, which proved to be the case during the brief year and a half of its longer existence.

I was present in St. George's Hall, as one of a large audience, on the 29th of December, when Mrs. Tappan's guides gave, through her, a very interesting account of her development and experiences.

In the July of that year, I had received a letter from Miss Pery, a lady unknown to me, residing in the Netherwood Road, Hammersmith ; saying that her hand had been guided by invisible agencies to do some curious drawings, and she had been told by a friend that I might possibly be able to give her some light on the subject ; which led to occasional correspondence between us ; she afterwards sent me one of her drawings to look at, and very beautiful it was, being executed in pencil with most extremely fine work, representing a multitude of small heads and faces, highly finished, and closely grouped together, there being sometimes a glimpse of a hand or a foot : there were also small crosses, and such other symbolism. The heads were varied as to size and position, and I admired it very much, but returned it without having been able to obtain any interpretation as to its meaning. Later on she gratified me by the information that she had commenced one to present to me. In the meanwhile she had gone to Brighton, but still I had not had the pleasure of making her personal acquaintance. On the 4th of March I received the promised drawing, of which the beauty transcended the one she had sent me to look at, although similar in character, the multitudinous faces seeming sometimes to gleam *through* the others ; and it was *explained* to me as representing a kind of section of what we should see, could our spiritual vision be fully opened, for just as closely are the faces crowded round about us, but as they are in most cases invisible to one another (for they only see those with whom they are in fellowship or affinity, or whom they may *descend* to help), they do not interfere with one another. I wrote her a letter of warm thanks; and kept the following record of her reply:—"*Brighton, March 6th*, 1874.—I ought to have said that I was 'impressed' or 'desired' to send the drawing to you, being a *Christian* Spiritualist, and so I did it. You are perhaps a *Head Centre* for the feeble folk, Christians who are at the same time Spiritualists." Her expression has reminded me of the same term having been applied to me at one of our evening meetings at Mr. Spear's towards the latter end of 1868: I have looked through my many manuscripts of communications given through him, in the hope of finding it, but my search has been in vain, so it was probably one of those of which I did not take notes at the time, and I know there was but a small portion that was of personal application to myself: it was on the subject of various centres (on which he touched more than once that winter), but that I was the true centre of all, and the term "Head Centre" was appropriated in our talk, more in a joking way, because of the then stir about Stephens the fenian Head Centre.

Not very long after I had received the drawing, Sir Charles Isham called here, and was so much struck with it that he said I ought to have it photographed, so as to enable others to share the privilege of its possession; I said that I had thought of it, only that I had not ventured to risk the outlay without some security of a return, so he at once ordered three copies, and I took my drawing to the photographer on the following day, to be done to the same size as the original, and the result was a grand success, being I think more effective than the drawing itself, and it has almost the effect of an agate or marble graven all over with minute heads. I had the pleasure of sending a copy to Miss Pery herself, so as to enable her to retain some remembrance of her own gift, and she afterwards kindly sent me another, yet more finished in style; that also had been done expressly *for* me, which I likewise had photographed, and it makes a good companion for the other. She sent me at the same time a collection of her earlier designs and fragmentary beginnings, which all, as it were, lead up to this more finished style. In August I had the pleasure of a visit from her of a couple of hours, on her way from Brighton into Northamptonshire. She afterwards came to reside in London, and five years ago took a house in this Crescent, nearly opposite me.

I met Mrs. Gray the evening that I was at St. George's Hall, and had a bit of chat with her before the proceedings commenced, and after they were over, she again joined me, saying that in the interval she had had a message for me, to the effect that although the clouds then overshadowed me very heavily, the path would soon brighten: she then added;—"but you will soon receive a new gift." . . I hoped and believed it might be that of sight, which was corroborated by what was spoken through her. (But the "soon" of the spirits is *distant* for us, for the hope is yet unfulfilled.) I then gave her the history of my having *worked* for that gift, about nine or ten years previously, by looking into the crystal for perhaps an hour every Sunday evening, according to the directions then given me by my invisible guides, who on each occasion told me when to leave off. I fully understood from them that I was not *then* to receive the gift, but simply to endeavour to fit myself for it in patience and faith: that it would not be the guerdon of my own exertions, but as a free grace in His good time from The Giver of all blessings. I do not remember for how many months I continued the practice, as I only followed out their injunctions; but, while looking into the crystal, I used to have some curious sensations in my eyes: at distant intervals, I have had similar feelings for a short time, when I have hoped that "sight" might be at hand, and I told her that such had been the case during the last few days. When I went on the 4th of January to see Mrs. T. I gave her the long history of all my byegone efforts, and my hopes, which had thus been again aroused. I made her another visit on the 25th, when I told her about my interview with Mrs. Marshall whom I had been to see on her 75th birthday (January 6th), and she was much interested to hear that the old lady, in the midst of our talk, had suddenly said,— "And *you* are going to have visions, and very grand ones they will be;" with more to the same effect.

Mrs. T. and I had a snug tête-à-tête after tea, and I had the feeling to mesmerise her, but asked first if she should have any fear of being entranced, as she is still so poorly, but on the contrary she said she should be glad of it, having had scarcely anything from her spirit friends since she had moved. At first it was all curative, but then we went to the eyes, when she soon passed under influence; and a rather long communication was given. Presently she opened her eyes, and I made a few passes, expecting that they were to bring her to, instead of which she again became entranced, and said: —"When, in fulness of time, the mantle shall fall from the shoulders of that aged pilgrim, it will descend to rest hereafter upon you. Even now she dimly sees a portion of your future life, and she will be constrained to prophesy of the link which has, and will continue to unite you together in this great movement. It is recommended that you set aside a small portion of time once a month to spend with her, but this is of course left to your sense of what is fit and right. Already the mantle is loosened." . . . She then awoke, and when I had read it to her, I mentioned that Mrs. Marshall had said to me; "It seems that I have often told you that we are *united* in our work:" to which I answered, "Yes, because we both look to the Bible as the original evidence of Spiritualism, and as still to be our land-mark."

It was decided by my counsellors that I should go always to my old friend for an hour or two on the first Tuesday in the month, to have a pleasant social chat, and

I was gratified by her delight when I told her of my intention, as hers had of late become rather a solitary life, her mediumship having so little of the phenomenal phases which are now run after, for excitement's sake rather than any seeking after truth. I went to see her on the evening of February 3rd, taking the small gift that my means admitted, and it did not seem to me as if much had come, but looking back to the fragments in the course of conversation, there certainly were some curious things. In the middle of our talk, she said—"The voice is saying Honour thy father and thy mother."—In the early part of my ministrations to her (when, years ago, her leg was bad, and I used to go and mesmerise her three times a week), that commandment used almost always to be said to her in my presence, and once she asked the spirit *why* that was said, and the answer was, "Because she *knows* it, and *does* it." . . . I mesmerised her on this occasion, curatively, several times; but the phrases spoken to her by the "voice" did not seem to be the result of it, but came incidentally now and then, and I will write them down as they arise in my mind. . . "I will bless you in your basket and in your store,—fear not." . . . "I am told we are *both* to work, and have much before us." . . . "You will have revelations the same as mine, and visions with them—revelations and visions." . . . "A great flood of power will be poured upon you, but you will not be overwhelmed, for you have already been enlarged to receive it, and it will fill you with a mighty power." I had to do a curious mesmeric action, striking one hand into the other, alternately, with much force, and she said: "It means,—I will fill you on the right hand and on the left, and I will be with you on every side."

I had a letter from Mrs. Spear, dated October 22nd, 1872, in which she says, "I met a few weeks since, a quite remarkable medium, and after reading a number of her communications, the style of which is very peculiar, I began to like them unusually well, and I felt like sending her one of your letters, and asking for what she might write while holding it. She sent me the enclosed."

I here copy the communication, although the style is peculiar, especially to our quiet English notions, but it conveyed some things that I knew to be true, and we can understand her singularities of diction as the outflow from her especial band of influences, and I feel that each variety from the *other side* has its own character of interest.

"Lovely life is before thee. Many heart homes will be blessed away from thy own land even by thy own powers.

"Banished art thou from the full life of realization: banished from the Loves as the moments pass along: banished from the Loves of heart-life as thy own soul would desire, but made white in the Living Life of Labour:—for thy form is habited in royal robes and thy feet are clad in sandals of Purity. One day-dawning for thy own life is near at hand, when tides of emotion will roll over thy soul lands, and musical utterances will be heard on the air waves of harmonies.

"Blessings are coming to thee—are coming as pearls of great price are coming, and fame shall be thine own. Blessed art thou. A home love thy heart giveth to all humanity. Thy sweet wave of love goeth out over all lands, and *heart* histories are the ones to be related to thee on a coming time. Beautiful soul language thy own life uttereth: home harps are thy own to give unto many. Dost know one lovely landscape seen around thy form speaketh of the starry orbs whose rays fall on thy own garments, and relate to earth dwellers. Thy love hath attracted the holy lives of the Celestials:—borne to thee are anthems from chimes afar. Borne to thee are heavenly songs from the lands of America, banishing fears of the laying aside of the garments of growth for humanity's uprising. Home loves must speak to thy soul of the vast work to be done. Oceanic waves roll over thy soul and master artists speak in love tones of the landscapes to be lain out.—Behind a door thy form has stood—seen no full forms of realization. Near at hand are fulfilments of prophecies, and beyond thy own seeing will love bless the lives of the true labourers. Bounding billows have been thy home—fears have attended thy form—hopes have arisen but to pass away. So Love hath promised thee heights to rest on : and so it shall be given thee to speak to the wisdom powers, and thy ears shall listen, thy soul respond.

"Bear ever in mind, compensation will come for all thy labours—*compensation*—and fully will revealments come according to thy own conceptions.—Below, on the ground, look and see the forms of lowliness arising ; see the open avenues, and love to gird on the armour sent to thee by angels of wisdom. Go forth laden with wealth, knowing mighty powers are in life assisting ; heralding the glad tidings that Peace and Harmony must become earth dwellers.

"Write one letter to this writer, and nearer can the lights come, even from the contact. Borne to thee Love from many hearts in the lands of America in the coming time. Let this be one greeting to thy soul."

Mrs. Spear added the name and address of the medium (the latter I suppose may have long been altered). "Mrs. Juliette Manley. Box 454, Erie, Pennsylvania, U. S. A." I wrote to her, enclosing a small fee, as my limited means precluded a larger one ; and the communication that resulted from it was written on the 5th of January 1873, and touched upon the innermost depths of my life, known but to few. The concluding sentences are as follows.

"One thanksgiving uttered in song, cometh readily to thy lips : one golden fruitage season is coming to thy own life,—owning large lands : the way will be over the mountains to places where rest, peace, and content will beautify your whole life-garment. One Harvester art thou called. . . . Blessed art thou, Oh woman of Love : a sweet willingness to do all thy duties well, hath endeared thee to many angels of growth."

I think it was towards the close of the last year that Mrs.

Hollis had come for her first visit to England, and I had known of the stereoscopic photograph taken of her and an Indian spirit by Mr. Hudson. Mrs. T. had talked with me of what we had severally heard, and she thought she would like to have a séance and wished me to accompany her, and also that I should write about making all the arrangements without mentioning her name in any way, and it was finally fixed for March 10th at half-past three, and I was to meet her there at the appointed time. She had had a communication from Mr. Spear that had made her rather anxious about her own health, but I had interpreted it as having a different signification to what she had done; however she gave the letter to me a day or two before and I was to take it in my pocket to Torrington Street. Mrs. Hollis shewed us her compact little table, which, as far as I recollect, could be folded up to put into her travelling trunk, but there was undoubtedly no wonderful machinery about its slight framework; and we were already seated by it when Mrs. Hollis covered it with a cloth; she then placed a small piece of pencil on a slate, and held the slate in the dark chamber thus formed by the cloth, which she however turned back so that we could see her wrist all the time, while her other hand rested quietly in her lap. We shortly heard the pencil busily writing, and when it was dropped by the unseen holder upon the slate, Mrs. Hollis drew it forth, for us to read whatever message might have been written; which was then rubbed out, and the slate was again held under the table, for the answer to the next query. I deeply regret that I did not write out each of those messages, so as to have been able to give the whole details, but I remember all the facts, and I think only one message had been written, when I took the letter out of my pocket and laid it on the table without a word of observation, and Mrs. T. asked if any information could be given as to that letter, and we immediately heard an invisible friend at work, and when Mrs. Hollis took out the slate, upon it was written, " What Miss Houghton told you was quite correct."

Messages were given about her expected infant, and it

was strongly impressed upon her that she was to be with *me* as frequently and as much as she possibly could, for her own sake, but more especially for that of the child, who would thus gather elements from me towards the formation of some of her attributes. It was also suggested that even when we were apart, I was to keep her and the coming babe as much in my thoughts as I could, so as to strengthen the link between us. The communications were full of deep interest. I then asked *who* was the spirit who was counselling, and the written answer was, " John, Miss Houghton." I said that we had several friends in the spirit world bearing that name, so we should feel obliged by a closer definition, and to Mrs. Hollis's surprise, when she again drew forth the slate, upon it was written " Patmos," and she said that no spirit of that *calibre* had ever written on that slate before; to which I rejoined that he was a dear friend to us both, and I told her of Mrs. T.'s vision of his presence with me on the 23rd of November 1870 : and thus our pleasant visit to her came to an end.

I know also that in one of Mr. Spear's letters to her at about that time, he had recommended that she should be as much as possible in the companionship of the Holy Symbolist, for the influences that might be thus garnered in.

CHAPTER XII.

The British National Association of Spiritualists was making its quiet advances in growth, although there were powerful dissentient voices, and one of the most curious arguments against it was that of its being likely to become a large body; some persons being of opinion that the formation of any amount of small societies all over the kingdom might be desirable, but it was *comprehensive* union that was objectionable. Others were of opinion that it might become too powerful, and that individual efforts might thereby suffer: but Spiritualism will ultimately embrace the whole world, so that surely there will be room for every variety and method of work, and the more closely the links may be drawn, the more perfect is likely to be the whole. In that early time, Mr. Blyton was the secretary, besides whom there were two most active and energetic honorary secretaries: Mr. Algernon Joy and Miss Kislingbury, the latter of whom exercised her great knowledge of all continental languages in correspondence with foreign Spiritualists in different parts of the world to enlist their sympathy in the undertaking. There must indeed have been an arduous amount of work in organizing and formulating so great a scheme; for there were so many points and questions to be taken into consideration. It had however been gradually shaped, and on the 16th of April 1874 a grand inaugural Soirée was held in Cleveland Hall, to which of course I went, and a very pleasant evening it was.

Two days later I accompanied my sister to the Dudley Gallery, when Mr. McNair told us that a new class of exhibition was in contemplation, for works of art in Black and White, and he suggested that I should do a drawing for it:—neutral tints would also be admissible. I scarcely thought much about it at the moment, for I knew that he only alluded to *secular* work, which I had given up ever since Zilla's death in 1851, and which I knew would never be resumed. But after my return home, I got into consultation upon the subject, and found that I should be aided to do a good-sized drawing, which was afterwards thus described in my book of interpretations.

A Monogram has been executed in the hope of its being accepted for the forthcoming exhibition of "Black and White," to be held in the Dudley Gallery. It was commenced with pen and ink, and was finished with brushes and water-colours, Chinese white and lamp black.

"B. N. A. S. Monogram of the British National Association of Spiritualists.

"Spiritualists have now united themselves under a very large and comprehensive denomination, and we trust that they will do their utmost to vindicate the title they have assumed, by merging all personal feelings in the one great bond of their acceptance of the fact that in these days open communication between the visible and the so-called invisible is again being granted to mankind. If they heartily concur in this, they must be content to bear with one another under the many points wherein they cannot fail to differ, for each man is individual, and therefore will accept only what shews itself to him as a truth. He is also under the dominion of earthly passions and weaknesses, and cannot see clearly, so that even of that truth he may at present be able to grasp but a very small fragment, but his powers will grow if he finds that those who have obtained a larger share, have thereby been filled with so infinite a tenderness to their fellow-men that instead of pressing them down for their misdeeds, they will strive to bestow upon them a portion of their own strength to enable them to resist temptation when it again assails them. Such is the full meaning of Association, and when thus linking itself with the British Nation of Spiritualists, it must take *all* within its folds, whether or no they may have enrolled themselves within its ranks, or it will run the risk of becoming a dominant power which might be injurious to those who have not united themselves to it.

"In the monogram we have striven to shew by means of myriads of interlaced threads, the lines of thought and life pursued by individuals, each having a specific aim, and perhaps in their termination uniting with certain others, although not following the same course, the very divergences being productive of harmonious results as to the formation of the whole.

"The S, in its fulness of size, represents Spiritualism itself rather than only those who have accepted its revelations, for the day is not far distant when all mankind will bask in some portion of the light thus shed upon them. The B shews how lovingly the true Briton embraces the blessing, and we comprehend within that term the multitudes in distant lands whose ancestors went forth to seek fresh fields of action for their indomitable energies, the N signifying those whose joy is in the nation to which they still belong or from which they have sprung. The A is like a bell, ringing its peal to attract the attention of those unheeding ones who know not of the manifestations now taking place in their midst, therefore a small portion of it extends beyond the S. It may not *toll*, like the mournful passing-bell, but must send forth a joyous sound, to teach that the gate of death is but the entrance into immortality, and that well-doing will lead to happiness in the hereafter: —but still the *whole* message must be given,—that sin and selfishness will meet with retribution, and that full expiation must be made for the evil deeds done in the flesh, but that there is One Who will ever hearken to the repentant sinner who truly seeks Him, even if long ages have passed in darkness and despair. This is the great lesson that Spiritualists have to teach, more especially to those troubled souls in prison, who are groping in what seems to them an eternity of misery, because they know not that even for them there may be a hope; although to many in the long ago past that message was carried by Christ Himself, and His followers must seek in this day thus to walk in His footsteps now that the way has been opened to them by the power of Spirit Communion."

I took my drawing on the appointed day to the Dudley Gallery, but it was rejected by the hanging committee, and I still think that, although doubtless that result *must* have been the best for me, as far as the exhibition was concerned, they made a decided mistake, for it had the advantage of being quite unlike anything else in the gallery, and would therefore have had the charm of variety. Perhaps they may have feared lest, by admitting it, they might be supposed to favour Spiritualism, but *that*, most assuredly, is out of the reach either of their favour or disfavour. I presume that the real object of its execution was that I should present it to the Association, which was what I eventually did. But I have still somewhat to say on that subject. I do not remember whether it was at that inaugural meeting that the announcement was made as to the Declaration they had drawn up of their Principles and Purposes; but it was published and disseminated, and I subjoin two of the paragraphs.

"The Association, while cordially sympathizing with the teachings of Jesus Christ, will hold itself entirely aloof from all dogmatism or finalities, whether religious or philosophical, and will content itself with the establishment and elucidation of well-attested facts, as the only basis on which any true religion or philosophy can be founded.

"The Association proposes, when circumstances permit, to establish a Central Institution, comprising a Hall, Lecture and Séance Rooms, also a Library for the use of Members, and for the benefit of all students of psychical and spiritual phenomena; to keep a register of Mediums or Psychics, with the view of affording facilities for investigation; and to promote co-operation and intercommunion between Spiritualists in all parts of the world."

I will grant to any caviller on that question that the language used with reference to Our Lord might have been in a higher strain, but He Himself says in S. Mark ix. 40, "For he that is not against us is on our part." And it was that paragraph, and that alone, that made me again consult the messengers from Above, as to whether I should *now* become a member of the Association, when I received an immediate affirmative. I do not expect that all my co-workers should be Christians as well as Spiritualists, for, alas! I know how blinded the world is; but by that Declaration I was ensured against *attacks* upon what I regard as the Central Truth of life; therefore I could join hand-in-hand with them to propagate as far as possible the new teaching in its multifarious forms, while in my home I may continue my own fuller life. One thing that always strikes me as so very anomalous is, that persons who consider themselves *liberal* in their views, would yet wish to narrow others down to their own poor level: they would let a person be as rampantly *ir*religious as they please, but the moment Christianity in any shape or form is acknowledged, *that* must be beaten to the ground:—and I would simply enquire *where* then is their liberality of belief? liberality of *un*belief it may be that they do possess.

I think it was through Mr. Bennett that I declared my adhesion, and on the 22nd of May I received my ticket of membership, and two or three days later Mrs. T. came to see me, when I told her that I had joined the Association. "Yes, I know it:" was her reply; which rather surprised me, for I could not think who should so soon have known it to tell her: but the intelligence had been communicated to her by her spirit friends, and that seemed to give some sort of importance to what I had done. I said I had no doubt but that she would some day do the same, although she did not then think it likely, for Mr. T.'s view was that he could do more good to the universal cause while unlinked to any one thing in the shape of a party— I however hoped that *this* would have nothing of a *party* character in it, but be as universal as he could wish. But still, the impression came to me strongly that a time would come when *she* would feel it, not only judicious, but imperative upon her to join, so I asked the promise that when such should be the case, she would accord me the privilege of nominating her, which she freely gave, although still thinking it very unlikely to come to fulfilment.

I was then elected a member of the Council. At that time, their meetings were held in one of Lawson's Rooms, Gower Street, where my first attendance was on the 15th of July and the next on the 31st. In those days there was still a large amount of preliminary work to be done, and a great deal of anxious discussion took place that every step should be the very wisest and best that could be thought of: there really appeared to be but one motive—the good of the work—and although there might be some differences of opinion as to the how and the what, there was no alloy of selfism apparent. But I understood that there had been rather hot debates before the "Declaration" had been finally drawn out, and it was still creating outside discussion: some of our Christian members withdrawing their names because of the *wording* of that clause, while others objected to it altogether; and the matter was again brought so much before the Board that it was finally decided to put it to the vote of the whole Association (by voting papers to be posted), as to whether it should be retained or withdrawn, and I am sorry to say that there was a very considerable majority as to its withdrawal. I again asked counsel as to whether that was to make any change with regard to my retaining my membership, and I was authorised to adhere to it, and to rest assured that that clause would still continue virtually effective, and I am thankful to say that such has been the case. I cannot carry back my memory to all the steps that were taken, but the great desire was to obtain a permanent home, so as to carry out the second clause that I have quoted; and those two energetic and hard-working members, Mr. Bennett and Mr. Dawson Rogers, tramped over a considerable portion of London, up and down no end of lengthy staircases in empty houses without number, until they finally decided upon the one we have in Great Russell Street; but I see it was not until the 23rd of March 1875, that we held our first Council meeting there; but of course even after the house was

M

taken, there was a great amount of work in seeing after the purchase of furniture, &c. &c., and the two most active in that respect were still Mr. Bennett and Mr. Rogers, although they had also the wise advice and aid of some of the lady members of the Council; for they not only had to furnish, but to do it in the most economical manner they could, as the funds never came in sufficiently to make it all plain sailing. There were some handsome contributions towards the establishment of the library by gifts both of money and books, so that gradually we have accumulated a most valuable collection; the larger proportion of which are our own, although at first a good many were lent, so as to form a good substratum; but I know that a portion of these have been recalled by their owners to do a work in other parts of the world, but at our monthly Council meetings we generally receive the addition of several presentations of the fresh works connected with our subject that are of value. There have likewise been many other gifts appertaining to Spiritualism, such as photographs, drawings, casts, and such like wonderful evidences from the invisible world. One great drawback to the rooms was the insufficiency of space for an evening gathering, or at least it was the inconvenience of the separation of one portion of the company from the other, for a dense wall separated the Reading Room entirely from the Council Room, and people could only go from the one to the other by way of the staircase landing. The landlord was then applied to for permission to take down that wall and replace it with large folding-doors, which will throw open to the fullest extent, when a fund was raised to meet the expense; and I must here add a word as to the unfailing consideration and liberal help always extended in one form or other by our dear President, Mr. Calder, who in all emergencies has come forward generously with aid.

I scarcely dare trust myself to speak of some of the impediments that have been thrown in our path, when the battle has been so fierce that once or twice it has seemed as if the Association must succumb, but, thank God! it has weathered through some desperate storms, although its expenses have been compelled to be reduced to the very narrowest possible limits, so that the work it would fain do in many directions is as yet utterly impossible; but it is rallying, and gaining fresh strength month by month in the shape of new members, so I trust we may yet see the day when it may carry out its original programme, and do great things in every department of spiritual work. One great trouble was in the last year, 1880, when my thought as to Mrs. T. was fully realised, and she felt that it was indeed a duty to strengthen us in our then struggle by the weight of her name, in becoming a member of the Association, and I had the promised pleasure of making the triumphant announcement at our monthly meeting.

During all this time, things had been going from bad to worse with poor Mr. Hudson : the winter had been densely foggy, which was not only prejudicial to photographic work, but was bad for spiritual manifestations that were in any way allied to the physical, and Mr. Williams said that there were some nights when they could not in their séances even obtain the raps. It was a season particularly to be remembered, for the fog so seriously affected the fat animals of the cattle-show, that many of them had to be killed, as it was impossible for them to breathe, and they would have died from suffocation. Gradually, from week to week, I noted the absence of familiar articles of furniture belonging to the specimen-room, which was the one I frequented, and at last I was greeted with the sad intelligence that there was an execution in the home of wonders in Palmer Terrace. Mrs. Guppy kindly took home one of the daughters for the time, and made great exertions in his behalf, drawing forth sympathy and aid from other quarters, so that in course of time he was re-established in a small studio at Notting Hill :—all of which I have detailed more fully elsewhere, but I must needs also allude to it here, as of course my own daily life was much affected by the change :—that occupation being gone.

It had seemed to me almost as if the drawing work were utterly set aside, it was so long since I had done any, the last having been finished in August 1872, and even the B. N. A. S. monogram of that spring, had been worked in pen and ink for the earlier stage. Now there came upon me the impression that perhaps I was to resume it, and I was confirmed in it upon enquiry: but I was to bring down a new drawing-block, twice the size of those I was in the habit of using, and I was soon again revelling among my colours and brushes; the subject also being a new one, and was entitled "One of the Many Mansions," of which I have never exactly received the interpretation, but, having been completed a day or two before, I took it with me on the 9th of July to Mrs. T.'s, and soon had the pleasure of exhibiting it to her and Miss Dornbusch; and after a time, Mrs. T. said: "It comes to me that the person whose home that is, is already dwelling as it were in that kind of oval on the left, and that there is but a very thin partition between that and the interior." She would have said more, but I saw she was almost passing under influence, so I prevented it, as I knew we should be soon summoned to tea, and that it would be injurious for her to be disturbed. Later in the evening, when she and I were alone together, I again placed it on a chair before her, and she soon said: "They are again telling me that the person whose home this is, is now dwelling within that oval, one side of which is thin, very thin, and when it opens a clear view will come to the person." (Then as if from herself, she said, "I do not see *how* the opening is to come, unless by death:" she then continued by impression.) "I see, as I look at it, that the light is going through the opening, so that the inhabitant is conscious of the *near presence* of the spirit world, but does not know of the life *in* it just separated by the wall. I think it is a female—a very feminine nature it certainly is." She now passed into trance, and thus continued:— "The rent in the wall will come by force, but it will close again, still leaving the inhabitant in this world, but *she* will have seen her home which is here pictured. The rupture will be closed by a direct spirit action, contrary to the usual order; for when such an opening is made, the spirit *must* pass through, and having passed through, there is no *return* without such aid. The wall is hourly growing thinner, and only a sharp stroke given at the weakest part is needed to break it. For the occupant it would be the highest happiness to go out and not to return, but there is further work here, which will be best accomplished by such an experience. God works in a mysterious way His wonders to perform, and *nought* is left to chance." She then awoke, and I read it to her. Before I came away, she said, "It seems to me there will be some change ere we meet again; I do not know whether to you or to me, but I think to *you*."—Perhaps I looked startled, for she added, "The change may be a pleasant one, so we will look forward to it." . . . The only change I can now trace out, seems to have been my taking a seat as a member of the Council of our Association, with which I have ever since been so closely united; may God grant to it more, and fuller prosperity.

After having finished the drawing, I had been instructed to enclose the painting-rag I had used to my friend at Guildford, authoress of the charming little volume of " The Songs of the Spirit," in the hope that although she had not seen the picture, she might through that influence be inspired to write a poem on the subject. At her own home she could not do it, but she went for a short visit to her brother-in-law and sister, when the following sweet poem was written through her mediumship:—

"*Spirit Homes.*"

" If Spirit homes are beautiful,
  What must the Spirit be,
Which wrought those mansions for itself
  So swiftly—subtle-ly?
Out-wrought those walls with gorgeous hues,
  Those windows tall and fair,
Painted those pictures on the walls,
  And wove those curtains there?

" Who made that stone of amethyst?
  Who carved those gates of pearl?
Who wrought those banners beautiful
  Whose silken lengths unfurl?—

With colours such as setting sun
    Dyes all the clouds above—
And on whose folds the words we read,
    ' His banner it was Love.'

" '*If* Spirit homes are beautiful?'
    —No earthly words can trace
The deep mysterious joy of things
    Which fills the heavenly space :—
We cannot into mortal speech
    Put visions which we see
Of piles of mansions glorious
    And wondrous masonry !

" Of colours of immortal stones,
    And jewels so set therein
That all the rays are seas of light
    In which deep voices swim—
Where *sound* is *colour*, *colour*, *sound*,
    And *form* partakes of each,
Where every *line* and *tint* and *curve*
    God's inward lessons teach.

" How can we tell of windows grand
    With shapes unknown to art,
From out whose casements all the scenes
    Of past life brightly start ;
Of organs pealing songs of praise
    Whose notes like silver gleam,
And stringèd Harps whose symphonies
    Are as a rainbow stream?

" And over all the fair light falls
    Straight from the Throne on high,'
Upon which beam the Angel hosts
    Pass ever swiftly by—
Each leaving as they go some gift
    For her who dwelleth there—
Some gift which garnisheth the home,
    And maketh *her* more fair.

" No ! mortal words *are* powerless
    To tell of homes beyond—
We can but send our echoes down
    Upon some heart so fond—
And this heart strives to put in words
    The echoes it has heard—
Echoes indeed—*faint* echoes too—
    Of beauty of The Lord."
              E. F. C.

" Written for Miss Houghton, on Sunday morning, the 12th of July 1874, by one who has seen her painting.   E. F. C."

I have never learnt to whom it is that this Home belongs, but I dare say it may one day be made clear, and in both the spirit communications the owner is spoken of as feminine. It carries no thought of a home such as *we* might conceive, but it gives the idea of arched corridors, and of infinite expanse, with a sort of entirely open entrance, like a proscenium.

Another Mansion was then done, but this appears like the outside front, and there is a closed doorway under an arch. Nor have I any idea as to its intended inhabitant, who evidently does not, while tabernacling here below, pass in and out of it. Another special difference between the two is, that the first appears to be bathed in full sunlight, while the second seems to dwell under moonbeams, with wondrously pearly rays of softest, sweetest tints. When it was finished, I was again directed to send the painting-rag I had used during its execution to H. H., who was staying with her sister at the time, but the poem could not all be written at one sitting, and in her accompanying letter she says:
—"The first poem expressed to me *form*, this one, *sound*."

"*Seraphic Gleams.*"

" A white-robed army praises sing
 Unto their Leader's name :
A seraph host in accents sweet
 Tell of their Master's fame—
A single treble faintly falls
 In droppings on my ear,—
A mighty band of instruments
 Pour thunder on the air.

" Above the army clouds are set
 Of purple amethyst,
Whose shape and hue no mortal heart
 Hath ever fairly guessed—
The seraph host upon their wings
 Bear streams of silver spray,
Which flash in brightness over them,
 Then fall in light away—

" The single singer round his head
 Bears rays of changing sheen,
Which rise or fall in gentle time
 Each varying note between :

The mighty band not *sound* alone
　　Pours on the trembling air,
But makes all hues of colour rich,
　　And forms—fantastic fair.

" They move along to notes alike
　　Passing *one* road the whole—
The road which leadeth up to Him,
　　The Lord of life and soul—
Passing with beauty richly grand
　　And music strangely sweet,
To gather with the Sons of God,
　　Around the Father's feet.

" Homes these have fashioned for themselves,
　　Each weaving out his own;
Wherein the work of life on earth
　　Is to the Angels shewn—
Bright dwellings of those serried hosts,
　　Full of their hearts' desire;
Wrought by the action of the soul,
　　And lit with soulic fire.

" Adorned with pictured walls are they,
　　And hung with clouds of air,
Which take the rapture of the mind,
　　And *fix* that rapture there.
Within these homes are companies
　　Of soul-entrancing notes,
Which wake that soul to melody
　　That ever round you floats.

" And *rest*—sweet rest of perfect ease.
　　Peace—rapture—rest—in one,
The blending of the harmonies
　　Long past—with those begun—
A never-ceasing stream of joy,
　　A murmur of content,
An overlying symphony
　　By life's deep breathing lent.

" An undesirèd thrill of sound'
　　(Desire *here* not needed),
Which passes down from heaven—below
　　To fall on ears unheeded.
These are but symbols of the home
　　Prepared by spirit power;
Spirit divine—which from the Lord
　　Flows down from hour to hour."

"Begun 25th, finished 26th August 1874.　　　　E. F. C."

In the following April I went to stay with Mr. and Mrs. Bennett from Saturday till Monday, and on one of the evenings two lady friends came in. Through the mediumship of one of them, in trance, the following communication on the same subject was given.

" *To All.*

" I wish to say that your mansions are being built up very quickly; Miss Houghton has added a great many rooms to hers of late.

" Day by day and hour by hour you build up. Time and space *are* not. Your work is not accounted by earth days. You may build a whole room in one hour of your earth time, or you may be weeks, months, nay years, and not add one stone.

" Love and charity to others build up a room of which the walls are one blaze of what you would call rubies. Most glorious are those rooms of which the lustre is ever changing, opaline colours constantly flashing through. That is where the daily work and the daily life are done *not* for self, nor for others, to receive human gratitude or approbation—but done for the Master's sake.

" You must pray,—for much prayer makes a window in the house. As prayer lets in the light of heaven in your souls, so prayer lets in the light of God's glory. Many people build houses up above, and there are no windows to let the light in. Prayer lets in the light of God's glory into your homes."

To Miss Houghton.

" I wish you to remember Elijah and the ravens. Day by day will the strength come. Day by day in the wilderness was the manna given. There was none to be gathered up for the next day. None to be left through the night— God means that thus you shall work for Him until He chooses to alter His way concerning you. When that time comes He will warn you beforehand. He needs many to shew to an unbelieving world that Faith is the engine that is to remove mountains. You will find His promises fulfilled in a yet more extraordinary way than any that has yet come to you. By hands that you know not will the help be given, *at the time* and not before.

"We shall be yet more faithful and loving because you have done your work tenderly and conscientiously, and have thought not of the applause of men, but that you should do it for your Master, Christ. 'To him that overcometh will I grant to sit with me on a white throne, even as I overcame.'"

Sweetly indeed did that message then come to my soul, for already was I beginning to undergo what, as other years have passed on, has pressed more and more heavily upon me :—the difficulty from day to day, and even hour to hour, of a something coming in that should meet my absolute needs :—but still the word has been—" Make no change in thy life's surroundings—Maintain still thy home in its apparent externals, however straitened may be thine inward existence; for even such is The Lord's Will. The time will yet come when the world will see and acknowledge that a wisdom beyond theirs has guided thine actions. Remember also that thy very trials give opportunities to God's earthly angels to come ministeringly to thine aid, and thus they fill their own lives with blessings by blessing thine. Receive each gift, small or large, as from Him, and grieve not that He hath laid upon thee the Cross of apparent humiliation in having to accept what thou hast not earned; He seeth thy work, and knoweth that the labourer is worthy of her hire."

CHAPTER XIII.

I WENT to see Mrs. T. a day or two after I had resumed my artistic work by commencing the heavenly mansion just alluded to; but the earlier part of our conversation had reference to the persecutions and trials undergone by Mrs. P. in her unsought communion with the invisible world; for her inner or spiritual senses seem to have been opened without any effort on her own part. Her experiences were indeed terrible, many details of which I have given in the photographic chronicles, but she realised that notwithstanding all her sufferings, the blessings conferred by the higher communion fully outweighed them, and on no account would she have returned to the mere earthiness of her former state. I had had a letter from her that morning, in which she had referred to a former message through Mrs. T. for her; but nothing came that evening, and I have only made this slight mention of her now, because I have reserved one of her communications for this volume.

We touched upon many themes, and especially upon my being once more established at my easel after so long a cessation of that class of work. After awhile I was impressed to mesmerise her, when she passed into deep trance, and said:—"Now, as in the earlier times, there are diversities of gifts but the same Spirit, which worketh with varied manifestations in the same person or other ones. The more highly organised the medium, the greater the susceptibility in every faculty of mind:—such an one can be influenced in several directions, and the spirit power passes with ease for the time being to that faculty which is exercised, and it remains there for the special manifestation, or is then, in such an individual, readily diverted to another channel. Hence you may have the gifts of seeing, hearing, perception, and speech, in the same body, and according to the natural development shall be the fulness of each form of manifestation. (Extending her hand emphatically towards me,) *You* may covet earnestly the best gifts, and it shall be granted to you to receive a very high form of manifestation of that gift you may seek, and it shall be shewn how you had best use the gift. You may, if you will, knock at the door until it is opened, and the whole inner condition of spirit life revealed, seen, apprehended, and if you so desire it may be expounded by you." [I desire only to do that which may be my *best* work.] "It is well.—Please bear in mind that only one faculty can be *fully* stimulated at one time. The power employed, if diverted into several channels, loses force, so we recommend that you seek the best gift for the time, leaving as you have ever done, the future to God. Behind a frowning providence He hides a smiling Face, and the veil shall be removed *soon*. If, in God's providence, it should be made clear that you could work more effectually for His glory in this world by changing your earthly habitation for a heavenly mansion, could you?" [*Most gladly*—but I can submit to whatever may be God's Will.] "Peace possesseth your soul, for you *know* that He doeth all things well. —The thought may rest with you, and will do its work." She then awoke, and I read to her what had been said, when she wondered *who* had given the communication; and the answer came that it was S. John. She then wished me to read it again, as she had been scarcely roused before; and when I had finished, she heard a voice say, "Peace, peace I give unto you, *my* peace I give unto you,—not as the world giveth, give I unto you."

In that year, 1874, two of my dear ones were most happily married. Arthur in Batavia, on the 16th of October, and his one loved sister in Norwich, on the 8th of the same month, when I went down to the wedding, and for the very first time since their institution, was away from home on a Wednesday! not even leaving my thoughts behind, for they were much too fully and joyfully engrossed with all that was going forward. Philie,—who for upwards of two years had been following his professional career at Swansea, with only occasional flying visits to London,—was of course bright, active, and energetic among the Norwich group; but from the time of his sister's happy wedding, he began to dream about seeking prosperity in distant lands, the struggle being so hard in this densely populated Albion, so I felt our tenure upon him very insecure, and could only rejoice when he obtained a Government appointment in the Survey service of our own Ceylon, for which fair country he sailed, in the beginning of 1878, reaching Colombo on the 7th of February, his own birthday—a good omen indeed; and I am thankful to say that he has been going on most prosperously, and is now, in 1881, looking out for a happy union with the lassie of his heart, who is just on the eve of joining him, under the chaperonage of a married lady friend of his who has been making a visit to her family in England at exactly the right time; so he, like his brother and sister, will also be wedded in October. God bless them all!

I continued my regular monthly visits to Mrs. Marshall, but I made no more notes of any *word* that may have come, for in truth it was not as for a séance but a friendly visit that I went, and we talked about all that was going on among the Spiritualists, but there was doubtless always a something, whether much or little. Also, as it became known that it was my custom to go, I was sometimes the bearer of a little friendly aid from others in addition to my own small offering—and the help was needed!—but she *did* put her trust utterly in The Lord, and He failed her not! And so it went on into the new year. Mrs. T. had accompanied me on the June Tuesday, when I did take notes, and a good deal was about the coming babe (who duly made her appearance in August), but much was political, and referred to our war in India. She now said she should like to go with me on the evening of February 2nd, when we found that the poor old lady was very ill, and confined to her bed, but she said she should like to see us, and we stayed with her for about an hour, for I think our visit was soothing and pleasant to her, although it was very clear that her appointed time to be released from earth's cares was near at hand. Mrs. T. heard the words,— " In thirty days,"—and we thought that probably that was the announcement of when the end was to take place. Mrs. T.'s kindly gift would have to be expended in absolute necessaries, for we learned from Mrs. Morris how complete was the destitution; and Mrs. T. went the next morning to enlist Mr. Burns's sympathy and aid in raising a subscription to supply her wants, and an instalment came quickly: the later contributions serving to defray the expenses of her funeral, for her time had indeed been short: she had lingered but ten days after our visit, dying on the evening of the 12th, and on the 15th' Mrs. T. and I went to have a farewell glance at her placid countenance in her coffin. I will here extract a few sentences from the *Medium* of February 19, 1875. "A few days ago we were informed by Mrs. T., a lady who is so active in every good work, that Mrs. Marshall was very ill, and almost destitute. Some needful help was immediately afforded, and a private subscription for her relief was set on foot, to which several friends subscribed as soon as it was introduced to them. In the midst of this work it was reported that Mrs. Marshall passed away on Friday evening last, but the effort to obtain funds was continued with the view of meeting the funeral expenses. The interment took place at Paddington Cemetery. The coffin was conveyed in a hearse, and in the mourning coach which followed were Mr. Sherratt, Mr. W. Wallace, and Mr. Burns. There was no opportunity for giving the funeral publicity, or no doubt a number of friends would have attended at the grave. . . . Thus the faithful servant of the spirit was buried by her brethren; and the wreath of immortelles which Mr. Sherratt kindly placed on the coffin will be supplemented by the sympathetic regrets of thousands of Spiritualists in various parts of the world."

I must likewise quote the chief part of Mr. Shorter's obituary notice of her that appeared in the *Spiritual Magazine.* "Perhaps the name of no public medium in

England was for a long time so much before the public as that of the late Mrs. Marshall. From her childhood she seems to have had the gift of communion with the dwellers in the spirit-world. . . . With none of the advantages of education, fortune, or social position, she was a simple-minded religious woman, who, in the words of the Catechism, did her duty in that state of life into which it had pleased God to call her. Faithful in the exercise of her gifts, she encountered with great good-humour the obloquy, ridicule, and abuse often heaped upon her by the ignorant and unthinking, especially by flippant, conceited writers in the public journals. Many, who were once sceptics and unbelievers in a spiritual world and an immortal life, have acknowledged that, under God and His ministering angels, it was to her they were indebted for the presentation of facts which brought home to them a conviction of those great truths which changed the current of their lives; which have become their hope and joy and strength; the sunshine of their Souls—a clear, constant light in the dark places of their earthly pilgrimage: and many—very many more—who have not made this open testimony, know full well how deep are their obligations to her in this respect.

"Mrs. Marshall had her full share of earthly trial and affliction, but through all, Spiritualism was her strength and stay and enduring consolation to the end. She had a simple, abiding trust in the care of God, and she knew of those things most surely believed among us. It were to be wished that a biography of her, with a full account of her remarkable experiences, could be written; but as no diary, or record of the séances, was kept, I fear that little data for such a work exists, other than is to be found in this and other Spiritualist journals. She had just completed her 76th year. It was the intention of a few friends to have placed a memorial stone over the place where her mortal remains are laid, but the shortness of time in which the necessary arrangements had to be made, combined with some misunderstanding, made this impossible. For the sake of any who may wish to see the spot, it may be mentioned that the grave is numbered 4004 in the Paddington Cemetery, near the Edgware Road Station of the North London Railway. (Mrs. T., since that time, has had a tree planted upon the grave.) But there could be no memorial of her who has gone like the ever-fragrant memory of her useful life and of the services she has rendered. Her best memorial is in the hearts of those to whom she has brought the assurance and comfort which the faith and knowledge of Spiritualism must bring to all who live up to the light of its revelation. As must necessarily be the case, the early workers in our ranks are year by year becoming fewer; but let us for our encouragement remember the words of John Wesley, 'God buries His workmen, but He carries on the work.' T. S."

No one can feel more warmly than I do, the full truth of all that Mr. Shorter has said, and I could not make up my mind to curtail one word of it. To her, most undoubtedly, I owe my own first knowledge of Spiritualism and its wondrous blessedness, which has been a boon beyond anything else that this world can give, and I am happy in knowing that I brightened up a little bit of the latter end of her life, for she always enjoyed my visits very much. She told me once that she had been writing some of the wonderful visions she had had, but I do not suppose those papers have been preserved. She had one weakness, poor dear, and that was aggravated by a weak head, so that a small quantity of liquor of any kind would, I understand, overcome her, but in my own experience, I have never witnessed any symptom of it, only I know that the accusation has been made.

On Thursday, March 4th, I was to go to Mrs. T.'s for the remainder of the day, after my visit to Mr. Hudson, and we both wondered whether there might come any evidence of the presence of our old friend, as that would be the thirty days from the time of our visit to her. I reached the Albert Road at about four o'clock in the afternoon, and I had not been very long with her before I saw that she was passing under influence, and she placed her hands in a peculiar manner, one hand, as it were, overlapping the other upon her waist. But it was some little time before she spoke, and said:—"Miss Houghton,—it *is* Miss Houghton, is it not? [Oh! yes.] But it is not *Tuesday*, is it?" Poor old soul! how she must have calculated upon my visits!—But that first day's communication was indeed a painful one. Of course my first question was if she were happy; and the sad response was *No*.——She had thought she should go at once to a happy heavenly home, but she had found no dwelling-place, and was just a poor, wandering, homeless spirit; and she plaintively said: "But I *did love* The Lord—I *always* loved The Lord." [Yes, dear, you always did.] And she had thought she should go at once to The Lord. But alas! as she whisperingly told me in shame-stricken tones, it was the drink. Neither could she find a resting-place here, for if she went to the rooms she had been living in, the same atmosphere of drink was there, and that harmed her yet more. [Could I not help her? Could she not come to me?] "No; my home was too sacred, she might not obtain admittance." [Could she not come to me when I was in the street, and thus gain strength and help?] "Perhaps that might be possible, if I would think strongly about her; at any rate my loving thoughts would go to her wherever she might be, and thus she would be helped, and gradually raised out of her pitiable condition." She told us that she had been to see her son Emanuel, and that he had done a number of pictures, and she also told something of what had passed with him. Dear, kindly-hearted soul, she wept sorely while making her confession, but I cheered and comforted her as best I could, and she said she could always come to me when I should be at Mrs. T.'s, and even if it should not be well or expedient for her to manifest, she should still be able to gain something by the intercourse. When Mrs. T. awoke from her trance, she found herself in a kind of half-sobbing state, and was deeply touched when I related to her the grievous history I had heard, which surprised us both, for we knew that she truly was religious, and that, as she said, *she did love The Lord*, but that alas! proved insufficient unless that love should shew itself by *self*-control. I fulfilled my promise, and kept her much in my thoughts during my short outings, although some weeks elapsed ere I received any information that she could be by my side, and that was not until I had again had a little message from her at Mrs. T.'s; when she told me she was happier, and in mysterious undertones begged me to try to forget the wrong things she had done, for that she was getting rid of the influences that had clung to her. On one of my visits to Mrs. T., having first been to Mr. Hudson's (for at that time the Thursday used to be her reception-day), cake and wine had been handed round, of both of which I had partaken; and when other callers had left, Mrs. T. was for a little while influenced by Mrs. Marshall, whose first signal was always that especial placing of the hands; but she then told me that she smelled my breath of the wine, and that it gave her a hankering for something of the sort! What a lesson that was! By our own self-indulgence we may arrest the upward progress of those who are striving to raise themselves out of the depths! But I did not again take an afternoon half-glass, although I had not in those days become a teetotaller as I have since done.—I have not taken the pledge, but I retired from the use of such things purely and entirely from motives of economy, notwithstanding that I almost feared lest at my time of life it might prove a hazardous proceeding with regard to my health, so the new habit was gradually assumed, small by degrees, and beautifully less, the old custom having always been a very moderate one, and no harm whatever has accrued, so that it will never be resumed.

I must now return to 1874, and transcribe a letter that I addressed to the editor of the *Spiritual Magazine.*—"SIR, —I was present on Tuesday, June 23rd, at a séance at her own house that Mrs. Guppy kindly gave, at my request, for the gratification of Mr. and Mrs. Brown, of Belfast, and just before the conclusion, the spirit Katie, in audible voice, asked me to write an account of it, which I have much pleasure in now doing.

"The circle consisted of Mr. and Mrs. Guppy, Mr. and Mrs. Brown, Mrs. Petman, Mr. Dodd, Mr. Volckman, Mr. Swinburne, Mr. Gale (of Hull), Mr. Hudson (of Leeds), and myself, and the door was locked as soon as we were all assembled.

"Mrs. Guppy has, by spirit direction, had a round hole about seven inches in diameter cut in her table, and the piece again fixed in with a hinge so that it can be raised up like a kind of lid, and that, in our first sitting, was just between Mrs. Brown and me. When we had sat for some little time, faintly glimmering lights, about the size of the glow-worm's lamp, were seen flitting about, and occasionally it seemed as if there were four or five together, but I think they must have been as it were attached to an opaque substance, for every one could not see them at once, only as if they turned about, and were thus shewn. We were then, by raps, through the alphabet, told to 'wish,' and in answer to our questions, that we were to confine ourselves to flowers, but we only received doubtful responses to any that were specified, and suddenly a mass of something fell upon the table, when we were permitted to have a light, and found a heap of fragrant roses, white and coloured, which were a grand delight to my four special friends, who had never witnessed such a manifestation. When again in darkness, 'Sit close to the door,' was spelt out, and we then ascertained that Mr. Gale and Mr. Hudson were to leave the circle, and place themselves in front of the door which was afterwards to be partly opened, thus admitting some light from the gas lamp in the hall; the ladies' dresses were then to be held up to the edge of the table so as to darken beneath it, and almost immediately the little lid was thrust up from below so as to leave the open space in the table. Mr. Volckman had before asked the spirits to bring him the branch of cherry-tree that had been taken to his own chambers at a séance a couple of evenings previously, and now up this aperture was thrust a long branch of cherry-tree (not his, but freshly gathered), and there was light enough for us all to see it rise; several other branches were passed up in the same manner, which we took from the invisible hands that gave them to us. Mrs. Guppy asked if they would take a rose from her, and on an affirmative being rapped out, she held a white rose over the hole, which after a time was taken from her, and it seemed to move backwards and forwards by its own volition and then disappeared. We were told to place a handkerchief over the hole, which we did, but just then there was a knock at the door, and another gentleman arrived, but as Katie desired me not to mention his name, I will designate him as Mr H., and his entrance seemed to alter the conditions, for we were then told to go to tea, after which we strolled for some little time in the garden.

"Instead of coming to the second sitting, which was altogether dark, Mr. Guppy and Mr. Brown went upstairs to the billiard-room, so that Mr. H. sat at Mrs. Guppy's right hand, while I retained my own place at her left. The table, in our movements, had been shifted round, so that the little lid, now closed, was in front of Mrs. Guppy. We had not been long seated, when the lid was flapped up and down, and I soon found it was being done in a sort of rhythm, and I exclaimed, 'Oh! it is Jim!' for I recognised the beat of Jim Ramsay's signal, and then three raps were joyously given with it, as if exulting in the recognition. I then said, 'But I have not had Môtee's signal to-night,' when immediately I felt her gentle fingers tapping the pearl ring. I asked her to go and touch Mrs. Petman, that she too might know the tender feel of a spirit hand, and she instantly complied. They told me that the General (their father) was with them. Each person was then touched, more or less gently, with the cherry-tree branches, and Mrs. Guppy wanted some one to wish for sea-weed. We all smelled perfumed water, and I felt the soft fingers bathing my upper lip and nostrils with it. 'Light' was spelt out, and on the table was a scallop shell filled with *sea water*, to which perfume had been added, but the flavour of the sea water was unmistakable.

"Mr. Volckman then had to leave in order to catch his train; when the door was again locked, and shortly after his departure, Mr. H. began to make convulsive starts, with exclamations of, 'Don't, don't! No, that's too much!' and we all wanted to know what was the matter. 'Oh! it's a pin!' he jerked out; and then the back of my hand was gently pressed with the point of a pin, so as to give me sensational information, and I asked the invisibles to do the same to Mrs. Petman and Mr. Dodd, which they did, but again the attack was renewed upon the sceptical Mr. H., who declared that the pin was being continually driven into him for about an inch. At last he sprang up, exclaiming, 'Oh! I have got him! a light, quickly!' 'Hold fast!' said Mrs. Guppy, 'and do make haste with the light!' But the first match missed, and Mr. H. was still struggling violently with the being he had caught, but when the candle was at length lighted there was no one in the corner, where Mr. H. in his impetuous rush had fallen on to the ottoman; but he declared that he had had his arms round some one who seemed as large as himself (and he is both tall and stout), and that he had *seen* something by the faint light of the match that had missed. I think he had felt sure that he had caught hold of a mortal who was playing a practical joke upon him, and therefore held him as firmly as he could, for he was quite panting and breathless with the exertion. Mrs. Guppy was vexed that he had not retained his grasp of the spirit, but that, alas! had melted from his hold, without leaving anything for us to see, notwithstanding which it was a very exciting incident, and after we had calmed down, Katie's voice made me the request I have mentioned, and 'Good night;' was rapped out. I had the pleasure of meeting Mrs. Guppy two evenings later at a friend's house, and was glad to find she had not suffered by the spirit's having been so roughly handled, and we again had a very good séance."

I made one of my most valued friendships during the

hiatus between Mr. Hudson's two studios, for, at a séance at Mr. Williams's, the spirit photographs came under discussion, and some who until then were strangers to that class of phenomena were desirous of obtaining specimens, which Mr. Hudson had not then the means of printing, so Sir Charles Isham, who was present, gave my address, saying that doubtless I might still have some on hand, and the 28th of May brought me a new visitor with whom I had a long and interesting conversation, touching on almost everything connected with Spiritualism and its teachings.

On the 2nd of July I paid my first visit to Mr. Hudson at Notting Hill, so as to have the pleasure of congratulating him, as well as seeing and hearing all the arrangements he was planning, for he had only just got in, and everything was in disarray. We both looked forward to better times being at hand, but as yet there could be no photography, and I did not commence my regular Thursdays until that day fortnight; but he had lost his *haunted* house, and there was not the smallest atom of spirit essence in the walls or belongings, so that it was some time before any sitters could obtain manifestations, all his outflow being *absorbed* into the deadly coldness of the building. I did not attempt to have any sittings, for in truth I had not the wherewithal to meet the expense, and I am sorry to say that I had but one professional sitter ere that year closed in; neither did Mr. Hudson have many sitters, although it had seemed probable that the extreme facility of access to his new place would have been in his favour. He was also disappointed in his hope that secular photography might here come to him in good proportion, but alas! Kensington Park Road was a *side-street*, and passers-by were scarce, so that scarcely anything came to him in liquidation of the *good-will* he had paid for, and from the negatives left with him by his predecessor, I think he had but *one single demand*, that of a boy who had since died. I cannot accuse him of any error in judgment in thus having been misled, because he had to take what he could get with the very limited means at his disposal, and his chief hopes were from the

Spiritualists themselves, stimulated now and then by some decided photographic success; as for example, when he had been there a couple of months the brothers Lamont with a couple of their Liverpool friends came, and the spirit face is as clear and substantial as any of their own, and he naturally concluded that all Spiritualists from the country would be sure to wend their way to him as soon as they reached London, let them be coming for ever so short a visit. My own first sitting with him was on the 7th of January, 1875, and was a grand success.

In September, Mr. and Mrs. Guppy, with their two children, went over to Ireland, and a month later he sent me a most admirable photograph taken in Dublin of himself and his wife, in which he looks as full of power and vigour as if he were at least ten years younger, and that is my last memento of him, for his death took place calmly and quietly in his sleep on the 18th of January, while they were staying in the neighbourhood of Cork, at Dr. Barter's hydropathic establishment. It came upon her quite as an unexpected blow, for he had seemed as if he might have had many more years of life. She came back to England as speedily as she could, and remained for some little time in apartments at Knightsbridge, where I went at once to see her. The term for which they had let the house at Highbury was still unexpired; but she resolved upon not returning to it, and eventually took a house in Victoria Road, Kensington, where she was more within the reach of her numerous friends.

Wonderful are the various phases of spirit power, and I am here going to narrate one of our Friday séances, which I was told to defer until now, although it took place in 1870. When Mrs. T. came in, on the 8th of April, she mentioned that a well-known friend of hers (in Massachusetts) had recently passed away, and that she had been a good deal engaged in writing on the subject to other friends.— After I had mesmerised her for some time, she saw a purple light, and presently she exclaimed: "Oh! I do think this is Mrs. D——, dear me!—It was only a glimpse; she seemed to pass just before me. She looked exactly as she used to look except that she stooped a little.—I see the main street at Hope Dale,—just as it used to look,—from top to bottom. I see a face I know so well, and yet for the life of me I can't remember the name. . . Oh! it is Edmund Soward; I think he is in the spirit world,—I am sure he is;—he died of consumption about fifteen years ago. Oh! yes: he had on something like a cloak, which he has taken off to show me his jacket of green baize. He used to be called the walking cyclopedia, because he knew something of everything.—He was a great friend of Mr. and Mrs. D——; he always dined there when they had friends who had need of intelligent conversation. He is going down the street from the school-house, and I am going with him. —I am passing some houses that I don't remember, where there used to be flowers and some nursery trees,—and the houses need painting very much. We go straight past where Mrs. D—— lived; straight down, till we come to a house with a large running piazza.—I see!—there is a circle, a spirit circle; I see the people sitting in front, I see four people whom I know sitting in this circle, and there are several others who are strange." [Can you mention the names of those whom you know?] "Mr. Eben D——, Mrs. George D——, Mr. B——, and a little girl called Mary, who is grown very tall, and many others: there are two coloured people.—I have lost my spirit guide:—we came in through the window, which opens like a French window." [Perhaps there is something special that you are to note.] "One of the ladies whom I don't know is gesticulating very much; she seems to be making a speech. There is some person in the circle from whom I feel such a pleasant influence. One of those black women is saying that she sees me.—It is old Aunt Johnson! so it is! Old Auntie Johnson! and she has got so much older. She sees me, and she thinks I am a spirit. They are standing up and pointing, and she is pointing;—and it seems to make me so much smaller somehow; I feel as if I must hide.—I am going into the corner of the room, close to a musical instrument, and it is open: I think it is a melodion; and there are so many keys, two or three ranks of keys.—I have got out of the room somehow into the garden, close to a rose-bush. I think old Auntie Johnson frightened me away; she wanted me to come close to her: she is calling to me: she says, 'Tell me about my boy Jem.'—Oh! she thinks I am a spirit. Poor little Jemmy was drowned a long time ago, and I don't see him anywhere. . . . I am going right up,—above the house." Here she awoke with a start, and she told me she was feeling frightened lest she should fall, and she reasoned with herself that it was only a dream, but the fear roused her, and the experience was curious and quite new to her.

CHAPTER XIV.

On the 21st of March 1875, I was agreeably surprised by a visit from my old friend whom I had known as Mr. Joseph Maurice, during the time of the enquiry into Spiritualism of the Dialectical Society, but who had now resumed his name in the original form, as Maurice Joseph, by which latter surname I shall henceforward mention him. I was shocked to see what a wreck he had become of his former self, but he had been suffering from various ailments, among them paralysis; and his nerves were still so unstrung that he could speak but few words and in a low tone, and even thus could talk but little at a time. By gradual degrees, he told me that he had been deeply under spiritual influences, and that his sufferings at times had been very intense, partly physical, but partly spiritually induced, and it is even possible that the paralysis itself may have been the work of malignant influences, such as might have been the case but for Mrs. T.'s timely warning, with another friend of mine, as I have narrated towards the close of the previous volume; and who may say how frequently such may be the primary cause of long and painful illnesses among those who believe not in the inter-communion between the two worlds, but who are none the less operated upon from the other side? Also, it is possible that if awakened to the truth, they might receive relief, even in the same way, from the invisible side.

It appeared to me as if he had been, as it were, a kind of battle-field for antagonistic influences, and he now came to me on a mission from very decidedly the wrong source, for it was with an entreaty that *I* should altogether give up spirit communion, which he was to urge upon me to the utmost. Of course, even such a step was only *permitted* by the higher influences in the certain knowledge that far from changing my life, it would lead to his own strengthening in his mediumship, as indeed was at once proved even on that very first day; after which he came to me with tolerable frequency, gathering both physical and mental strength by each visit. Many people say,—Oh! the spirits who come to people teach always the religious dogmas of the medium him or her-self, whatsoever may be their creed either of belief or unbelief.—His was most undoubtedly an evidence of a very contrary character. Be it remembered that he was a Jew:—he had been developed into trance mediumship long before this illness commenced; and even in the earlier days he told me, that to his rather horror, once on awaking from one of those trances, he found himself praying to the Virgin Mary! nothing could *possibly* be farther from his own religious views! and I consider that even that one circumstance is sufficient to topple down the theory as a dogmatic fact, although I do grant that the spirits that surround a person are likely to be those whose views are in harmonious accord, but they may nevertheless become gradually remodelled either for better or for worse according to the influences to which they may yield themselves whether for higher or lower instruction, and we also know that the thirst for conversion is as strong among some of the dwellers on the other side, as it had been with them before quitting this earth.

In his case, the struggle was very much upwards, but his was a peculiar mission, therefore it was fought against with such deadly virulence by the evil angels. He had had wondrous visions of which he had in those days kept full records, but in one of the *dark* moments he had been induced to burn the manuscripts. (Like Emanuel Marshall with his pictures, and other instances that I have known.) He was not a student of Scripture, and therefore could not realize the special grandeur of some of his own visions, which in his many visits he would relate very fully to me, and I could frequently shew him in the Bible the full meaning and interpretation of what he had passed through. I wish I had had some of those destroyed records, for the visions, with the light thus thrown upon them, were of deep interest; but it would have been too much for me to attempt to write down any of them after he had left me, for my own life's work has always been too close for me to have had such time to spare. . . . The truth was that all unknowingly he was being led up to Christianity. Even on his first visit he told me in how many things he had already made a change : for instance, instead of *standing*, according to the custom of his nation, he would *kneel* to pray. . . and the words he employed were those of The Lord's Prayer, retiring to his own room three times a day for that purpose. A large proportion of his visional teaching, was to shew (which comes to me to and through so very many sources) the rapid approach of some great change taking place in the spirit world, and the intense effort being made to raise the unfortunate ones in the lower spheres—and also that the antagonism between good and evil is stronger than has ever hitherto been the case, consequently the conflict between the two powers becomes more and more fierce. Do we not see it even here on earth?—look at drunkenness, what a fearful scourge it is!—and see the mighty efforts being made in all the land to contend with and utterly subdue it: efforts chiefly made with religious fervour, seeking help from The Lord, and how wonderful in the last year or two has been the realized improvement. In Mr. Joseph's own seekings after higher light, I never attempted in any way to lead or to bias him; I simply answered any questionings he might put to me, of course according to my own views, but I was always tenderly careful to say no word that should even hint at controversy. His nation had received the truth in the earlier ages, and to them we are indebted for our own Scripture evidences as far as *they* went; and a portion, too, of that same nation gave us the written records of the New Testament, but—could they all have received that fresh revelation, the olden prophecies would have been falsified—therefore we are their debtors both for what they did believe, and for what they did not. As a nation I honour and esteem them highly, as well as being firmly convinced of their close kinship, and that we, sturdy Britons, are likewise lineally descended from Jacob—of the tribe of Joseph—of the tribe of Ephraim. My faith is centred in The Lord, and I can trust all whom I love or care for in His Hands, secure that in His good time they shall be led into the fulness of truth; therefore it is that I am not given to proselytising, either into Christianity or into Spiritualism, although I am ready and willing enough to speak whenever the words may be called for. I have been asked—Oh! do talk to so-and-so about Spiritualism.—No: let them seek from me, and I will tell with open heart, but were I to speak at the wrong moment, I might do more harm than good. I was once enquired of by a dear but sceptical friend, as to whether I looked upon the refusal of these new truths as a sin, therefore I sought for *advice* how to answer her judiciously;—and the written message was —" In Our Lord's time there were many of the Jewish nation who *could not* accept Him as the Messiah. Therein were they guiltless while they persecuted Him not either by word or deed. It was the active antagonism that formed the sin to be visited upon themselves and their children, even according to their own cry. So now, in these latter days, there are some who walk blindly on, unheeding the wonders vouchsafed :—for their blindness they may be pitied, nor will sin therein be imputed to them unless by scornful word or bitter action they may wound those who are God's appointed agents in disseminating the fresh truths He is now shedding forth." Although I have applied the word sceptical to my friend, I must do her the justice to say that she knows but very little on the subject, for she dwells at the antipodes, and during her visit to England was only twice able to spend a few short hours here, when we had many other things to talk about, so that Spiritualism could have but a small share of our time.

The awakening that God is now giving to our senses, is to teach us of the influences that have ever been around the path of humanity, whether acknowledged or otherwise, while at the same time we receive the unmistakable evidences that the *possessions* spoken of in the Gospels were literal facts, however much the *intellectual* world may desire to class them under medical terms of disease, such as epilepsy, &c.;—and perhaps even in these days, their so-called epilepsy might be driven out by angelic ministry. In the Chronicles of Spirit Photography, I have given copious extracts from the letters of Mrs. P., a lady who had suffered in many ways from the malignity of untoward and low-class spirits. She had obtained much relief through the photographs I sent her, because the portrait, thus filled with their own emanations, became a link whereby she could implore the spirits' presence and aid when her tormentors became absolutely unbearable. I have saved one of her communications for this volume, and will here transcribe it, premising that I had sent to her (by direction) some frankincense (gum olibanum), for her to burn in case of any strong emergency, so as to "purify by fire," as I had been instructed to do at Mr. Hudson's when untoward influences had clung to the studio in consequence of the mixture of visitors.

"*September 25th*, 1874.—MY DEAR MISS HOUGHTON,— Again, thank God! having returned home, I am able to write to you, and to return you thanks for *all* your kindness, and for your last most thoughtful present of the frankincense which proved most useful to me. How well the dear kind spirits who favour you with their presence understand my position and the class of some of the spirits that haunt me. How happy you are with such friends, not, thank God, that I am friendless, for I have, and always have had, powerful spirit friends; indeed, were it not so, I do not know what would have become of me. I assure you I have often been snatched from the hands of spirits who I am quite sure would have caused my death. If you were to read my spiritual diary you would see that such has been the case, and at one time I was actually afraid to have the power of leaving my room, so awful was the temptation to suicide. On one night in particular I was nearly wild with terror; I never ceased praying to God, although I was so

exhausted that all I could say was—' Oh! God save me!'
and a sneering spirit man kept continually whispering,
'Ah! you will find your prayers are of no use; you'll find
that the evil spirit who is beside you is stronger than the
God who is far off.'—I then fell into a magnetic doze, and
I saw a dearly loved spirit-uncle (who was as a father to
me, my own father having died while I was an infant)
approach me and take my hand, speaking kind and encouraging words, and assuring me of safety and protection.
The wretched wicked spirit fled, and I never again was so
awfully beset. But nothing can be clearer than the protection St. Stephen affords me by means of the photograph."
Here follows her account of her burning the frankincense,
which I have narrated elsewhere. . . . "A lady, a Spiritualist friend of mine, has told me that the house I have
been staying in, had been, prior to my relatives living in
it, inhabited by a very dissolute man, and that he and
his two mistresses (or as they call them, his wives) are
the spirits who haunt it. I used every night to be awakened
in terror conscious of an evil presence, and then I would
always see some one at the bedside, either leaning over me
with outstretched hand, the fingers pointing to my forehead,
or else some strange object more like a withered stick with
a bunch of twigs at the end which would point at me in the
same way. One night I saw a thing like a dark cloud at
the further side from me about five feet high; at the top
was what I at last saw was something like a human head—
the size was tremendous, and it was covered with dark
brown fur, which hung before the lower part of it in jagged
ends: there were two fiery bloodshot eyes also of tremendous size, which steadily glared at me; the other features I
could not distinguish. This thing remained quite still until
I drove it back by adjuration and prayer; but the injury to
my health you could scarcely credit. Often have the voices
said in cruel mockery :—'We are vampyres, we live on
your magnetism, and the cause of your ill health is mainly
occasioned by *us.*' They used to say, while I was in town,
to each other: 'Are you hungry?'—The other would

answer: 'Yes, I am; I think I would like some,' then they would mention something that I could get; and I assure you I would get ravenously hungry for the thing specified, *nor could I rest till I got it.* They would make me in this way eat or drink what they pleased:—was not this awful? but never did they have any influence to cause me to take anything but what *was* suitable; but so alarmed have I often felt, fearing they might make me do something contrary to my habits, that I used always to be in prayer to God for His divine protection. What a field for thought is thus opened up! how awfully near is that world of temptation that Our Lord warned us against! How much to be pitied are those who fall! How various must be the causes of our falls! What a light those things throw on the sudden acts, the crimes sometimes committed by persons who previous to this act had lived blameless lives!"

"April 21st, 1875. . . Be assured, dear Friend, that among the many who are indebted to your philanthropy, there can scarcely be one that needed your help more, or who is more grateful to you than I am. Even last night those precious spirit photographs were, *as ever*, a source of peace and safety to me. In my spiritual diary I have noted down with ample details the several occasions on which they released me from the attacks of what in aspect and according to their own account were 'Fiends.' Last night I was told with bitter mockery by two of the 'voices,' that *they* it was who had prevented me from writing to you, and that it was *they* who had made me as ill as I have been and am. Also they added, 'Not to make such a fool of myself as to think they were unhappy spirits: that they were *devils*, and far from being unhappy that they were very jolly, and would rather be where they are, and where they enjoy their liberty, than imprisoned in Heaven where there is no amusement but flying about; also that they are quite sure of having me with them, and that their delight was in thinking how they would torture me for not always listening to them.' I drove them off in the name of God and Christ, and now they are vowing vengeance against me. I spoke to them about the 'pit,' the 'abyss,' the horror of darkness, in which the Bible tells us impenitent sinners are finally engulfed. They seemed affected for a moment, but afterwards they seemed as usual.

"During the time I was unable to write to you, my two daughters were away from me; the eldest being in very bad health, and the other went for a week to take care of her; and I really think that but for the photographs and the frankincense I should have died one night; and after that I was obliged to drag myself out a little every day. *I felt the air thick with spirits:* they were principally historical characters (English), about the time of the Tudors, and more especially James 1st. The poor spirit who calls himself 'The White Rose,' that Sir Andrew Melville talks of, has been about me from the first time my sight was opened. I could not rightly understand him, other spirits so often interrupted him, but I think it was he, who after escaping from the Tower, was retaken by the treachery of a woman, and something about an apparition. All these and many more pressed on me, actually stifling me night and day. At last I was seized with violent and continual retchings, which lasted until my younger daughter returned. We again sat at the table, and *at once* the retchings subsided; but whenever we give up the sittings the sickness returns. I have an impression that this is caused by my guardian spirits, for my foes, the ' voices,' have always done their utmost to make me give up sitting in circle, as that brings me into relation with other spirits, and *weakens their own influence*, and I have been seized with such an unaccountable *disgust* to Spiritualism that I dare say I would have desisted, and so have given them more power."

On the 17th of May I wrote to her, enclosing the painting-rag I had used while engaged upon a drawing of "The Eye of The Lord" which I had just completed, with directions to use it for *health* purposes, by placing it upon the spot where she might at the time be suffering pain, specifying also how long it was to remain (I think only half an hour, but I am not sure, and only followed the directions given to me at the time by my *teachers*), and that it was afterwards immediately to be replaced in the envelope—also that it was not to be applied too frequently, so as always to come with fresh vigour. Her answer was: "MY DEAR GOOD FRIEND,—How can I thank God sufficiently for sending you to my help? What a consolation it must be to you to think of the forlorn and bound creatures that you have relieved! That piece of calico which you sent to me has relieved me more than once *instantly* by following your directions. Another thing is that your remarks about *hostile spirits* causing a feeling of dislike and repugnance to Spirit manifestations in order that they may retain the sufferer under their own control, has often been remarked by me. I always noticed that when my mediumship was low, I was ill, out of sorts, every way miserable; I could not refrain from giving you this information, but I can write no more at present. May God's blessing be ever about you, you good woman, and believe me, even in your earthly life you will be blessed, for the blessings of those you have so disinterestedly helped will surround you like a halo of light. Believe me ever your faithful friend, E. P."

My suffering friend (still personally unknown to me) was removed from this life some four or five months later, and her daughter adds: "Her end was so peaceable that we did not for some time perceive that she had passed away. I trust that we shall all terminate our pilgrimage here as happily as she did." She had frequently assured me that notwithstanding the persecutions she had undergone from those malignant ones, the higher spiritual communion was so transcendant a blessing that the trials were comparatively insignificant, so that on no account would she have been again shut up from it. I have often since been conscious of her presence with me, and she has her own signal whereby she makes it known.

In one of our very far-back Friday séances, Mrs. T., after having been mesmerised, passed under influence, and said:—"There is a spirit I do not quite like. He has followed me here, and he says I am to tell you that he came, so that I could see him, last night about twelve o'clock. He represents himself as a catholic priest:—he is shewing me the back of his head, which is quite shaved at the crown: he has black hair, which is combed forwards; a long flannel dress tied at the waist with a black ribbon; last night his dress was black." [Perhaps he wants help from us.] " He means to make converts. His face is not at all nice. He can't get very near us; there is a crimson light, and he cannot get past that:—he reaches his arms over, but it is of no use. He says he got nearer to me yesterday. He has a book in his hand; it has a cross on the cover. His face is covered with wrinkles, and has quite a yellow cast; if it had but a little more wickedness in it, it would be something quite frightful. He says he is appointed to go to Australia with that young man I told you about, and that we have no power to prevent him. He will do his best to convert him to his own faith. He says he comes to tell us because he thinks it right to acquaint us with his intentions, which he considers judicious, and for the good of the young man, whose mind cannot be led right without high authority such as is only found in the mother church. He says if he did not take him in hand, he would be open to undeveloped spirits who would control him, and affect his mind again." [You are now uttering things that you know to be *false*, and striving, in Jesuit-like spirit, to give them a favourable colouring. The young man will be granted better guides than you are.] " He says he needs *control, authority*.—He has lifted his hand, and says— You see I can control *your* friends." [Here I was spoken through quite strongly to the effect that he knew it was only *by permission*, for some especial reason that he was allowed to come, and that he was a *false, lying* spirit.] " His face has turned quite black, Oh! Oh!" (Shuddering.)

"Some odours are being brought. The spirit whose control I generally feel, tells me I am not to fear that such a spirit will be allowed to control me when I am alone, because there is a line which he cannot cross." On returning to the normal condition, she still seemed uncomfortable, and said, "I feel so shaken." I mesmerised her for a short time, when she quite rallied, and passed again under influence. "I am in a cloud.—Why, there is Grandmamma! I thought I saw her face just before. Can you see Miss Houghton, Grandmamma?—She says, Yes.—I do not come often, but I am come now because you appeared in trouble.—She is shewing me her hair: it is like it used to be, as I remember it; I had forgotten it was cut off a little behind in the neck, and she is shewing me the place; I had quite forgotten it. . . . Here is the spirit who has a special interest in our séances." [Oh! can you help that poor young man, so as to prevent him from being influenced by that Jesuit priest? you, as having been perverted to catholicism, and then brought Home again, may have more influence over him than others.] "He was not permitted to come *near you*, and the same power will guard the one whom he is seeking to win. There is a Will stronger than *his* will. It is foreseen that the priest will have no power while the youth keeps his reason. He cannot unaided reach his mind with his religious views: that is his only aim, to proselytise, though why he should have made known his mission I cannot tell, without he was *compelled* to do so by some power stronger than his own. What is called insanity is frequently only another name for obsession, and such spirits as that one, are sometimes strong enough to overturn the undefended reason." [Was it he who influenced you?] "It was in his likeness. Oh! Oh! Oh!—I could have resisted the power at first if I had sought help, and had believed it was evil, but I was self-willed, and it grew too strong for me; it took my reason. A circle should be always conducted in such a spirit that it may be impossible for any of those to enter who go up and down seeking whom they may devour. Part of my work now is to help poor mortals to resist their influences, and when my strength is insufficient, more is given to me." [It must be consolatory work for you, dear.] "Sad, sad, but it is useful work." The remainder of the séance diverged to other points, and has already been recorded.

In *Human Nature* for August 1870 is a long article bearing upon the same subject; written by J. H. Hall, giving an account of strong physical manifestations, which I will curtail wherever I can... "I went at once to the house, No. 972, 6th Avenue, New York, and found out from the family the following particulars.... It consisted of a girl (medium), eleven years old, an uncle, also an uncle just deceased, and two aunts. They appeared to be people in middle circumstances, catholic persuasion, with strong prejudices. They were ordinarily intelligent, but the girl was unschooled. I happened to get there just after the spirits had made a raid.... Entering the parlour, the various pictures from the walls were strewn about, *except the catholic pictures*, which were not touched. Behind the sofa, and under it where one could not go without lifting the sofa out, lay every movable thing in the house, not very heavy, as nicely and in regular order as could be; then in the pantry lay upon the floor perhaps 20 dols. worth of china, plates, tureens, dishes, all emptied out of the cupboard at one time, in a heap, and smashing nearly every one of them. A large fine looking-glass broken all to pieces; a sewing machine, thrown over, lay on the floor broken; a large bell in the hall, which had been rung furiously. In the bedrooms, articles were found stowed away between mattresses, and the uncle said he had had 4 dols. taken away from him. These people are strong catholics and unfriendly to Spiritualism. The rappings began at the door and in the house before the old man died, but nothing so terrible as the above. They could not punish the girl for it, because it occurred in *broad daylight*, when the girl was not near the places where the destruction was going on. A spirit seized the girl's hand one time and hurled something at an aunt, for which she was whipped; she seemed to love her aunt, and is said to be affectionate and kind. When the girl was sent away the manifestations were less violent.... Various were the surmises.... We convened a circle on going home (Mrs. Marquand was the medium), and to our mental enquiry 'What does this mean?'

we received a written communication in the following words:—

'The end justifies the means.'

"The remark made by the lady was not a foolish one about the catholic pictures, they remained while the others were taken down.* There is a battle going on at all times with catholic spirits against liberal religion, and there is a force of two kinds of spirits to gain possession of that child where you have been; the catholics have so far had the sway. A host of catholic spirits were around the man that died in that house, and the doctor brings his, used as a force, also in that direction. There are no spirits here who desire to injure any one, but they have a wonderful power through the force in that house, so many mediumistic combinations; they will leave no means untried to get that child into their power, so they are taking this course in order to frighten the relations and to get them to place the child in a convent for safety; then they have all they want, and then they will wield the child, after they have got her, with her powers, to accomplish their own purposes. Other spirits have also been there, but as soon as these catholics see and realize the approach of other spirits that they know are as yet not strong, they overpower them, and the result is these terrible physical manifestations. The uncle that has passed away had more to do with it than they know, but not consciously; that will soon be proved. They cannot approach very readily when those present are well balanced in their spiritual and temporal organisations, but as soon as they are those whom they can overcome, whose organisms can be controlled or laid by, they shew their power. Two young priests (spirits) together with an old cardinal have been around and amongst them many days. They care not what is done so they drive them to do what they want, and then feel that a mighty lift

---

* I remarked to the catholic lady who had said "It was evil spirits," because the catholic pictures were not molested hanging upon the walls, "Madam, that is a foolish remark, they could take *any* pictures down."

or power. They are doing or shewing their powers as spirits, and it is only on account of the trouble they make that there need be any sorrow. Let them work, let all the spirits work in all the ways they can. The greatest spiritual battle ever fought on earth will take place between catholic and liberal Christians. They watched you out of the house, and stood by you when you picked up the glass off the floor. The child is a powerful physical medium, and when brought under schooling, in herself, and the spirits that use her are of a more liberal and loving kind, these manifestations will change. Take a few select individuals who have faith in physical manifestations, and hold a circle up there, several physical mediums, men and women, a select few, and you will have some tremendous manifestations, unless these catholic spirits withdraw, and then they will not be so violent. It is an effort for catholic supremacy." *nonsense!*

CHAPTER XV.

A FRIEND came to see me on Whitsunday, May 16th, 1875. She was suffering terribly from toothache, and lay down on the sofa. In the hope of giving her some relief I mesmerised her for some time, and although her eyes gently closed, I was not sure that she had lost consciousness, until I saw her move her right hand upwards in rather an emphatic manner, when it struck me that it might be the first manifestation of her development as a trance medium. I waited patiently for *permission* to address her, and then asked in a low voice what she saw. The sentences seemed to come by fragments, with little spells of silence between. "Oh! it is beautiful! . . . so beautiful! . . . all glory and light . . . so beautiful!" [Do you see any one?] "The light is round her" (then, as if whispering to some one), "shall I tell her? shall I tell her what I see?—I see them coming . . . so many people . . . they are bringing leaves . . . oh! there is a ship! . . . Oh! how beautiful, and there are such sweet faces." [Any that you recognise?] "No, I do not know them." [Perhaps there are some who know you.] Here she extended her arms yearningly as if to embrace some one, while her countenance assumed a very restful expression; then letting her arms drop, she said, "Now they are all gone." . . . She then took my face between her hands, fondly stroking it, and said—"Fear not, fear not, all will be well—all *is* well. Little mother!" (her pet name for me), "little mother, the light is all round you, you are *in* the light." [What colour is the light?] "It is white, but there are lovely rays from it, bluish rays and golden ones ; so bright:—and they are giving you a book." [What is the book?] Looking attentively, as if reading,—"From Helen." [Is the other name there?] "Helen, it is only Helen . . . Now there is the ship again." [Who is in the ship?] "People: the ship will come safely into port; *Helen* is there." [Dear Aunt Helen!] "Yes—she smiles so sweetly: she has such a sweet face." Here she rose from a recumbent to a sitting posture, and was silent for some time : then, taking each of my hands firmly in hers : " Your faith is sufficient :—your strength shall be great :—your health shall be good :—all your needs shall be supplied ; fully supplied ;—*as* you need. Oh ! there are mountains, such beautiful mountains—in the North, and there are so many people, and they want you to go." [What do they want me for?] Whisperingly, "They want her to teach them:" then aloud, "You must not go, you must stop here ; you must finish what you are about ; you must finish that picture ; you will sell it." . . . [Can you tell me about those leaves that you saw them bringing?] " Wait a minute . . . oh ! I see, they are palm leaves, and they are bringing them to you :—and flowers, oh ! what flower is that? it is not clematis—oh ! jessamine ;* yes, jessamine : they are putting them on you—it means purity : they are covering you all over with them—in the bright light :—they are like a mantle . . . Oh ! there is a young girl behind you : she is tall and very fair ; now she bends over you very lovingly." (Being fair, it could not be my dark-eyed Zilla.) [Is it Môtee ?] " Oh ! yes : she has been wanting that. She has her hand on your shoulder." [Is the General with her?] "No." [Jim?] "No. There is a little girl with her ; she pats her on the head, and now she sends her away. Now she is fanning you, and it is so pleasant, I feel the warm breeze. . . . Oh ! now I see some children at play : there is a little boy with a hoop." [Has he anything on his head?] " Yes, a flower ; it is like a lily ; it is a crown of lilies : oh ! they are playing, and they seem so merry :—dear little things, they are so happy. . . . Now there are people coming again—and they are bringing you things—and they are pouring money into your lap." She was silent for some little time, and then I was impressed to mesmerise her slightly, when she opened her eyes, saying,

---

* This charmed me very much, for jessamine is a perfect passion with me : I always long for it wherever I may see it.

"How dark it is," for the daylight had faded away during her trance, and she was much surprised when I related to her all that she had been saying. She was also much pleased that she had passed both into and out of the trance without any kind of twitchings or convulsions.

I wonder whether the *Book* thus spiritually given to me by Aunt Helen might be the premonition of this very one I am now writing!

I must not forget that one of the efforts made to raise funds for our Association was a Fancy Bazaar, held in the Co-operative Institute, Castle Street, Oxford Street, on the 26th, 27th, and 28th of May, and had, I believe, a very fair success. The General Annual Meeting was held there on the first evening of the three, and was very well attended.

I had been at Mrs. Guppy's on the previous evening for her first séance in her pretty little house at Kensington, but, I am sorry to say, I made no notes.

Soon after this, Mrs. Hardy came for her first visit to England, and I had heard her so highly spoken of by Miss Ingram and others, that I was glad to have several opportunities of meeting her:—first, at a reception at Mrs. T.'s: then at Mrs. Guppy's on the 13th of July for a séance, when her table with the hinged lid was especially suitable for Mrs. Hardy's class of manifestation. We sat in a tolerably good light: the little flap was pushed up so as to lie flat on the table, and we were told to lay a cambric handkerchief over the opening, thus making the needful dark chamber below, and in a short time we saw the handkerchief pushed up by fingers; after which it was grasped by the fingers and drawn away, to be presently tossed out through the same aperture. The lid still remained open, and white lilies in abundance were then handed through it to us, allowing us to have a glimpse of the white fingers that held them, and from which we abstracted them. I wish I could have remembered more of the details, for it was altogether an interesting séance. Mrs. Guppy had engaged Mrs. Hardy for every free evening that she had left (for her stay in England was but short, and she was in great demand), and she shewed me her list, for me to select the one that would suit me best to go again, and we fixed the 28th inst.

In the interval I went with a friend for a private séance, and Mrs. Hardy was soon entranced, and spoken through by the spirit Willie (I believe a little Indian). The sitting was my friend's, but I had bits here and there, between the answering of her questions. The name "Arthur" was mentioned with reference to something, which reminded me to ask Willie whether he had noticed the picture of *my* Arthur on Sunday when Mrs. Hardy had called upon me, and had been wonderfully struck with what she termed that beautiful and *good* face. "Oh! yes, I saw his photograph *then*, but since that I have seen himself. I went away to Java, to Batavia, to see him. I went with his father, who took me to the right place; and he is so good, *real* good in every way, he has no tricks." [He is like his father, is he not?] "Yes, something; but much better—nicer—everything. . . . Oh! there is a spirit belonging to you. He is William, he is very close to you. . . Your Mamma is here . . . she says she does not want to *die*." [But she is *there*, on the other side.] "Oh! yes, but she says she does not want to die *again*. She says some of them told her she must be re-carnated; but that is all *trash*, *dreadful* trash, you must not believe any one who tells you such trash." . . In which I thoroughly agreed. Then something was said about my home. [But *can* I keep it?] "You *must* keep it; you must not leave it to be wandering about the world like a poor little pussy cat." [But shall I have anything to keep it with?] "Yes, it will come; you will soon have a cheque." (Which really did unexpectedly come, even before I copied the messages into my book.) Again turning to me. "Oh! have the spirits told you that you are to go about more? you have been still and quiet for a long time, but now you are to go out a little." [They have not *told* me so, but the fact seems to be so, for you see I am out to-day, and I have several engagements which I have been counselled to accept, and indeed have liked to do so.] "Well, that is all right, and has its purpose." He finished by telling us, " Brighter days are in store for both of you." So that was a cheering termination.

I also had the pleasure of meeting her at the house of dear Mr. and Mrs. S. C. Hall, when I think there was a circle of about sixteen, and the dark chamber was formed by leaving a vacancy of about four or five inches between the leaves of the large dining-table, and shawls, or some dark things, were covered over the crevice on each side, so as to make a sort of square hole in the centre; the light in the room itself being rather subdued. I think Mrs. Hardy's invisible friends regulated the position of the sitters, at any rate I know that my seat was next to hers, and at that part of the table near where the opening was thus contrived. Some persons who understand nothing of the necessary laws for the formation of circles make an outcry at such regulation of the sitters:—but—if they are musicians they must know that it is necessary that an instrument to be played upon must be made with the notes in proper sequential order; *not* placing F next to C, or in any other random fashion. Each individual in a circle is, as it were, a musical note, and must be harmoniously placed and *attuned*, for full melody to be produced. Such rule holds good all through creation, and if wantonly broken, discord must be the result. On this occasion the meeting was very concordant, and the sweet voice of Katharine Poyntz indulged us with sacred song, when we would see the white spirit fingers creep up just above the opening, and occasionally wave in rhythm to the notes we were listening to.—Messages also were rapped out; and one gentleman felt a ring which had belonged to his mother taken from off his finger (he had been apprised that she was present), and shortly afterwards a hand quietly rose to our view *with* the ring on one of the fingers. I do not remember the method by which the ring was restored to its owner, but I know that somehow he did have it back; nor do I recollect anything more about the séance itself, for such things slip away from us if we make no memoranda, but it was a very pleasant evening with highly valued friends.

Fortunately I wrote the account of my last séance with her, and sent it to the *Spiritual Magazine*, and now copy from its pages.

Before giving the account of the séance held at Mrs. Guppy's on the 28th of July, I wish to state the particulars of a singular circumstance that took place earlier in the month. Mrs. Hardy, during her late visit to London, has been so fully engaged that she found it impossible to come on the Wednesday as she had wished, to see me and my many spiritual curiosities; she therefore sent me a message by a friend, requesting admission on some other day. I wrote to suggest that as she would be at liberty on Sunday (July 18th), she should come to me quite early on that day; which she and Miss Fletcher accordingly did. We had a very pleasant chat while I shewed her some of my spirit-drawings and other objects of interest, but she several times mentioned how very strongly she felt the spiritual influences in the room. At last she exclaimed, "Oh! I never did feel anything like this! it seems as if everything in the room was being moved about by spirits." Soon after that they took their leave, and I began to put away my things, when, glancing at the mantel-piece, I missed from it a small china vase, and a little Madeira curiosity— the half of an orange-peel, painted yellow inside, and crimson, with yellow flowers, on the outside. They were both very valuable to me, as having been gifts from dear friends, so I at once wrote a note to Mrs. Guppy, that in case they should be brought to any one at a séance, she should know whose they were.

Well, it seems that on that very morning, while Mrs. Guppy (who wears herself out in the service of her friends, and in the cause of Spiritualism) was endeavouring to recruit her strength by a little extra repose, she felt the touch of small cold things, so she pushed them farther from her in the bed, but when she got up they had vanished, and were not to be found. My letter on the

Monday morning explained to her what they had been. On that same evening she held a séance with Mrs. Hardy, as medium in conjunction with herself, and during the course of it, my little treasures were placed in the hands of two of the sitters; but our spirit friends had, with pencil, written a message for me inside the orange-peel, which will remain there as a testimony to the character of those invisible ones, who manifest these wonders through Mrs. Guppy's mediumship—"Excuse us, we only borrowed them, *we never steal.*" My little ornaments are now back in their own places.

Mrs. Guppy has been indulging her friends by engaging Mrs. Hardy for a series of séances, and has thus given them the opportunity of witnessing the marvels resulting from the combination of two such powerful mediumships. Her invitations have been eagerly sought for, and most liberally granted, and on the 28th of July the assembly was unusually large, for we numbered about forty persons, among whom were some very distinguished guests, so instead of adjourning upstairs into her séance room, we remained in the drawing rooms, of which the windows had been properly darkened. Some of your readers may not be aware, that in her séance table Mrs. Guppy has had a circular hole cut, of about nine or ten inches in diameter, the piece being again replaced with a hinge, so that it lifts up like a lid. Mrs. Hardy arranged the sitters, selecting those who were to be at the table, while the others formed an outer circle. She placed Mrs. Guppy on her left, and me by the side of Mrs. Guppy, so that we three were just in front of the lid.

There was a dark séance, when a few flowers and some large branches of lilac and other shrubs were brought; then the wax candle was lighted, and over the opened lid was arranged a piece of black calico in which a slit had been cut, thus forming a sort of dark cabinet under the table, and the candle was taken into the back room, so as to throw but a very subdued light into the one in which we were. Presently we saw one finger of a hand gleaming up at the aperture, then all the fingers, when each person in rotation asked, "Is it for me?" they moved *once* for *No*, and at a third or fourth the answer was *Yes*, by a threefold movement; the lady stretched forth her hand to touch that of the spirit, and there was thus a little interchange of question and answer. Other hands were afterwards seen, but they scarcely rose above the aperture of the table. Mrs. Guppy asked a gentleman for his silk handkerchief, in the corner of which she tied a knot, which she passed down to be taken hold of, and many of the sitters in succession held the upper part of the handkerchief, pulling against the Spirit-hand, and thus realizing its strength; Mrs. Guppy asked leave to place her ring on one of the fingers, which being granted, she did so, and the finger was held up several times, shewing the ring upon it, and raps were made with the ring under the surface of the table.

A small bell was held over the hole, and the white fingers were seen to clasp it, after which it was rung under the table; a second bell was passed down with a similar result. Mrs. Guppy has a curious musical instrument called Turkish bells, formed of eight metal cups ranged one above the other for the octave, and very weighty. We held this with the handle downwards, and we saw it taken between two middle fingers of a hand, and thus carried down, and I do not think that any *mortal* fingers could have held the heavy instrument in that way. The upper part of it was then projected, and answers were given by rapping it against the hands of those who approached closely enough, and some of the blows were pretty strong, but they were *discriminately* given. Mrs. Ramsay then passed me her bracelet, and asked me to hold it at some distance *above* the hole, which I did at about five inches, and suddenly, almost like a lightning flash, the hand sprang up and seized it, and after a short time threw it out on the table.

We were then desired to go and have tea, and on our return the table was moved out of the room, and a large circle formed, still with a second circle beyond, Mrs. Hardy being seated on a chair in the middle, and she requested a gentleman to place his feet one on each side of hers, to be assured that she did not move from her place, and the light was then extinguished; she then mentioned that during the séance she would continually strike one hand against the other, more for the purpose of stimulating the outflow of influence from herself by which the spirits work than as any kind of test, for any such test would be quite superfluous, as many persons in the circle were being touched at the same time by warm and firm spirit fingers. Mrs. Hardy (whose back was turned towards us) is occasionally clairvoyante, and said, " I see three young men, brothers." She partially described them, and the lady by my side whispered that they belonged to her; and Mrs. Hardy continued, " They are for the lady on the right of Miss Houghton, and there is also a little girl." [Yes, quite right, also my child.] Then Mrs. Hardy said, " There is a spirit saying, 'I am Ferdinand.'" He was claimed by the gentleman who guarded her feet, and some messages were delivered from him. Suddenly she cried out, " Oh! I am smothered! strike a light quickly, Mr. Hardy, make haste." When he had done so, we found she was completely enveloped in a large table-cover. We disentangled her, and the light was again put out. One gentleman's chair was taken from him, and Mrs. Guppy, who was in the outer circle, made several exclamations that different things were being done to her, and Mr. Burns said he wished the spirits would bring Mrs. Guppy inside the circle; presently she was quite silent, and Mrs. Ramsay, whose seat was next to hers, said, "Oh! be still and quiet, for Mrs. Guppy is *gone!*" In about a minute she said in a faint voice, " Where am I?" and she *was* within the circle, but they must first have entranced her. But again she was lifted up, and now in her normal condition, for she spoke several times, and her voice was heard close to the ceiling. Suddenly she was placed on Mrs. Burns's lap, but was quickly removed, and was carried swiftly round and round the circle, her dress whisking against us, brushing firmly against Mr. Sergeant Cox (who was seated next to me) and myself, and at one time I took hold of her foot above the level of my head; then for an instant she was on my lap, and next, at my request, on the lap of the friend by my side. She described it as the most delicious feeling of *dangling*. They afterwards floated Mrs. Hardy in the same manner, then Mrs. Guppy again, and they then seated her on the floor by the side of Mrs. Hardy in her chair. Some little squeaking sounds were heard, after which a spirit spoke with the direct voice, and told us we might ask for some things to take away. Mrs. Hardy mentioned one or two, and among them a butterfly; one gentleman asked for a stone, which was brought: also two dead butterflies in a box: which I hope Mrs. Hardy has taken with her to her transatlantic home. There were several other things brought, but nothing of any importance. The voice wished us "Good-night," and when the gas was lighted, we found the carpet within the circle all strewn over with visiting cards from a basket in the corner, and the letters Mrs. Guppy had received during the previous week.

It was certainly a wonderful séance, from the great variety of manifestations, and was a grand finale for Mrs. Hardy, who gave us some hopes that she may pay us another visit next year.

Gummed into the magazine I also find a cutting from the *Medium* on the same subject, so there can be no indiscretion in my reproducing it. "A brilliant reception was held by Mrs. Guppy on Wednesday evening, the 28th ult., at her house in Victoria Road, Kensington, the occasion being in compliment to Mr. and Mrs. Hardy, now on their return to America. Mrs. Guppy's pretty residence was filled well nigh to overflowing by her friends, amongst whom may be named, in addition to Mr. and Mrs. Hardy, Prince Albert of Solms, Countess Poulett and Miss Vere, Count and Countess Von Wimpffen, Count Bastogi, Hon. Mrs. Ramsay and Miss Ramsay, General Brewster, Captain James, Mr. Serjeant Cox, Mrs. and the Misses Schletter, Mr. and Mrs. James Burns, Mr. Gledstanes, Mr. and Mrs. Stack, Mrs. Wiseman, Mrs. Fitzgerald, Miss Houghton, Mrs. Petman, Miss Douglas, and Mr. Bentinck. Mrs. Guppy's recent receptions have been much sought after, and have been amongst the most interesting events of the London season."

We little thought that Mrs. Hardy would never revisit us, for she was at that time but eight and thirty, but I think it was even before the twelvemonth had come round that she was removed from the land of mortality to join the workers on the other side, and I have no doubt she is very active there, for she was a lively, energetic little woman.

The trial of strength with the handkerchief reminds me of something that took place in 1863. Shortly after Papa's death, Mamma and I went to stay at Beckenham with Mr. and Mrs. Varley. They had some friends one day to dinner, during which the subject of Spiritualism was broached, which was quite new to, I think, two of the visitors; so in the evening a séance was proposed, and some half-dozen of us sat round a small table, one of the neophytes being placed between Mrs. Varley and myself. My spirit friends lifted my hands about five or six inches, so as to be *above* and not resting *on* the table, when Mr. Ansell raised his in the same way:—" Oh ! *you* are not to do it," said Mrs. Varley, "you must put your hands flat on the table." "But I can't help it," said he, "I am trying to put them down, but I cannot." He clearly was struggling against some power, which suddenly was loosed, and his poor hands came down upon the table with a most violent bang, which left them tingling for some time ; shewing how great was the effort he had been making against a something that he neither felt nor saw, for the only thing he had been aware of, was his utter inability to lower his hands. It was indeed a singular manifestation to receive at his very first sitting. I have never since met him, but I should think he must have had the germs of strong mediumship.

On the day previous to Mrs. Guppy's séance, I had been present at the most extraordinary exhibition I have ever witnessed. Madame de Sievers was going to give, in her own rooms in the Queen's Road, a concert for the benefit of the poor sufferers by the floods in France, and invited me to go for the purpose of seeing what she termed "*Les oiseaux médiums.*" I of course declined, because it was out of my power to contribute anything to her fund, but she urged me most warmly, saying that that was quite unimportant, for there would be sure to be plenty of supporters; so I accepted her cordial kindness, and as soon as I arrived she introduced me to Mademoiselle Van der Meersch, the elegant possessor of the marvellous birds, and placed me in the very best seat, exactly in front of the low table on which they were established. I think there were six of them, all foreign, and beautiful in plumage; one, I remember, was a bishop, but I do not recollect the others, only they were all known to me in their kinds, for I have kept a great variety myself formerly, but I never attempted to train them in any way. They were in a long low cage, divided into so many compartments, and in front there was a kind of trough or tray along the whole length, of a size to hold a row of cards on their edges lengthways towards the cage, and thus the cards made a little platform or promenade level with the door-sill of the cages. Mademoiselle held a little wand in her hand, with which I suppose she was accustomed to playfully threaten them, but she seemed exceedingly fond of them, and I daresay they were charming little companions for her; and I believe she had upwards of thirty, so that some stayed at home, to take their turn on another occasion. When we were all assembled, she took one little package of cards from the tray, and shewed us that upon them were the names of months, in French on one side, and English on the other. She then begged <u>that some one would say</u> which was their favourite month. She had replaced the cards before saying so; and when <u>the answer had been given</u>, she opened one of the little doors, scattering a few grains of seed on the cards, and desired the bird, who had trotted out immediately, to select the said month, giving him many injunctions to be sure and choose rightly: but he went up and down picking up the seed before he paid attention to his duties, and then he touched two or three of the cards with his beak, and finally drew one well up, and lo! it was the very one that had been named. She said they were fond of a little applause in guerdon of their success, and we willingly bestowed it. She spoke to the little creatures quite as if they were rational beings, and in the same way they gave the day of the week, and of the month, and she would each time take a cluster of cards out of the tray to shew us what words or figures were inscribed upon them. The questions became more and more puzzling, for she would ask you to mention two numbers, for them to do an addition sum, and their calculations were always correct, and they would in the same way subtract. She was very amusing, too, in her ways with them, impressing upon them that they must be sure not to make a mistake, and they never did! One of the packages of cards consisted of different colours, and then we were to fix upon some one's dress, or bonnet ribbon, or necktie, that was to be matched, and the feathered mediums invariably pulled out the right one, and the cards were put in so closely together, that I, just in front, could not have told which was which. In some instances we had to whisper a word one to the other, with reference to the cards she then shewed us, so that Mademoiselle herself could not know, and the result was equally sure; and it seems to me utterly impossible that any amount of training could enable them to do it, so that I quite agree with Madame de Sievers that spirits must have been the instructing powers, and have guided the little beaks to the right place, for their mistress herself often did not know, and therefore could give no clue to what she was unaware of, and I was quite close to her and her birds, and made several of the suggestions myself, as did also Mrs. Ramsay, who was by my side. Once Mademoiselle omitted to sprinkle the seeds on the platform of cards, and her knowing little subject did not choose to work without his hire, so he scornfully trotted straight home again: they were the most amusing little creatures, and I should very much like to have another matinée with them, although I do not care for dissipations in the usual way. Mademoiselle had an album, in which were the signatures of many of those who in different lands had witnessed her wonderful exhibition (among them many crowned heads), and there were also artistic sketches added by some of those who had shared the enjoyment, and in several of these sketches, a spirit-hand is seen leading the sensitive bird to the card which is to be drawn up: and any one may understand that they are pretty closely packed, or the grains of millet seed would fall between them, and the little creature would jerk its head knowingly on one side with two or three little twitches at the card so as to loosen it. I believe she was only in England for a very short time, but if she should return, I would advise every one who can, to go and see the performances of her marvellous pets, of which I have given but a poor account, as it is so long since that I have necessarily forgotten the full details. Mademoiselle Van der Meersch contributed likewise to the pleasure of the concert by singing two or three songs, and it was altogether a delightful afternoon.

CHAPTER XVI.

THERE are so many curious ways in which I have been helped, and it has only been by comparing all the circumstances that the full force has been realized, so I hope to be excused if somewhat prolix in what I am now going to detail, as another evidence that there is always a *purpose* in what may seem accidental.

On Trinity Sunday, June 8th, 1873, I had the pleasure of a long visit from Sir Charles Isham and Mr. Sutherland, when we entered very fully into the photographic work, which was then the chief object of my life, and I had out my large collection of photographs for them to see, giving full details of each and all; so that the hours flew unheeded by them and by me, and it was past five o'clock before they left. As Ann let them out, in the letter-box (which fortunately has a glass in front) she found a letter for me, which she brought up with full speed: it had *not* been there when she admitted the gentlemen, nor had the person who brought it rung the bell; and I imagine that it must have been delivered the night before to the wrong address, and that whoever had received it had slipped it into my box during their Sunday afternoon walk. The letter was from Mrs. T., telling me that Miss H. had just arrived from America, and was staying with her for a few days, would I therefore go there to tea *that evening* at six o'clock! Fancy my rush! to fly through my dinner and be off like the wind, leaving my turmoil of photographs in a confused heap on the table as they were. If that letter had reached me, as in due course, the evening before, I should have ordered my dinner at an earlier hour, and should have felt fidgety and unsettled with my visitors, with half my heart in the Rochester Road; yet that interview with Sir Charles was of more vital importance than I could at first have imagined, for it was in consequence of the strong interest thus awakened in his mind that he was led to think of the stereoscopic camera, and to offer the gift of it if I thought it would be serviceable

All hinged upon the detention of that letter.

Mrs. T. had wondered at my non-arrival, and thought I might perhaps be from home, but the spirits said *No*, and that I was coming; so they waited tea for me, and the delay was not very great, for I exactly caught the omnibus. We occupied ourselves for some time in looking at the spirit drawings in pencil and colours that Miss H. had done during the time of her absence from England. I had taken a few of the latest photographs with me, and we three then established ourselves for a séance, having placed them on the little table before us, but instead of Mrs. T.'s taking them up, as she usually does in such cases, I was impressed to mesmerise her, when she passed almost immediately into trance, and presently said with much emphasis: —" Thank God!" (taking a hand of Miss H. and myself,) "I greet you all.—My body is being refreshed with sleep; in spirit I am here—John Murray Spear (then turning towards Miss H.): Did I not tell you, Mary, that my spirit must go out with you, even to the waters?" [Yes, indeed you did so], answered she, and he continued, "Your meeting to-night has brought me *across* the waters. My body passed into a deep sleep at one o'clock this day, New York time, in which sleep it still rests: (it was 8.20 by our time). Two hours have passed, and I have waited to observe the great work there (pointing to where Miss H.'s drawings were lying) presented to *this* mind (placing the right hand on my shoulder), before making myself known. Thank God for this manifestation, which from this time may occasionally be repeated." Here she awoke, and I read to her what Mr. Spear had said, and we had only made a few observations about it when a gentleman visitor made his appearance, so we had had exactly time for the intended communication and the séance was at an end. Miss H. had said how strongly and frequently Mr. Spear had spoken upon the point, expressing his strong certainty that he should thus be able to communicate when the conditions on this side should be favourable.

Twice in the earlier times Mrs. T. had *seen* Mr. Spear, but then it had seemed like her going forth, not his coming to us. I was at her house on the evening of November 21st, 1869, and in the course of a séance we were having, she, in trance, said: "I see Mr. Spear, he is lying on a bed: there is a window at the side of the bed.—The bed is very low. He is thinking of us, and I think he sees us. The rain is coming against the window, which is shut: it is quite light, and I see his hat in the corner on a chair. Mr. Spear looks pale, but I think it is weariness, because his face does not look in pain or suffering. He seems to need something: he is troubled, perplexed, and we must write and say that the cause of the perplexities will pass away in *five* days from this time; and that will be a test to him that he will value. He is lying on the bed, dressed." Mr. Spear was at that time in California. Two months later, on the following January 21st, on one of our Friday afternoon séances, when I had mesmerised her, she said:—
"Violet clouds are surrounding me; they roll quite close to my face, the edges are of such an intense violet, shading off into light tints: they are thrown directly into my eyes. —I am looking into something shaped like a telescope, only made entirely of these clouds, and there is a face at the end that I shall see presently.—How very curious! it is Mr. Spear's face! he is looking so intently up it, but he does not look as if he saw me as I see him.—I am told that I am to speak of the vision that I had on Wednesday night. It was partly relating to Mr. Spear, just as the clock was striking twelve. I had been under influence from a very dear friend who is often with me, and suddenly I saw every part of Mr. Spear except his head: his hands were shewn very distinctly, and his head was in a cloud. He made some passes over me, lifting the curtain for the purpose, and I was given to understand that he knew I was not well. The spirit is saying, 'Now you have seen his

head, so that it is a complete picture.'—Mr. T. heard the rustling of the curtains before I told him who it was, but he did not see him.—The spirit says:—'He will be aware of having been here, but will think it a dream;' and he also adds—'Tell Mr. Spear the time of these séances, and he will devote an hour in sending his thoughts to influence in this direction;' and the spirit hopes that in time those sitting in this circle may all see Mr. Spear and perhaps converse with him. It will give Mr. Spear great delight to be thus in communion with you, and he will at any rate be with you in spirit." I sent out the communication to Mrs. Spear, and from that time he did, when it was possible, devote the appointed hour (making the necessary calculation for the distance) to being with us, but we do not then seem to have received any evidence of it. Later on came the vision of his apparent death, which I have already narrated.

Miss Kislingbury read a paper before our Association on the 3rd of February 1879, on the subject of "Apparitions of the Living," finishing with a circumstance that Mrs. T. had long ago related to me, but as I had not recorded it, I am glad to be able to give it here in her own words: Miss Kislingbury says: . . . "Since concluding the above, I have received from a lady, well known to this society, a letter containing an excellent example of the class of spiritual manifestations I have been speaking of to-night. With your permission I will give it as it stands:—

"I have myself had an exceedingly interesting experience of the apparition of the living, viz., my own appearance at the supposed death-bed of my sister, when we were three thousand miles apart. She was attended on this particular night by another sister, who distinctly saw me go into the room, and lean over my darling young sister. The latter was too ill to speak, but she whispered, 'Mary is here, now I'm happy.' I ought to mention that my elder sister is not given to visions, and is indeed a very practical, matter-of-fact person; but she has always since declared that she saw me from my knees up, and the very dress was plain to her too. At this time I was just recovering after my confinement with my son, who is nearly seventeen. He was between four and five weeks old, when one night I fell asleep, thinking how much I wished to see this sister. I knew of her illness, and that she was not expected to recover, and of her intense desire to see me. Between us the most tender attachment had always existed, and it was thought that her illness had been much increased through grief at our separation. The previous summer, when we came from the United States to this country, I had purposely kept from her and my mother the knowledge of my expected confinement, and they were only informed *after* the birth of the child in a letter from my husband. I mention all this to shew how impossible it was for me to go to her, as she intensely desired. On the night referred to I had a most vivid dream of seeing her, in a bed *not in her own room*, and of seeing my other sister in attendance. I leaned over her, and said, as I thought, 'Emma, you will recover.' I told my husband I had been home, when I woke, and my impression that she would recover. This dream comforted me very much, and from this night there was a change for the better with my sister, and she gradually recovered from what was supposed to be an incurable illness. When we came to compare dates, we found that my dream and my appearance to my two sisters occurred at as nearly as possible the same time. I was so lifelike to my younger sister that she thought I really had arrived on a visit; but, as I said before, to my elder sister I was shadowy below my knees, but perfectly natural in appearance. She afterwards remembered that I did not notice her as I passed into the inner room, although in my dream I saw her, nor did I seem to see anything but the one object of my love." Although no farther reference is made to the *room*, Mrs. T.'s sister had at that time been removed out of the one she usually occupied, so that even that fact had been correctly noted by her spirit (or soul) when on her distant visit.

In the spring of 1875 I went to stay with some friends

in the country, from Friday morning till Monday night. On the first evening they had some visitors, but on the next we were alone, and I had recited the following verses, which I had copied into my scrap-book many years ago, but I know not the name of the author.

> " Oh ! there is a dream of early youth,
>   And it never comes again ;
> 'Tis a vision of light and life and truth
>   That flits across the brain.
> And Love is the theme of that early dream,
>   So wild, so warm, so new,
> That in all our after dreams, I deem,
>   That early dream we rue.
>
> " Oh ! there is a dream of maturer years ;
>   More turbulent by far—
> 'Tis a vision of blood and of woman's tears,
>   For the theme of that dream is war.
> And we toil in the field of danger and death,
>   And fight in the battle array,
> Till we find that fame is a bodiless breath,
>   That vanisheth away.
>
> " Oh ! there is a dream of hoary age,
>   'Tis a vision of gold in store,
> Of sums noted down in the figured page,
>   To be counted and counted o'er.
> And we fondly trust in our glittering dust,
>   As a refuge from care and pain,
> Till our limbs are laid in that last dark bed,
>   Where the wealth of the world is vain.
>
> " And is it thus from man's birth to his grave ?
>   In the path which all are treading—
> Is there nought in that long career to save
>   From remorse and self-upbraiding ?
> Oh ! yes ! there's a vision so pure and bright,
>   That the being to whom it is given
> Hath bathed in a sea of living light,
>   And the theme of *that* dream is Heaven."

Even while I was speaking, S. passed under influence, and what follows was taken down in short-hand by E., her husband. "I want to say that I heard you. 'The theme of that dream is Heaven.'—And yet you do not say it quite as it is. The dream of youth is a promise of what the dream of life, completed, shall be. That is, the dream of youth is the dream of inexperience. The vision is clear, but the battle of life has not been fought. The dream of youth is a selfish dream. It is love for oneself,—mostly for oneself alone. And the battle of life teaches you that the selfish love will not stand the fire,—that all which is selfish must be burned up. If life is lived rightly and beautifully, the vision of the youthful soul is all fulfilled:— the discipline has crucified the self-hood, and the true eternal love begins: the love which has no dross in it. Then it is no longer a dream; it is a fact which makes the soul full of melody for ever. . . I want that the young should never think that they leave anything behind them that is worth carrying forward. The end of life is better than the beginning, if the life is lived rightly. It is sad for the young to feel, that the flower-time of life, the love-time of life, the poetry-time of life, the music-time of life, is left behind when youth is gone! *It is not so.*—There are always to be found better things before. There is better music, better poetry; there are brighter visions, there is truer hope; there is infinitely more perfect love to be found on before. For the soul that walks upward, looks upward, lives upward, finds that to-morrow is more beautiful than to-day: that the end of life,—the grey hairs, the withered wrinkled form, which to selfish youth seem sad: —that even in this state of decay of the body, the soul is brighter, has more abundant hope,—is living really in eternal youth: for there is no decay over that which—what shall I say?—Decay holds dominion *only* over that which was born to fade away; which is just the outward. I want the young to see this. The old are younger than *they* are, in all things which make young life beautiful. Nothing that is really of value is left behind. All things grow brighter and purer unto the perfect day. The only youth which is worth having is eternal. The pleasures are pleasures for evermore." . . . [Who is it that has been speaking?] "I will ask *them*—I am a long while ago." (He who was the Roman Catholic priest now speaks.) "You do not know her. She has not spoken before. She wanted to come, and it seemed best. It is difficult to fix their names; they do not retain the double earth-name as you do. They say 'Jane Thatcher,' but this may be entirely wrong. She does not often come through us. But that is enough about her.

"I do not see where you are." [In our usual sitting-room in S.] To G. H. "I thought *you* were with *them*, *out* of the body. Are you speaking *through* a body, or are you living *in* a body?" [Yes: I am living *in* the body.] To E. "Then that is clear: your friend is like you, and your Her.* Sometimes I can scarcely tell. It is clear enough in most cases, but sometimes I cannot tell whether people are in the body or not.

"I cannot say much, but I should like to say quickly about last night, which I am quite cognisant of. It seems sometimes to you—as we see clearly—that there is no use in fighting with opposition, but if I could tell you what we see, it would help you. . . . We long that *all* should come to the knowledge that WE ARE, and that we are intimately connected with your daily life. It is as if you were in a room signalling to others in another room—to those who would take no notice of you. This is our abiding feeling: —that we hope for the time in which *you*—speaking generally—shall recognise *us*. Feeling this, you see, we know that we have no power over those who are in a *material* state unless you help us. So that we take pleasure in your work—selfish pleasure if you like so to call it. That is, that through you we may get to these people. When *you* feel that it is not much worth while, *we* often feel that it is *very much* worth while, and we wish that you would try, your Her does not do enough in this. That is, it does not seem worth while to mar the harmony by entering into, by discussing the subject with inharmonious people. But *we* watch and wait, and know that, so to speak, our only chance is through you. You can tell a little how we feel. You never lift up your standard without, as it were, blessing us: that is, we rejoice through you when we can reach any

---

* They speak of S. (their mouthpiece), E.'s wife, as his Her.

soul which is, so to speak, dead, in material thought. We as workmen are powerless; always in a sense without tools. The carpenter looks at the dead rough plank, and he longs to fashion it into something: but without his tools he can do nothing. We in this way look to you: and when we see all around, the rough material, the plank, the log of wood, we *beseech* you to let us use you, if so be that we can fashion something which shall contribute a little more to the glory of God, and to the good of man, than that being can do who is dead in material thought. *You* are the tools now in earth-life, because *we* have passed onward, and our hands lie still. We often entreat you with earnest entreaty to let *our* spirits, through *your* fingers, *your* tongues, *your* strong arms, do that work which we see needs doing, but which we without you are powerless to perform. Does not this shew you what I mean? I know that spirit power is sufficient for all things:—but we reach them through you, and when you will not let us work, and think it is not worth while, you disappoint us, and you darken yourselves." (G. H.) [Was there any good done last night?] "Yes:— in this way. It helps us to get nearer to them, and being nearer, we can more readily use our influence when there is a favourable opportunity. Distance is not it exactly, but it is being brought nearer by you, our influence abides there. They see a light which they long after, that draws. You can dispel all things by acute argument—'There is nothing, nothing is anything, and all is nothing.'—But when light which is shewn from the righteous is seen and recognised, it is longed after. Last night there was a torch of spiritual light upheld, and to the light that streams from that, they *cannot* close their eyes. It remains the light-giving witness that there is something after which it would be good to strive, and for which it would be good to live.

"Now I shall say one text, and then go. This is God's promise to you, and you must feel that it is true, and say after me in thought:—'Thou SHALT GUIDE me with Thy counsel, and afterward, in a little while, receive me into glory' (Psalm lxxiii. 24). It can never fail, if on your part you simply look : God, *through His ministers*, but still God, shall guide you by His counsels and afterwards receive you into glory,—which eye hath not seen, for mortal eye must dull before it can behold it : which ear hath not heard, for mortal ear must be hushed before it can hear it :—neither can it enter into the heart of man while in the body to conceive those things which God hath prepared for those who love Him, and who help Him to help His suffering ignorant children : for you do help God when you help another. . . . God, through His ministers it may be, will *certainly* guide you—there is no mistake,—and afterwards receive you into glory."

I think there is in these messages an infinite pathos that I have rarely seen equalled. The humble, earnest pleading of the spirit to be assisted to aid humanity, shews a tender lovingness almost beyond our conception, while even the alloy of selfishness (the selfishness of *unselfishness*) is urged in argument. Often have I reverted to that communication while listening to the futile talk of the materialist, and thought,—well, it is even possible that this wooden head may have the capability of being chiselled into shape by higher hands, if but one little notch may be pierced,— and that remembrance has soothed one's impatience, and strengthened one to say yet a few more words.

I have already spoken of the power of the emanations from my drawings, impressed thereon by the influences who have aided me in the work, and I am always careful that there shall be if possible no human intermixture besides my own, by never allowing them to be touched by other fingers, and I therefore supply knitting needles to my visitors in case they should desire to point out any particular portion that may interest them, although I know that they sometime consider it a whim on my part, and cannot conceive that a mere touch can leave anything behind which might even remain ineffaceable ; and yet that evidence is clearly given by any substance that has a strong odour. At the time of my amateur photography, I painted some of my pictures in oils, and used a kind of tiny cup for the turpentine in which to clean the brushes. Twelve years afterwards I used that same little cup daily for another purpose, and although I tried every expedient, even putting it (filled with water) continually on the hob, I never could free it from the original taint. . . When I was in Madeira, I saw a beautiful sort of small beetle on a shrub, but fortunately I did not touch it (not feeling very secure as to the nature of the creeping and flying things there); for my cousin told me that if I had, I should not have been fit to come near any one for almost the whole day, because of the odour that would have remained upon my fingers in consequence of the contact; I think the Portuguese name for the insect was *frade*. There was an article in the Edinburgh Review for July 1869, which gives an evidence of a similar nature, an extract from which I copied, not for its scientific, but its spiritual value, and I here subjoin it.

From " Mrs. Somerville on Molecular Science."

A series of remarkable researches by Dr. Tyndall on the absorption exerted on radiant heat by minute quantities of gaseous matter, points out most forcibly the active agency of these smallest particles. . . . The odours from plants and flowers are shewn to act as most powerful absorbents, and the most minute conceivable trace of many of these perfumes produced marked effects:—" The perfumes during the experiments adhered to all parts of the apparatus so pertinaciously that after a continued stream of dry air had been pumped through the tube until the exhaustion seemed to be complete, and the needle stood at zero; after a few minutes' repose, the residue of the perfume came out so powerfully from the crannies of the apparatus as almost to restore the original deflection. ' The quantities of these residues must be left to the imagination to conceive. If they were multiplied by billions they would probably not obtain the density of the air.' "

CHAPER XVII.

DURING their autumnal trip on the Continent, Mrs. T. had a communication given through her by Mrs. Marshall, which Mr. T. took down at the time, and which she then forwarded to me. The poor old soul was anxious about my pecuniary matters, and suggested a plan that she thought might be advantageous, and finished by saying, "If she were *here*, she would need neither house nor food, and she has plenty of spiritual riches." In Mrs. T.'s accompanying letter, she said she had been looking through it, and did not think the advice of any value. Indeed it was utterly unfeasible, but it was most characteristic of Mrs. Marshall, and was of the class of suggestions made to me by both her and her son at different times in their normal state; it therefore had its value as proving how much we shall all retain our idiosyncrasies in the hereafter, at least during the earlier period of our existence in the spirit world.

My second visit to her after her return home was on the 2nd of December, and in the first part of the evening she had just a momentary glimpse of Mrs. Marshall, which led to some little talk about her and the message she had sent, but we had then no further manifestation. Later on I made some allusion to its being Papa and Charlie's birthday, and Mrs. T. said, "That is what they are telling me about, and that there are so many of them here." I spoke of feeling something like S. John's signal, and yet the sensation was stronger and more forcible than that, and then she exclaimed, "Oh! here is the old lady again, trying to speak to me." That reminded me of the time (May 6th of this year, of which the account is given in the "Chronicles") when Mrs. T. had seen my forehead as it were lighted up with a flame which seemed to go up

Q

from the eyes, the forehead, and the front of the head, and I also remembered that I had then felt the same peculiar glow; and as Mrs. Marshall had on that occasion been summoned to look at it, I thought that perhaps she could now see it. "Yes," said Mrs. T., "she is speaking to me, saying—I see it, I see it." The expression of her countenance changed, and I saw that she was passing under influence, and soon it was as Mrs. Marshall that she turned towards me, giving me her hand in greeting, and saying, "I am so glad to be with you again, dear Miss Houghton :—your head is all lighted up and shining . . . Thank God, I am *quite* happy now. The Lord is very good to me. . . . I can go *anywhere* now." [Could you come to me?] "I think I could if I were *asked*." [I should be glad to have you whenever you can come.] "I should like to come if I can, and perhaps I might help you, for I do want so much to do it : you were always so good to me, and you have done me so *much good*. You see you are so spiritual, and all those about you are so spiritual, that perhaps such a material body as I am, might attract material things to you. But I don't know—only The Lord knows, and He *might* let me work for you in my way . . . I *must* do something ; I can't *rest* without I do something. Oh! I ought not to have told you that, because you may think it is only for my own sake, because I *must* not rest till I have done something for you, but I do want to help you, for I love The Lord, and I love those whom The Lord loves, and I think He *will* let me. I think I see something coming to you soon ; and may I come to see you?" [Oh! yes, if you can.] "I think I can with her," pointing as if meaning Mrs. T., so I suggested that she should try to make her come to my house, and the sooner the better. "Yes," continued she, "but I had such a trouble to come through her now, I could not get into her head ; it seemed quite, quite full, and all in a whirl like this (moving her head round and round) full of everybody's troubles, and I had to spoon, and spoon, and spoon it out before I could get in. . . . Good-bye, and God bless you."

Mrs. T. here awoke. She had told me in the earlier part of the evening, that the *tree* had been planted on Mrs. Marshall's grave, and I referred to her having expressed her anxiety about that when she had influenced her while in Pomerania, but she had not remembered that, having only glanced through the communication before forwarding it to me.

The following was sent to me by a friend in the country.

"Message given through—W—Christmas Day, 1875. Coming a new year of your earth time: to you of many changes. Change brings life :—with life, Hope and Courage stand on each side of Faith :—thus shall you be supported through all, through *all*. . . . Those whom God counts worthy to do His Holy Will must pass this gate of discipline :—to some in one way, to others in another:—whatever each can least bear is sent; then these are strengthened *in* the trial and thus grow strong.—Strong to endure, strong to counsel, strong to sympathize.

> WILL YOU BE STRONG AND SUFFER ?—OR
> WILL YOU BE WEAK AND LIVE AT EASE?

Lo! this day we place these two before you, which ye shall choose! We are able in God's Holy Will to give you which you will have. Between God, yourself, and Us this alone stands. We aid you either way, and seven days are given for you to decide. . . . By order of St. Michael and other Six, this is written for Georgiana Houghton."

To this there could be but one response; that I would seek for *strength*, whatsoever might be the suffering appointed to me. But the very message itself brought me comfort, by proving that hearts were beating in sympathy with me, and that the same high intelligences who guide my own life, could give me such tender assurances through other channels. How true it is that to each one is sent the trial that to them would seem the most difficult to be borne. To me has come what in former years I have said I *could not* endure, and yet, thank God! I have been enabled to do so, and to drink the bitter cup to the dregs :—these *have* been years of trial in many forms, but yet they have been years of blessing for the wondrous ways in which, in the moment of deepest need, help has reached me from the most unexpected sources: "heaviness may endure for a night, but joy cometh in the morning," and although the "heaviness" may return again and again, the "joy" is ever new and sparkling.

Mrs. T. came to see me on the 26th of January, and at one moment she was almost passing under influence, but I checked it because she had not been well: she had had a gleam as of a form coming between us. All at once I felt the peculiar sensation of my head lighted up, when it seems to glow, and it again reminded me of old Mrs. Marshall, who had never yet been able to make her entrance here; and upon my saying so, Mrs. T. heard the answer "Yes." . . . Poor old soul! I *am* glad.—Mrs. T. had been asking me in the earlier part of her visit for the date of the old lady's death, for she is going to look at her grave, and see if the *tree* planted there seems to be flourishing,—but after that bit of talk she had passed out of our minds, but it was *then* that she was admitted into the room.

I went to the Albert Road on the following day, and while we were in quiet talk, I noticed that she was looking very earnestly at me, so I asked if she saw the light, for that I was feeling the sensation on my head. She said no, but would I describe to her what the feeling was like—was it as if of a strong pressure? I pointed to the clear, bright fire, and said that it seemed to glow like that, but that at the same time there was a feeling as of air circulating, or, as if one might be in front of a glowing furnace with delicious vibrations of air tempering it; but still there was a perception of *vitality* in it that neither of those descriptions could give. While I was yet speaking she saw the light. . . . Then she said: "Now *I* feel it, what a pleasant sensation it is!"

On the 14th of March (1876) came a grief to me that will be well understood by any one who has had a pet, for when I came down in the morning I found my Dove dead at the bottom of the cage. Although she had at different times had illnesses when I had feared I might lose her, such had not now been the case, as she had appeared quite well, and had been in her small conversation with me the night before until within a short time of my going to bed, so that it was utterly unexpected. She had been my dear little companion for nearly eight years, with her cage by the side of my easel, and her general place when I was at work was on the lower perch, and as close to me as she could get. I must confess that it was a sore trouble to me, and I missed her sadly for some time. On the 5th of April Mrs. T. came to see me, and of course the first feeling was that of missing the Dove from her accustomed spot, and while we were gently talking on the subject, I suddenly stopped to *listen*, and so did she, in the same moment, and then she asked, "Have you got *another* one?" to which I said, "Then you heard it also." "Yes," she rejoined, "I heard three distinct coos, at about the farther end of the table;—have you any feathers or anything of hers there?" No, I had not; but the sound which we both heard so distinctly, almost as loud as her own living coo, thrice repeated, came from just beyond the place where the glass containing her eggs usually stands, only on that occasion they were removed into the back room, as I had had the gift of a hyacinth for this one.

I took my poor pet to Mr. Gardner, in Oxford Street, to be stuffed, and he was struck with the fine condition it was in, both with respect to plumpness and plumage: he executed his commission very satisfactorily, and I have hung her case just over my portfolios. As soon as Mrs. Guppy- (now with the addition of) Volckman, heard of my loss, she came to me at Mr. Hudson's, to insist upon bearing the expense of it for me, and another kind friend had also done the same; so that in that trial I had received the immediate help as to the pecuniary difficulty, and Mr. Gardner fulfilled his promise of having it ready by the 6th of April, when an entertainment had been organised in Cambridge Hall for the benefit of poor Mr. Hudson, with whom matters were again going very badly, for however careful a man may be, if *almost nothing* comes in, it is not enough for a family to live on. I had thought that probably I might have shewn the Dove to the audience in general, and given in a few words the history of the Whit Sunday séance when she had been brought to me, but Mr. Burns's programme was already made out, so my information on the subject was limited to those persons who were seated near me.

Mr. Joseph was very anxious to replace it to me with another dove, or to give me some other bird instead, but although grateful to him for his kindness in proposing it, I felt that any other would rather recall my loss than give me any gratification, so I entirely declined his proffered gift. Indeed, very few people seemed to realize how differently I felt with respect to her than merely as a pet bird; not only from the wonderful circumstances of her being brought, but also as such a link between Mamma and myself: the evidence of which was so strongly given by my obtaining two such good spirit-photographs of Mamma when I took the Dove enclosed in its case to Mr. Hudson's; and it has seemed to me that the dear little creature's death took place at exactly the right time, so that I could take it for the Maundy Thursday sitting on the 13th of March. Also the length of time that I had had her was in conformity with my own *number*, for the eight years were nearly completed.

On Saturday evening, May 13th, I had a curious manifestation which lasted at least three hours, beginning just after I came up from dinner. It was like a gentle tapping on or near my portfolio-stand, almost as regular and as continuous as the ticking of a clock, although with occasional variations: sometimes it would be an even beat, at others it would have the alternating time of a pendulum. While I was drinking my tea, it gave the beat of Jim Ramsay's signal. Sometimes it would give only five beats, and stop; but it was *not* as the request for the alphabet. Of course, lasting so long, while I was busy drawing, I did not take constant heed, but twice it attracted my attention by stopping, and when I said aloud, "Now you have left off;" it recommenced. Finally, it seemed to have finished, but just afterwards a post-card from Mrs. T. was brought up to me, when it began again with fresh vigour. The only information given to me on the subject was that many spirits were concerned in it, and that they were gathering power, but whether that power was to distribute among others, or to be used in my own work, was not revealed. Since that time the same tapping has come to me at intervals, and Miss Ingram has likened it to the sounds heard in mines, and considers it a token that my portfolios are to be to me as a mine of gold where the spiritual workers are still busy until the right time shall arrive for the contents to be brought forth to the full light of day, and be productive of wealth to their anxious-hearted possessor.

I had then so little photographic work that only my Thursdays were given to it, in my visits to Mr. Hudson, therefore I had for some time gone on steadily with my drawing; that of the symbolism, for alas! commissions did not come in, although I must acknowledge that it was the sacred work that was always the most charming to me, unless indeed it might be a character of especial sweetness that had to be delineated through me. A series of drawings had been (in the course of years) completed, wherein *each* sept of the Archangels had symbolised the Eye of The Lord; ten separate pictures, and in the same way, another series was in progress, representing the Shield.

Mrs. T. came to see me on *Monday*, July 3rd, and about an hour before she came in, I had finished "The Shield," No. 4, upon which I had been occupied for twenty weeks. It has a peculiar effect, not giving our earthly ideas of a shield, which is only to ward off blows from any particular spot that it may cover at the moment, whereas this looks like infinite arches, under which one may be entirely sheltered; and during the early work of the drawing it had continually expressed the thought of countless wings, waving above, around, and in every part.

I did not expect any visitor, but had been told not to

remove it from the easel, so when Mrs. T. came in, my first thought was to shew it to her, for which purpose I put it in my favourite point of view on the sofa, seating her in the chair where she could see it best. Almost immediately she gave a little shiver, and said, " Did you not feel that? it was like sharp steel, passing swiftly and cuttingly." Then she assumed a listening attitude, and as if repeating the words she heard, she said, " Take to yourself covering, and be hidden." I saw she was passing under influence, so I got out the porcelain slate in readiness to write, when she once more said, with much emphasis :—" Take to yourself covering, and be hidden, for the day so long foretold draweth near, in the which they shall say,—Rock and mountain fall upon us, hide us from the eye of The Lord. . . . Already the Eastern sky reddens for the birth of a sun of righteousness. A sun shall come through throes which shall shake the earth to its centre. The wicked shall surely perish, but the righteous will be gathered into the kingdom of The Lord. . . . So the wicked will then say, Rock and mountain fall on us, and cover us from the eye of The Lord,—and thou shalt say, Inasmuch as ye have *chosen* to be naked, no covering can be given you." Here she awoke with a start, as if roused by the force with which she had spoken. This led us to talk of the Eastern war which is even now beginning, and I reminded her of Mrs. Marshall's fall, which had been said to be typical of a blow to England. . . . On that occasion, June 2nd, 1874, we had been together to Mrs. Marshall's, when after much interesting conversation, Mrs. T. had passed into deep trance, and had said :—" The blow was typical of the crushing weight which shall come to this nation *steeped in luxury and wickedness.* Behold in the East a cloud no larger than the hand, but it shall overspread the heavens. Before the storm descends a way shall be made for my people. *To* the land cry aloud that my people be gathered in spirit, so that no division come. The nation shall be purified as by fire, and the righteous shall possess the land. (Turning tenderly towards me she added)—A host no mortal can count encompasseth you, and your vision shall be opened to see, and all fear shall depart from those who are the chosen of The Lord."

In our youth we often do heedless things for which we have afterwards to suffer. While I was in Madeira I had a quantity of pretty grey seeds given to me, called Coix lachrymæ, Job's tears; they were of a good size, and I pierced holes in them to enable me to thread them into necklaces for my two younger sisters. But some of them were exceedingly hard, so that it was with great difficulty that the needle could be induced to perform the operation, and I had frequently to bring my teeth into requisition in pulling the needle through, and in so doing, I made a small notch and a slight upward crack in one of the front teeth; which however did not trouble me, but it made me rather more cautious for the future, and finally I brought home my necklaces in triumph. But as the years rolled over my head, the upper part of that damaged tooth shewed serious symptoms of decay; and Mamma had made me promise that if I should lose it, I would have it replaced by an artificial one, for it would be indispensable for the clearness of my utterance, and she had never contemplated that I should have any difficulties as to worldly matters . . . One day when I was quietly eating a piece of bread-and-butter (not crust), I found something in my mouth that ought not to be there, at least not exactly in that situation, for it was that large unhappy tooth that had snapped right off, and I thought,—well, Mamma, I suppose I may have the new tooth at some future time, but *now*, it is undoubtedly impossible. . . . On that afternoon, a friend who had been at the sea-side, returned to town, and came in at once to see me; and she had not been here many minutes before she exclaimed about the loss of my tooth, and I told her she was very unkind to discover it so quickly, but that I had no doubt I should gradually get accustomed to the vacuum, and that then it would not be so perceptible, and I joked over my misfortune.

She came in again early the next day, and her first greeting was that *she* must give me that tooth ! ! Was it not wonderful that she, who had been away for seven weeks, should have returned to town on the very day of my calamity, and should so lovingly have come to my relief? And what rendered the circumstance yet more striking to my mind, was that it was on the 19th of July that my tooth broke off, and on the 20th that she promised me the new one :—the anniversary of my drawing-mediumship day ! God does indeed frame my life into one perfect whole, and finally converts each trial into a new source of thanksgiving.

About a month previously the dearest friend of my girlhood (the Kate Hills with whom I had had my earliest experiences in Spiritualism), who had been away in South America for about nine years, returned to England. She had remembered my love for birds, for in former times I had a magnificent aviary for which I had given ten guineas, making a happy home for a variety of pretty foreigners : and she had brought me a cardinal, so that all-unsought as it were, another bird was to be mine. He was the wildest little creature, scarcely bearing to be looked at ; I suppose it was but young when caught, and not even the long sea voyage had tamed him. Being thus lovingly bestowed upon me, I could only rejoice in the gift, and I formed a sort of fancy that added to his value as especially appropriate to my home, for he sets up his little crimson crest just like a flame. I had great difficulty in at all taming him, especially as I never have any time to devote to such a purpose ; but Mr. Joseph recommended a little judicious starving as the only remedy, assuring me that it would not harm him, and he was thus gradually brought into good behaviour, and is now universally admired. My dear Kate passed into the spirit world more than a year ago.

Communion with Mrs. P. . . . For some time back I have occasionally felt a touch on my foot, but have usually been stayed in my enquiries as to who it was, beyond the fact that it was some one whom I had not personally known. On Saturday (July 29th) the feeling came much more strongly than it had ever been before, and I was impressed to pursue my questions, when I learned that it was Mrs. P.; at least I was corrected, and told "Emily P." She said she came to "sit at my feet," in the apostolic sense—I then felt her nestling against my knee. I asked whether, on her first passing from mortality, she had been troubled by her cruel tormentors, who had seemed to threaten something of the kind, but she said No, that she had been entirely protected from their assaults; and that those who first surrounded her were the spirits whose photographs she had received from me,—my dear brother Cecil, St. Stephen, Hannah the mother of Samuel, and the damsel named Rhoda; and her earliest consciousness was of being in this room with me. After that, she saw, and gradually recognised many of the brighter spirits with whom she had so long been in communion. She is very happy, but she has not yet attained to her spirit home, although she does gain occasional glimpses of it, but she will have much to do in the world's spiritual movement; although requiring to be strengthened in many ways ere she will be equal to the work allotted to her to perform, and much of that strength will have to be gained in the atmosphere of this room, filled as it is to overflowing with the aroma from the pictures, which forms a kind of material medium through which the influences who have guided my hand in their performance, can link themselves with those who are seeking to rise upwards; and I am told also to add that it is impossible to explain to mortal comprehension the value to the spirit world of this same home of mine and its varied contents.

On the 15th of July, I went to a séance at Mrs. Guppy-Volckman's, which I believe to have been the one of which I have the following reminiscence. We were a party of about a dozen, and we went up into the small room appropriated to her sittings. In the first instance we had a dark séance when flowers were brought, and the spirits gave me some beautiful white lilies. We then went down to take tea, and re-assembled in the hope of another class of manifestation. We had no light *in* the room, but the gas was burning brilliantly in the lobby, and our door was partly opened, so that there was sufficient light for us to distinguish clearly one another's features. A vacant chair was placed at my right hand; Mrs. Volckman being seated on the other side of it, and Lady A. was next beyond her. There was not much talk, for we all watched the vacant place in a kind of breathless expectation, and gradually we beheld a sort of white cloudiness which by slow degrees became more and more substantial, until finally it had exactly the appearance of one of Mr. Hudson's photographs :—just a bust, and with the head draped in a similar manner to theirs. Mrs. Volckman asked me to speak, so I put two or three questions, to which he responded by gravely bowing his head, three times for yes, or once for no. He was above the seat, at about the same height as we ourselves were. I then asked if he could approach closer to me, which he gradually did (the motion being so gentle as to be almost imperceptible), until his face was within about three inches of mine. He had a closely trimmed brown beard, and I think his eyes were blue, although at this distance of time I cannot be sure, but I *did* notice the colour and remembered it when afterwards telling of the séance, but unluckily I made no memoranda. Several others round the table asked questions, but he did not seem to hear their voices. When he approached me so closely, he had floated towards me above the level of the table. I then asked if he would move over to Lady A., so that she might see him clearly, with which he at once complied; passing on yet a little farther, but not much; and he gradually floated back to his original place above the chair, where we still saw him for some little time, flickering stronger and fainter at intervals until he faded in the same gradual manner that he had appeared to us. Mrs. Volckman seemed very nervous all the time, and her hands were quite cold and damp when she afterwards gave them to me to feel:—but it was a most interesting apparition.

I went to Mrs. T.'s on the 3rd of August, and in the evening, while we were in quiet conversation, she passed gradually into trance, and said with great impressiveness, making sometimes lengthy pauses :—" My words that I speak unto you, they are spirit and they are life: hearken therefore unto the words of My voice, for therein is life. . . . By the small gentle voice the way shall open. . . . Where two or three are gathered in My name, there also am I :—as it was in the past time, so it is now. . . . Hast thou not read? sorrow may endure for a night, but joy cometh in the morning: does My promise *ever* fail?—My peace I give unto thee, that peace which passeth man's understanding, but which thou canst receive, for lo! thou knowest that I am with thee always. . . . These thoughts are given now to strengthen thee through the troubles that beset thy pathway." She awoke gently, and as I had all the time felt most strongly the sensation on my forehead; I asked her if she saw the light. "Oh! yes, but you seem *all* lighted up (and she touched my dress as if she thought she should be able to feel the light), and all behind you there is light." Then she appeared to be listening, and as if repeating the words she heard, said: "I am the Light that lighteth the world."

In the course of our conversation in the afternoon, she told me that she had latterly had some figures very constantly shewn her: first there was one eight, then another; then there would be two ones; and they would be grouped about in various ways.—"1881," answered I,—"the same date as that given in Mother Shipton's prophecy." That was an entirely new idea for her, as it had not struck her as referring to a date: she had only thought that perhaps figures had been troubling her brain because she had been helping her daughter with her arithmetic in preparation for the examination she is going up for. Shortly after the manifestation of Light that I have recorded above, she said: "Now I see those figures again, on your face, 1881, an eight on each cheek, and the ones outside." At that time, in 1876, the date belonging to this year was not so much thought about by people in general, as it has been since its nearer and nearer approach. It is now upon us, and certainly, as far as my own life is concerned, the figures might well be manifested in forms of light upon my countenance; therefore that in that instance it might be considered as a *personal* prophecy (little as I then suspected it) which has most assuredly been marvellously fulfilled, for even in the opening of this year, my pathway looked most densely dark, but in the very worst moment, the light suddenly irradiated it, filling me with wonderment and gratitude; and only now has this solution presented itself to my mind, for although I have often reverted to the date having thus been seen on my cheeks, I had never recollected that it had come in combination with the previous words of comfort that had been spoken to me through her.

She wrote to me from Malvern on the 21st of September, saying: "I often think of you, and dreamed the other night of seeing you in such shining clothes; they seemed like what you wore at your Exhibition, but to be shining like mother-of-pearl. When I got up in the morning, I opened for a verse for you, and it was S. Matthew xvii. 2: 'And He was transfigured before them, and His face did shine as the sun, and His raiment was white as the light.' I had just been telling Mr. T. about my dream, and he was as much struck as myself when I opened to the above verse."

CHAPTER XVIII.

THE outside public had been most wonderfully stirred in the course of this year by the visit to England of Dr. Slade, whose mediumship attracted more attention than any had done since the first appearance here of the Brothers Davenport. I did not have the pleasure of witnessing any of the phenomena myself, for the guinea fee (even had it been fractionised to the smallest degree) was quite out of my power; but my cousins went to him, and received not only the slate-writing evidence, but, in the broad daylight, Mrs. Pearson *saw* and *felt* her mother's hand caressing hers, and Mr. Pearson in the same way was patted on the chest by his father's hand, which they both of them saw. Those parents also were the spirits who dictated the messages written for them on the slate, and thus they were characteristic ones. We Spiritualists know that we are sure to get the best manifestations when we go to mediums, although we may be utter strangers to themselves personally: *because* our own atmosphere is already in harmony with the invisible world, therefore we can easily forgive those outsiders who are disappointed that nothing of importance comes to them:—but we *cannot* forgive those who therefore make an outcry of fraud; and the foolish conduct of *Professor* Ray Lankester and Dr. Donkin will remain as a dark blot on their lives in the history of Spiritualism, for their persecution of an innocent and gifted man. I wended my way to Bow Street on the 10th of October, in the hope of hearing some portion of the trial, but the crowd was far too dense for me to have a chance of penetrating through it, or finding a place within the court, so I finished my day in Harpur Street with my cousins.

Although the case was not absolutely taken up by our Association, for our funds would not admit of our undertaking law proceedings; the committee who did work in his favour, consisted of many of our own members, and the use of our rooms was freely assigned to them for their meetings. I will not attempt to go into the law details, as I might make a blunder; but I know that the ill-used man was set free, but with sadly shattered health, and that his friends at once took him abroad. But his persecutors then took some other step, so that he should not dare to return here, or he would be again incarcerated. I know likewise that he afterwards wrote to Ray Lankester, offering (if he would ensure his safety under the circumstances) to come to England for one week, so as to give him several opportunities for testing the phenomena, to which he *received no reply whatever.* Such conduct was not only ungentlemanly, but makes it clearly evident to me that it was not truth in any way that was sought for in the first instance, but just some opportunity to victimise the man through whose instrumentality the proofs of a Hereafter might be given. Those two gentlemen *may* be scientific, but I am thankful to say that we have many *Englishmen* of unquestionable science whose judgment is not limited within the narrow boundaries of their own profession, whatever it may be; or we should be put to shame by the more liberal conduct of foreigners, as for instance Professor Zöllner of Leipzig, whose "Transcendental Physics," translated by Mr. Carleton Massey, is an entire and grand refutation of the accusation brought against Dr. Slade,—whose innocent table, by the bye, remains at our rooms for the inspection of everybody; and even the most weak-minded antagonist must acknowledge that it is free from anything in the shape of trickery. A few months ago, after vainly trying for Marcus Ward's foreign paper all down Oxford Street, I called, *en route* to our rooms, upon a stationer named Lake, in Great Russell Street, and after a little talk about what I wanted, he offered to get it for me, as I said I should again be in the neighbourhood on that day week and could call for it, mentioning where I was going. He then told me that it was of him that Dr. Slade had been in the habit of buying his slates, and at first he had thought he must be a schoolmaster from his needing so many, but that gradually Dr. Slade had entered into conversation with him, and he had thus learned something on the subject of Spiritualism. When the trial came on, the prosecutors, having heard that he had supplied the slates, came to subpœna him to give evidence in the case, but when they found that the slates were just common ones with no contrivances of any kind, they *did not* summon him to shew up innocence! all they had wanted was proofs of fraud!! the manifestation of truth was by no means their object.

Mr. Joseph's health had gone on steadily improving; so much so that in the April of this year he had had a very charming spirit photograph taken at Mr. Hudson's, which forms one of the illustrations of that work. But now the visions given to him were chiefly of the boundless ocean, which he interpreted as a sign that a long voyage would be the best recipe for his recovery, and he finally decided upon going to Melbourne, and thought he might be absent perhaps a year or two, but he hoped I would write frequently, so that my letters might convey a something of the beneficial influences that he was always conscious of obtaining when within my home; accordingly our correspondence was very steady.

I spent November 21st at Mrs. T.'s, and in the evening was telling her about Mr. Joseph's approaching departure on the 27th, when I saw that she was in some degree receiving influence, so I enquired what it was; and she said: "They are telling me that you two are to be brought together again, for that your work is most closely united, and as it were dovetails into one another.—It is very curious! they are shewing me a saw, and now another, with the two edges fitted exactly into one another, to express how complete is the union of the work."

Again to me at this Christmas of 1876 came a message through—W—

"To Georgiana the well-beloved! Blessing and glory and honour. . . . Days come when the cloud and the shadow shall be no more remembered, when Faith shall triumph in the Light of the All-Holy, as she now uplifts the banner of the Dove in the midst of the dark night of unbelief.

"The Holy Watchers are watching, and the morning Star rises in the dawn of the year that is coming up. As birds fly swiftly, so shall many changes come, and glad new tidings from the East are at hand. . . . Take new courage, oh! thou tried and faithful one, for the glory of The Lord shall suddenly come upon thee, and the days of thy mourning shall be ended!

From the Holy watchers."

I have spoken in the other volume of the small pen-and-ink monograms of which I had done so many as birthday gifts for friends, on cards the size of those used by ladies when on calling expeditions; and at the latter end of this year one of those friends enclosed me a half sovereign, with the hope that I might be aided to do one for her of the same size in colours. I well understood the tender delicacy of her suggestion, and that she was desirous of thus sending me all the aid that her finances would allow, and I was exceedingly glad when my *helpers* not only agreed to it, but selected for me at Roberson's a block of drawing-paper of nearly five inches by three and a half, and a very lovely monogram was done, which was placed in a good-sized sunk mount; thus it made a very pretty picture, far beyond anything she had figured to herself, and she warmly hoped that I might receive many other commissions of the same class.

It is not usual for me to have any messages written through me for others, although fragmentary bits of advice or comfort may sometimes go in any letters I may be sending, although seldom as given by any one but myself; I was therefore surprised when a friend wrote to me from the country that she had been told that I should receive a communication for her from Michael the Archangel; which was given that same evening, and I am here to copy a portion of it, as being also partly to myself.

"I, Michael, the Arm of The Lord—sent from on high to muster the forces of earth, to work together with the heavenly host,—for the dire strife which is now close at hand—do summon you, ⊙, to don your armour of proof, and to be prepared to take your full share in the warfare which now approaches. You will say, How can I work? In what way can my feeble hands avail?—But lo! I tell you that you will have much work to do, and you will see ways open to you, leading you apparently into new paths of life, but they are *not* new, inasmuch as that you have been gradually preparing to walk therein during the hours of mortal slumber, when your spirit has been guided by mighty ones along sure paths, whence you, looking down, have seen trembling mortals falling down precipitous rocks which you have passed in safety, because you trusted not in your own strength, but knew that your hand was held by God's own appointed agents; therefore you could walk steadily on, looking ever upwards, whereas they, weak but self-sufficient, thinking that they could themselves remove all obstacles from their path, thus lost their balance, and fell into the abyss. Understandest thou, my daughter, what I fain would teach? That thou must follow without fear the leadings given unto thee, even if they may seem in some degree not to tally exactly with what might appear the most pleasant to thee:—but thou hast many trials known only to thine own heart; but also thou hast blessings many and great, as well as that peace which the world cannot give: and in the forthcoming conflict with the evil hosts now pursuing earth's sons and daughters more hotly than ever, it will be given to thee to confute many of the lying statements poured forth through their human mouthpieces. . . . May God's grace ever shine upon thee, thou faithful one, MICHAEL, ARCHANGEL.

"*January* 21*st*, 1877."

On Wednesday, February 14th, Mrs. T. came to see me, and as Miss Creighton was my only other visitor, we had a nice quiet talk, while they were both seated in admiration of the (full-size, commissioned) Monogram on which I am engaged, of which the two letters are M and M as if one within the other. Presently I thought Mrs. T. looked as if she were either hearing something or likely to pass into trance, and she said that as she came along, she had seemed to feel the presence of Mrs. Marshall, and at one time the omnibus had appeared to her to stop to take some one up, and upon looking, she saw an old lady being helped in, who took her seat near the door, whom she seemed to recognise as our old friend—and then, upon rousing herself, and looking again, there was no person there whatever!! After a little more talk, I saw she certainly was passing under influence, so I got the slate. Then came the words :—" Do you think she's asleep ?—I'm afraid she isn't asleep, for she never will go if she can help it." She then took Miss Creighton's hand, and gave her a message of some length : after which she addressed herself to me. " I am *her* sister :—perhaps you do not know me." [*Whose* sister ? Who are you ?] " *Her* sister (pointing to herself), I did not have any name.—But that old lady ; she came when we came—she wanted to make her go to sleep . . . she couldn't, and *she* can't talk now. The message is like this from that poor old lady, M M; (the letters were said with rather strong emphasis, as if dear old Mrs. Marshall had felt very proud that we should be doing a monogram with similar initials to her own). She works, too, for you, and will do all she can." As there was a slight pause, I said, [May I be permitted to ask if you are the sister who was photographed with Mrs. T. as my first professional sitter ?] " Yes.—I am one year younger than she is, in some things but not in all." [You will pardon my interruption, but I wished to ascertain whether I was right in my inference.] " Quite right, and I am glad you asked." [May you now continue your message ?] "She will do all she can to help you through this time— and more will come. I can't give you the words, but it comes as a picture. There is a stick, like this (extending her two hands horizontally about a yard), and here there is another stick, *so* (putting her hand down perpendicularly about midway of the other stick as if joined to it, and about half the length downwards ... as I now understand, it would thus represent something like a pair of scales)—then here (on the right) is something very large, like a saucepan—it is nearly full, but not quite—it is black : and that means *trouble*. And on *this* side (the left) there are flowers ; and books—and long shining—cloaks I think they are." [Raiment ?] "Yes,—raiment ; and all bright and beautiful things. And there will be *as much* here as there : but not quite ;—for there is so MUCH there. But there will at *last* be enough here to *balance* it, and this old lady's work is to help to make that balance. When she has done that, she will be happy, and when she and *others* can get as much *good* for you as will make that balance on this side, *she* can rest, and then you will have rest." [Has that saucepan of trouble to be made *quite* full ? Is there *more* trouble coming?] "It must *boil*, but it can't hold any more." [In point of fact, then, have I got pretty well to the end ?] "There is just the difference of fulness in a quiet state *outwardly*, and fulness in a turbulent state, which will be harder to bear. But as a compensation, all dross will be purged away, or taken up, or given off in vapour, so that what remains after the boiling process is completed can be utilised in many happy ways for others. In fact, it is shewn that *you* do not need that this should pass through the boiling process except for purification—*not* for *yourself*, but for those who are to follow. In one sense it is a sacrifice, but it is of the nature, and is the same through which a mother passes, in giving birth to something better, brighter, and more beautiful—a something which adds a new link to life, and death, and all that is to come. . . . The old lady does not know what we say : she says,—Is that Miss Houghton ?—tell her The Lord walks on the face of the deep : His footstep even now approaches, and nothing can be hid : even now He waits for those who are to be gathered into His Kingdom, and those *are* called. Think not that His vision faileth, for all things are His : from the beginning He knoweth the end thereof. Cast thy care upon Him, for He shall be thy strength and thy shield and thy comforter.—Even so, for He cometh quickly." She then gently awoke.

How fully I did indeed learn to realise the boiling of that saucepan of trouble, and how much harder it truly was to bear when the external world had to know somewhat of my privations and trials, although even then there was of course much that none could know or guess: but in all my worst straits, in passing through a class of difficulties of which I had indeed heard, but *could not* have had any experience, I have never failed to feel that painful as it might be, it was *only so* that one could learn the fullest sympathy for others: and even thus I trust that the dross of self may have been in some degree purified.

The whole spiritual atmosphere has been for these several years full of prophecies of woe and change, to which the date of 1881 was given by that denominated Mother Shipton's. Whether hers or not is unimportant now that it is passing on, bringing much trouble in its train; but I wish to refer to some that are not so definite. The Rev. Mr. Barrett thus wrote to me, *May* 17*th*, 1877 :

"MY DEAR MISS HOUGHTON,—I was glad to hear from you, and should be still more glad to see you. . . . Have your guides given you any intimation that tremendous changes are coming, or already upon us? An uneducated clairvoyante, medium, or ecstatic, whichever is the right term, has told me that a *divine air*, or *breath of God*, is shortly coming, and already acting in the world, which will change everything, open spiritual vision, cause thousands of deaths, and bring living judgments. . . . She also describes what seems to answer to what Swedenborg would term a judgment in the spiritual world as now going on; and as the places of suffering are cleared, and the persons there, raised, so are the judgments to come upon the earth. . . . The published accounts through such and such writers (whom he named) differ much. My authority is the Bible, and I test all theories and doctrines by that. But it is a comfort to me to be told that my time is now short, except that one does not know what *short* means, when used by beings who have been in existence thousands of years." . . . (His *short* lasted four years.) I wrote to tell him of the prophecies of the same character coming to me from so many quarters, as well as given to myself almost from the beginning of my mediumship; but of which I have kept no written records. In his answer he says: "What you tell me is curious, and all corresponds with what this clairvoyante has told me, and like you, she says that we shall see the departed walking upon the earth, but not with the eyes of the body, but those of the soul." Later on, in answer to a request, he said : " I have no notes of revelations that any one could make out, but merely what might serve to refresh my own memory. They are barely legible, and mainly written in abridged Latin words, for the sake of conciseness, but they might help me if I had time to go over them. When I am able, I will try to put down some short analysis of them. They are by an uneducated person, who when in trance believes that she is employed by *angels* in preaching under *their* direction to spirits in suffering :—says many other trance subjects are thus employed. That it is not the work for spirits in Paradise, and that, until more progressed, the spirits can understand a lower person, like men, better than they could angels. After a certain amount of work, the angels and spirits in Paradise talk to her, and shew her the places there. They tell her that as these places of suffering are cleared, the final judgments will come on the earth. They are nearly cleared. Before long, the spiritual vision of many will be opened to see and talk with the angels who are always with us. The angels don't know the day of Our Lord's coming, but they know from what is now being done above, it must near. Wickedness will increase terribly, also the good be better and more active ; vivisection among other iniquities will be put down by terrible judgments from God. An air is coming, and already is in the world, which will bring terrible heat : it is (as I understand) some emanation from the sun, and a modification of God's love, which is the source of heavenly heat ; when the wicked breathe it, it will destroy many in an instant. To the righteous it will open their eyes, give spiritual vision and great joy. . . . <u>A new remedy for illness they have told me</u>—I generally use mesmerised sugar for mesmerising patients, as it saves me, and prevents me from suffering from unhealthy emanations. I was ordered to place sugar for two hours in the sun for two days running, and then use it, and was told it would give strength to my body and open my spiritual vision. I have done it for about a fortnight, and I think I have derived much good from it, but it is to be done for about six weeks to produce much effect. Do you know anything about such a remedy? They say it is a very strong one, stronger than mesmerism—and to be used cautiously. I put a little of this sugar in the hand of a clairvoyante when asleep—it took her to a new and beautiful place—and partly took away the use of the hand for two or three days. This was to shew me the effect of it." . . .

"Directions for solarising the sugar. . . I find I had not made clear to you the use of the sugar. The solar power is distinct from, and not to be used with, mesmerism. I was told to put a pinch of it in the clairvoyante's hand, merely to shew that it had a strong power *sui generis*. It is to be white pounded loaf sugar, the finer the better. The least a person should take *to do much good* would be about three teaspoonfuls a day for about five or six weeks. The best way of taking it is at your meals in your food, tea, puddings, or whatever you like. The more a person takes the better. . . . When you have the opportunity of a fine sun, *do a lot of it.* Spread out as much as you can in the sun, on paper, plates, or what is convenient, for two or three hours.—Do this for two days: the *same time each day*, as the sun has different powers at different hours: *i. e.* if you put sugar in the sun from 11 to 2 on one day, *don't* put it out from 2 till 5 the next day, but from 11 to 2 or 11 to 1.—We keep it in the same things: finger-glasses I find convenient, and then cover them with silk in a drawer in the dark. Thus, when well charged, it would preserve its power for a month, but you might repeat it at times. . . . As far as I can judge, I have found the sun sugar do good."

The revelations thus given through this clairvoyante are exactly in accordance with wonderful visions that I have heard related by Colonel Andrew Jackson Rogers of the United States, with whom, during his residence in England, I had the pleasure of being very intimate. The opening of his spiritual vision came upon him seven or eight years ago (I do not remember the exact date) quite unexpectedly and unsought, and he remained in his normal state, while during a whole night he both saw and heard marvels beyond his conception. Prophecies as to individuals (some of whom he scarcely knew even by name) were given, some of which prophecies have already been fulfilled, while some are still in the future, but the realization of a portion gives the probability that in due course it will be the same with the others. It was then foreshewn that a time was at hand when the surrounding spirits would be beheld by the mortals among whom they are ministering; but for the wicked the sight would be overpowering and many would fall down dead, stricken as it were in an instant, whereas for the upright and true the visible presences would become a source of strength. Many things were told to him which he was forbidden to reveal, but there were others that he might mention in confidence, and I believe that he wrote them all out very fully, so that in due time they may be given to the world.—It must have been a most marvellous night! After that he had similar experiences at distant intervals, and during his visit to this country I think they were stronger than ever, but he was not allowed to acquaint us with the details, although there was always much of interest to communicate, and I look forward to his future return here, and the renewal of our pleasant intercourse.

Mr. Joseph's visions had been more of the character of those communications referring to the clearing of the lower spheres of spirit life, and the help that has to be given to uplift the unhappy ones there, as being the most important work that Spiritualists have to perform. During his years of illness and suffering, he seems to a great extent to have been labouring in this field, whether wittingly or unwittingly : and he had even, during his childhood, had visions of the same nature ; and I almost regret that I should not have written any of them down, for they contained a multitude of small lessons, but I have always been so very closely occupied in one way or another, that I have returned to what I was previously engaged upon as soon as he had left me. I subjoin an extract from one of his letters from Melbourne, dated *June 25th*, 1877 : "About a month ago I visited a small watering-place near Melbourne, where I remained three weeks, and accidentally made the acquaintance of a small community of about 30 souls living together in perfect harmony under one roof, with a prophet at its head. (I mean the community.) They get their living by fishing, and the prophet, who of course is really a medium, but knows little or nothing of Spiritualism, was told by *voice* and *vision* some time ago of the *approaching advent*, which they await, and lead a very religious life with frequent prayers and explanations of Scripture, which the prophet inspirationally delivers. . . The séance with Mrs. T., of the 'saucepan of trouble,' interested me much. It appears indeed that the X must be passed before the crown is obtained. God knows how to deal with us, and I trust that your afflictions are nearly all passed. . . Sometimes I wonder how and when that great power will again descend upon me. From a vision I received a few days ago, I judge it will not be long. . . It is strange that lately the name and love for Jesus has been getting a strong hold of me ; I look upon Him now as a Father ; almost as a part of myself.—Once upon a time I should have laughed at the idea, yet now it seems to me quite natural."

I had many intermediate letters, but one of about a twelve-month later contains further allusions to his changed views, so I will make a short extract, although I can only begin, as it were, in the middle, as the previous part was in reply to something I had written with respect to—to use his own term—"Jesus of Nazareth, in the fulness of time. Things have so come to pass with me that what was once the impossible and most improbable have either become verified facts or amongst the certainties of the future. . . . Mrs. Britten is lecturing here now, and is much liked:—indeed she is a marvel of eloquence and a fund of knowledge, and is doing, I believe, a great work in Spiritualism; but her guides have not the *Highest* truth; at least do not *as yet* preach it. And yet all she says is in a measure true, but she *wants* the *Key* that will reconcile her truths with the *Bible truths*—and it is so *easy*. In God's time it will be done. But she and others are laying the foundation for a grand superstructure, and believe me that it is under God:—although they preach not the full truth, yet on that foundation the X will stand—and they know it not—They are busy *underground*, and therefore in partial darkness, laying the stones for the glorious building; the new dispensation, the new era, and the new kingdom which will shew forth in the brightest light of God's countenance—Therefore may God speed them. The reconciliation of these different forces and powers will *come*, and their wisdom though opposed to each other will be made manifest.—The *Cross* is in possession of the Highest knowledge: it is feeding the children, but it gives the food best adapted for the *season*, palate, stomach, and life of the creature to make a new spiritual constitution."

About the latter end of the January of this year came the final break-up with poor Mr. Hudson, who felt that he had no remedy but to give up his studio, and go away to a small house where there were no photographic possibilities; so that great gift was let to drop for want of the efficient human aid that ought to have sustained it. Of course cameras and such-like apparatus were sold, to enable him to hold life together in some degree, and he strove hard to obtain employment in any shape or form, but only occasional temporary fragments came, for in this age of struggles, he, with his infirm health, could have but little chance when even the young and active have to seek other lands to earn their bread. But still he in some way lived on; he had kept his printing frames and a portion of his negatives, so that he has occasionally had orders for photographs that have brought him in a trifle; and I am happy to say that he has latterly received more substantial help, so that he is looking better in health than I have known him for years.

With regard to myself, my friend's kind wish respecting the small monograms had been partly fulfilled, and I had received various commissions for them, and I must gratefully add that for some of them my remuneration had gone a good deal beyond the limit of the original fee, and in one instance my heart was rejoiced by a cheque that helped me through a painful difficulty. The dear giver is now gone to where she will reap the full reward of her beneficence, and I learn that she is now by my side, sympathising with the tears that the recollection has drawn forth. Dear tender-hearted soul! I little thought when last I saw her that she would so soon be taken hence. In some cases more than one commission would come from the same quarter, and one dear friend has had quite a collection of them done, many of them being of persons eminent in our own day; and then, after enjoying them for a time at her own home, she has lent them to me back as specimens to shew to my visitors. But they were wonderfully various, each being in some degree illustrative of the individual represented. An exceedingly beautiful one was B. D., typical of the now deeply lamented Lord Beaconsfield; and much as I had always admired his talents as a writer and as a statesman, I thus learned to realize them more fully, for I was much struck with having to use an especial colour in the course of the working that I have scarcely ever needed even in the larger monograms, for in these miniature ones only the predominating characteristics are given; and the quality that had here to be expressed was what my teachers term "adjustingness of mind," by which they mean a mind that is capable of balancing the pros and cons of a question with such nicety, that it can find the true best to be acted upon under the most conflicting circumstances. Such a man was indeed a loss to the nation, and England might well mourn him. While doing *personal* drawings of any kind, the most wonderful insight is often given to me of the *depths* of the nature that is being portrayed, but in many cases that passes quite away from me after the picture is finished, unless at the time I should make some memorandum, which I rarely do, for it is not desirable to be burthened with the specialities of other people, and I know that if required the reminiscence will be brought to me by those who have originally shewn it to me, and whose advice I always take as to whether I shall make any record. Among those I had the pleasure of delineating in 1877, were Mr. Berks Hutchinson, of the Cape, and his sweet wife.

One of the battles fought with respect to our Association, especially by a portion of the ex-members, has been as to the numerical size of the Council,—and in deference to some of the opinions, it was reduced a year or two ago, but not to the absurd extent that had absolutely been suggested. For my own part I hold with making it as large as can reasonably be done : for in any way, there will be but a certain few who will really attend the meetings or do the work, and I should like to see in the published list the names of Spiritualists in all parts of the kingdom, so that in whatever town travellers might find themselves, they might know *where* to seek for information on our subject as soon as their interest in it was awakened. An incident that occurred to myself has given strength and substance to the idea. Some years ago, just as I was finishing dinner, a lady called, saying that I should not know her name, but would I kindly see her for a little while ? So she was walked up to the drawing-room, whither I immediately followed her. She then told me that she had quite recently lost her husband, under very painful circumstances ; and she had been told that through Spiritualism she might obtain some comfort.—But—she knew no Spiritualists, nor where to seek for them : however, she had also heard there were newspapers connected with the movement, so she enquired for one of those, and bought a number of the *Spiritualist*, which in those days contained our advertisement including the list of the members of the Council with their several addresses; among which she found my name and abode within an easy distance of her own home, so she thought she would venture to call upon me, trusting that I would pardon the intrusion. I was heartily thankful to be able to give her all the information she sought, and she did indeed find comfort therein, and has since become a steadfast Spiritualist. I do not mention her name, although I know she would be quite willing that I should do so; but I only speak of it as a proof of the advantage granted to outside seekers by such a clear evidence of our willingness to enlighten them, shewn by the publication of our names and whereabouts.

What a gratification it would be if we could make the acquaintance of all our foreign adherents whose names are conjoined with ours; this pleasure was granted to us in the course of one short visit to London made by the Baron and Baroness Von Vay; and although it was in the empty season of the year, August, we mustered a tolerably fair gathering in Great Russell Street for their reception, when they gave us a hope that at some future time they might make a longer stay in England, and thus give us fuller opportunity for intercourse; in which there would be no lingual difficulty, as the Baroness speaks English very well; although her husband was not quite so fluent in it. Since that time we have occasionally had glimpses of some of our foreign members, but we should like more.

CHAPTER XIX.

JUST about that time a friend, whose life is devoted to establishing the fact of our identification with the Israelites, told me of a work by Piazzi Smyth, the Astronomer-Royal of Scotland, entitled "Our Inheritance in the Great Pyramid," as containing the prophetic proofs, by accurate measurement, that some great change was to take place in 1881, and I at once had the book from Mudie's, and read it through with deep interest in all the details there given as to our own weights and measures, but was disappointed *not* to find the special information I was seeking, which I then learned had only been published in the *second* edition, *not* possessed by Mudie. I then heard of a pamphlet referring principally to the one point under consideration; "Philitis," by Charles Casey (published originally only in Dublin, but now to be had of Hamilton, Adams, & Co., price 2/.), and that I did succeed in borrowing. One may well marvel at the mysterious system within which such great truths were enwrapped, only to be elucidated in the "fulness of time" by one who should fully realize that the wonders of creation could only be the product of ONE COMPLETE MIND, with whom every *small* detail is as needful in forming the Whole as what we may consider the large ones. I must here limit myself to the one subject, and as I have lately been fortunate enough to have the *brochure* presented to me, I am able to make extracts from itself, instead of clothing the ideas in my own imperfect words; I will do so as briefly as I can, but I would advise all those who feel an interest in such vital truths to study the small book for themselves.

"The pyramid .. presented from the hand of the builder a solid-mass surface without any visible opening, and .. about 3000 years after its creation, the Arab, Caliph Al Mamoon, broke in an entrance on the north side with the hope of discovering the vast treasures which tradition had said were concealed in its chambers. The result of his labour was the discovery of the true passages and the chambers to which they led, but no such treasures as he hoped for. . . . It may be thought that this is not the place to allude to the ethical readings of the pyramid. . . . yet I may be permitted to hint at some results which have been communicated to me in advance by a devout and eminent thinker, as they are of such a nature as to profoundly interest all believers in Revelation.

"The *descending* passage is typical of that dispensation after the dispersion, in which men *descended* to the depths and abomination of idolatry; when, following their own inventions, and rejecting patriarchal worship and revelation of the true God, they pursued a course which could only end in the bottomless pit (exhibited in the pyramid by a deep subterranean chamber without any finished flooring).

"But the foreseeing mercy of God commenced a mode of salvation to man, first by separating a peculiar people, under Moses, unto Himself, from the rest of mankind, at a particular date—a peculiar people, through whom was introduced, in the fulness of time—*i.e.*, a particular date, the Saviour Christ, and the Christian dispensation. This first separation of the peculiar people, without at the same time interfering with the sinful course of the rest of mankind, is typified by the first *ascending* passage, actually leaving the course of the descending passage, which still goes on descending as before to the bottomless pit.

"The first ascending passage, moreover, or the Hebrew dispensation, having begun an ascent, continues to ascend for a period equal to that from Moses to Christ, and then merges suddenly into the still ascending but incomparably more capacious and more solemnly constructed 'grand gallery,' typifying the Christian dispensation of the First Coming, as at present, and for the last 1872 (the date of that portion of the book) years, in existence.

. . . "Let us take the pyramid's unit of measure in our hand, and faithfully reading off Philitis's work, we shall find that he has foreshewn accurately, as 985 years, that part of the first dispensation—from the dispersion to Moses—in an inch to a year, on the length of the floor of descending passage, from its beginning to the point of its intersection by the floor of the first ascending passage (produced). And following up this good man's work, we still further find the Hebrew dispensation of 1542 years given precisely, on floor of first ascending passage, in an inch to a year, while still more upward, in the grand gallery, the present Christian dispensation is recorded as intended to contain 1881-2 years, on the same scale.

. . . "But there is another date of a totally different kind which may be appealed to, and this is the pyramid's own memorial date of foundation, as recently computed by modern stellar astronomy and the existing calendar, and thence found to be 2170 years before the acknowledged birth of Christ. . . . The date will be evidently . . inside the mouth of the slanting entrance passage; and there, remarkably enough, in a structure usually supposed to be without any markings, and certainly without any *written* language, or sculpture, the usually rectangular joints of the great stones forming the inclined, sloping walls are made vertical or nearly so, in two successive instances, and in no other throughout the whole passage. These two, however, are only to arrest attention . . . so the two strikingly visible vertical separations of continuity in the walls are followed by a *thin, fine,* but *exquisitely true* line, ruled at six inches behind the last of these separations, and in that line— evidently the work of a master-hand, and of that period— is contained the position answering to 2170 B.C., or indicating that, after the drawing of that line, 2170 years were to elapse before the Redeemer of mankind should appear. . . . It is a very glorious revelation, and test of divine guidance in a prophetic structure, inspired in the cause of the true God and the mystery of His purpose respecting the human race.

"But that is not all, for on entering the grand gallery we come upon a square sepulchral aperture, partly in its floor, from the bottom of which a passage leads westerly for a short space to the edge of a dark, almost perpendicular, abyssmal shaft, which leads down, down, down, into the deep and dismal subterranean descending passage, just before it falls into the Hades chamber or pit, which lies some 180 feet down in the living rock. Now, at an inch to a year along the line of the floor of the grand gallery, this sepulchral chamber shews the date of Calvary in our Lord's life. The inhumation of His body in the tomb and His resurrection therefrom are exhibited (in the stone that covered the entrance to that sepulchral well being burst out or rolled back with triumphant power from its mouth) in mechanical features, which speak as incontestably to the eye of science as eloquently as to that of faith—that the grave could not detain Him beyond the appointed time.

"Thus and here we have the death, burial, and resurrection of the Messiah shewn.

". . . To those who believe in the divinely-inspired character of the Hebrew and Christian Scriptures, it will be refreshing to know that here, in this pillar of witness, seven hundred years before Moses wrote the Pentateuch, did Philitis record, not in written characters that might or could be defaced or mistranslated, but in metric characters, fixed and unchangeable as the earth's axis, the three notable dispensations of our race—viz., that from the dispersion at Babel to Moses, the Hebrew dispensation, and the Christian dispensation, foretelling to a year the date of the birth of the Messiah."

My extracts have extended to greater length than I had contemplated, but I could not have omitted anything that I have given without weakening their force, and they seem to me of inestimable value, most especially when the actual year of 1881 is on its journey towards becoming a date of the past, and people will perhaps exclaim—Well? and what has it brought in its train?—Yet even the most unobservant may have noticed that in many respects it *has* differed from the generality of years. But that is all unnecessary to prove that it may define an epoch. One

version of Mother Shipton's prophecy, copied I *believe* from
a book of ancient date, was worded—

> " And finally the end shall come
> In eighteen hundred eighty one."

No modern prediction that has come to my knowledge, has
in any way foretold *destruction* (unless of the wicked), but
renovation—The opening of a new dispensation, *not* the
closing up of a previous one, any more than took place at
the birth of Our LORD. We must bear in mind the history
of the inauguration of *that great change.* Who among the
wise and great knew aught of that humble birth in an over-
crowded inn that was eventually to revolutionise the world?
A few shepherds tending their flocks heard the angelic host
proclaim the wondrous power thus shed upon the earth, but
imagine a similar knot of uneducated men in this our day,
walking into this City of London with the announcement of
a parallel marvel!! who would heed them? They would
be scoffed and jeered at!—Revelations *do* come—the voices
of the angels *are* heard,—and the air is burthened with the
whispers of the unseen throng who are telling of change:—
but that change may come with tread as soft as the previous
one, and a hundred years *may* pass away before it becomes
clear to the human intelligence in the aggregate, that 1881
has in truth been the entrance upon a new era, *belonging to*,
not separated from, the previous ones.

In now looking again over the earlier portion of the
pamphlet for a something that I thought was there, I have
come upon a mystery which I believe forms a kind of prophecy for these present times. After *ascending* the grand
gallery, the first *level* floor is attained, which is that of what
is called the Queen's chamber, which must be the beginning
of the era upon which we are now entering, and here I will
again quote from its interesting pages.

" Mr. Waynman Dixon also has had the honour of
making a discovery in this chamber which is mysteriously
inexplicable, viz., the existence of two channels seemingly

similar in design to the air channels of the King's chamber, but which were evidently *not* meant by the architect for ventilating purposes, because they are hermetically sealed up by the inner or chamber-lining stone, giving no indication of their existence, until broken into by cold chisel and hammer, when it was found that they reached some seven feet into the wall horizontally, then rose N. and S. at an angle of 32°, and likewise that they were cut through the chamber-lining block in its entire thickness, save the thin tympanum which was left to conceal their existence on the inner surface. The question, then, is—As they were not meant for ventilating channels, what was their use? It strikes me that they were meant for acoustic purposes, as the slight covering slab would serve as the veritable tympanum of an ear that led—where?—possibly, probably, almost certainly, to another yet undiscovered chamber, . . an idea supported by the fact mentioned by Mr. Dixon, that although the smoke of a fire lighted in the southern passage went away, its exit was not discoverable on the outside of the pyramid. And when we reflect that a slight tap, given on the stone tympanum by a small metallic or other hard substance, would be faithfully transmitted through the length of the channel to its exit — the conclusion seems reasonable that those passages had an acoustic use, and were *not* meant for ventilating purposes."—Now, how do I read it? As an evidence of the communion now opened with invisible agencies, whose slightest tap may beat in harmony with those who have ascended so far that they may almost be said to place their feet on level ground.

In one of my letters to the Rev. Mr. Barrett on the subject of the 1881 prophecies, I mentioned Professor Smyth's work, which I thought would interest him exceedingly, and also " Philitis," but he did not allude to them in his answer, as he was shortly coming up to town, and upon his visit he surprised me by the information that he had absolutely] been with Professor Smyth and his intrepid wife during a considerable part of their arduous labours at the pyramid, of course assisting them in the various measurements. And it was he who told me (what I thought I had also seen in the book) that the ascending gallery had been formed of one class of stone, limestone I think, but that you then come upon the harder and closer material of granite; and he considered that as a fact full of significance, although he did not attempt any solution thereof.

A soirée was held at the Cavendish Rooms on the 17th of October, for the benefit of Mr. Morse, which was very well attended. It is always my custom on such occasions to wander about as much as I can, between the parts, so as to have if possible a few words with all my friends : thus in the course of my peregrinations I had a bit of talk with Mr. Towns, who said he had seen a spirit near me while I was sitting down, who was still by my side, whose name was Samuel; and he proceeded to describe him as having a fine presence, and wearing an ancient costume, so that he seemed to him to be one of the Biblical personages; in fact, *the* Samuel of the Bible :—had I ever had any communion with him? Oh yes! from an early part of my mediumship. He went on to say that he had a new design for me, at least it was a drawing; and that he was either working upon it, or he would be present while it was being done. As he commenced a description of what he appeared to be seeing, I recognised that it must be the Shield, No 5, which is now in progress. He saw towers and towers as it were endless, with light streaming through, which must apparently emanate from a glorious Sun within it, whose rays should pierce through everything; but that, beautiful as it has been all through the work, the finishing will surprise me by its especial glory. He had a vision of sparklings far beyond those of diamonds, as if showering down the front. I told him I thought it was almost finished, and that there *had* been an unexpected change; but he was of opinion that there was still a surprise in store for me before it should be quite completed.

The picture, as it has been worked, has seemed to be formed of many substantial columns, making vistas of arches, while ever and anon, there have been what I term "water-works" forming as it were in the background a grand centre shield (sometimes threefold), which has always brought to my mind the text, "For The Lord God is a Sun and a Shield," and the drawing throughout has had a kind of golden glow, which is still more apparent in its present state. It has already had an immense amount of work on it, but it may be that there is a great deal yet to come.

I was introduced on that evening to Miss Mancell, a normal clairvoyante, who has been developed about a year; and she came to see me on the following Wednesday, but, as she arrived rather late in the afternoon, the fading light would not admit of my shewing her much, so after letting her have a cursory glance at the one upon which I am engaged, I deposited it on a chair, to make place on the easel for another, with which she was much struck, but presently she said she saw a beautiful spirit form passing round and round the unfinished picture. I now seated myself on the low chair near her, when she turned towards me, and almost immediately said; "I see the face of Jesus above you, with a wonderful glory all round Him. . . . Now I see Faith as she is represented in old pictures, with a cross in her hand as if for a staff." She then saw an elderly lady bending tenderly over me, describing Mamma very clearly, and two or three other spirits. "Oh! I see a glorious sun, with wonderful rays above your head, so bright I can scarcely look at it; and now there is a shield! what *can* that mean? a sun and a shield?" I answered that I understood the meaning, for that it referred to the drawing on the chair, the one I am now doing.

She had a wonderful succession of visions: they were mostly fragmentary; but as a curious phase of mediumship, I will note the larger proportion of them, which I had to write down as fast as I could. . . Several lights and stars, and one very brilliant star just over my head, then streams of coloured light pouring down upon me, blue, scarlet, and golden. She then saw my two dear little sisters, one holding a lily in her hand, which she was placing on my head;

then that lily became the centre flower of a garland with which the two were crowning me. Then she saw spirits with wheat ears, some of which were formed into a sort of tiara on my head, with small clusters behind my ears, while a horn of plenty was showered over me. . . King David, with a golden crown on his head and a harp in his hand. . . "Now there is a ship in full sail upon beautiful clear blue water." [Can they shew you what that means?] "Jesus is guiding the helm. . . Now there is a dove descending over your head. . That lady whom you recognised as your Mamma is standing behind you, holding a lovely crimson rose, and I see written up,—'Go on, my dear child, go on in the good work.' . . Now there is a beautiful church, and in front of it a magnificent white throne, on which sits One surpassing fair, Who looks like Jesus, and they are all bowing down before Him, a concourse of beautiful angels. . . A very aged gentleman with very white hair, leaning on a staff, a pilgrim he looks like,—he has a great deal of hair, and a very long heavy beard: he wears sandals and a long robe." [Will he give his name?] "'Never mind my name,' is written up, 'The Lord is my Shepherd.—Cast thy bread upon the waters and thou shalt find it after many days.' . . . You are surrounded with doves, they are all round your head. . . Now a circle of stars is coming down on your hair, like an ornament with a large one in the centre. . . There's an angel blowing a horn, and it is written up—'Oh! lady pure and gentle, your trials have been many and great, but in the end you will come off victorious.' . . A beautiful little boy, he has got a lamp in his hand, and oh! such a bright light. . . A beautiful angel with a pencil or paint-brush in his hand, and there is an easel and a lady sitting at it—oh! it is *you!* he has on an azure robe and a golden girdle, and he is guiding your hand; and now there is the Sun and the Shield round you." Just as she was finishing this sentence, Mr. W. came in, but he seated himself quietly by my side, and the séance continued: "An elderly gentleman who looks like a lawyer; he has a paper in his hand, with three or four rows of red sealing-wax on it: he is counting some money; pieces of gold. He went to a desk and took out some money: and he is holding a pen towards you for you to sign something. You are shewing him a picture, and he seems to be admiring it very much; he is putting some money in your hand, and you are signing something in a book:—you are shaking hands with him: he has taken off his—oh! it has all vanished now. . . . There's a large place; it looks like some place of entertainment; there's a large table, and they are all sitting round it:—oh! they are sitting in séance, and you are with them, in darkness; there are some very beautiful birds, like canaries, they are being presented to you by an elderly lady; there is GUP over your head." I told her it was a vision of a séance that had taken place (at Mrs. Guppy's, as already narrated); and then she had another, also of a past event; then a series of short fragmentary pictures. "There's a beautiful white Cross.—There's a beautiful Dove, and it says—' I come from the Holy Land.' . . There are two men bringing a large chest, oh! it's so heavy: one man is kneeling down and taking out some old musty-looking parchment: it does look so old and dusty this parchment they are bringing out, as if it had been there hundreds of years:—it says, 'On this schedule '—They have shut down the lid now, have shut it in."

I now suggested that she should have a séance with Mr. W., and a great deal came for him, containing various tests, and I gave him the paper on which I had scribbled it all down.

Miss Mancell was at that time in very great straits, but I was able to recommend several visitors to her for séances, and I also had her here on another occasion, with Mr. W. and his daughter, who received some remarkable tests, and I had plenty of writing to do. A good deal had come for me before their arrival, as well as fragments afterwards, but I will only give a few short extracts.

"Such a bright light came down from near you just while you were saying The Lord's Prayer. . . There's an elderly lady just by your feet with very white teeth; her hair is rather dark, and done with combs in an old-fashioned way: she is either kneeling or sitting on the ground." I believe her to have been Mrs. P. . . "There's the Sun and Shield again." [Can you describe them?] "The Sun has bright rays, and there's a hand holding the Shield out, as if something were coming against it: the hand and arm seem passed through the back of the Shield to hold it out. . . . Now there's a very high ladder reaching up, oh! so high! it's such a wonderful ladder, all gold, you are climbing up it, and now you've got to the very top :—there's an angel crowning you with a gold crown, the angel was by the top :— and now you have vanished above it. It was a gold crown, and you looked somehow changed, you looked quite *translated*; I never saw anything so wonderful."

Later on, I was able to assist her to a comfortable home, so that she does not now exercise any professional mediumship.

Mrs. T. came to see me on Friday, January 25th, 1878, and of course my first thought was to shew her "The Shield," No. 5, which had been so lately finished, and to read her the memoranda I had made on the subject, a sort of compilation of what I have already narrated, with this addition: "The picture, as I look back in my mind to its commencement, seemed at first as if it might be the interior of a strong castle, with a surrounding wall of full rich crimson, giving one the idea of a bulwark of mighty power that nothing could penetrate; of which the gateway was a cerulean arch, type of The Lord Jesus. Then were designed many substantial columns, making vistas of arches, as of a tower of strength, terminating finally with a grand archway spanning the whole, that was sprinkled over with myriads of sparkling globules of light." She was much struck with its beauty and profundity, and she said it seemed to give her so much the idea of *creation*, as if that were what was signified by it,—after a time adding ;—"The words come to me—'I will create a new heaven and a new earth;' that is a text, is it not?" "Oh! yes." So I sought the texts, Isaiah lxv. 17, 18, and lxvi. 22, 23.

She had not purposed coming to me when she left home, having had to go into town, where she had found much excitement and commotion, in consequence of Lord Beaconsfield having declared his war policy; and she then felt that she *must* come and talk it over with me, especially as she had passed a singularly uncomfortable night; each time she had slept undergoing acute pains, which she had felt were symptomatic of fresh trouble coming forth to the world. That the pains were a spiritual sign was evident by their ceasing whenever she fully awoke. Also, several times in her sleep she wept and sobbed, so that Mr. T. aroused her, but she had seemed overwhelmed with pity for some upon whom heavy trials were coming : but she had not realized the political source until her visit to the City, not having looked at the papers before leaving home. All this talk led us to revert to the prophecies given and spoken of when she had been looking at the *previous* "Shield." I was then impressed to hand her the Bible, which with much solemnity was opened at Isaiah v. 1, 2, 3, 4, 5, 6, 7. When she had finished reading; my hand was pointed towards the picture, and through me was strongly said :—"*But*, I have built a Tower wherein the righteous shall find refuge."

She said that the allusion to the "tower" in the 2nd verse had struck her very much while reading it, as referring to the drawing. I was then influenced to seek a text, and it was opened at Isaiah ix. 8, 9, 10, 11, 12, 13, 14, 15, 16 : and when I had read those denunciations against pride and self-sufficiency in the nation, Mrs. T. again took the Bible in her hand, but instead of being led to a text, she passed under influence, and said, "Blessed are they who have reached the fulness of time in which they may rest from their labours, but woe unto many in these *coming* days. The Lord is a tower of strength to those who trust in Him and who keep His commandments, but the wicked shall perish from the face of the earth, and for the righteous a new heaven and a new earth shall be created wherein shall dwell righteousness. Even now the seed is planted :—it shall grow, it shall increase by night and by day, nurtured by the will of The Lord, until it become a habitation for the faithful; in it they shall dwell, and no harm shall come nigh them." For some little time she spoke not, still remaining deeply entranced, while I cogitated as to whether I could put any personal question, although feeling that I was to do so, when she turned fully towards me, and said : —" Ask, thou faithful one, if thou wilt, and I will answer." [May I ask of earthly hopes ?] "According as thy day is, so thy strength shall be." [Thanks be to The Lord, but matters press upon me.] " No sparrow falleth to the ground, neither shall any hurt come to thee.— Wouldst thou choose to come *within* the veil, and be for ever sheltered from earthly cares, or wilt thou still strive—wilt thou *still* strive to live thy appointed time ? Thou mayest choose, for life and death are within the hands of The Lord, and I am bidden to say thou mayst *choose.*" [Dear Lord, I choose to do Thy work, in the path Thou hast appointed unto me, I seek not to quit it.] " Thou hast chosen well.—Nevertheless, as I see that the thorns press sometimes heavily on thy brow, if the pressure become too great, it shall be lightened before it become unbearable." She was silent for a time, and when she again spoke, yet more comforting assurances were given me. . . . " Thou hast been faithful over the things committed to thee . . . thou hast not buried thy talents, and when The Lord comes, thou shalt receive thine own with usury. No promise is forgotten, though the fulfilment may be *long* delayed." She now stood up, and said with great tenderness, " And now, may the grace of Our Father, and of The Lord Jesus Christ, and of His Holy Spirit, rest upon you and be with you for ever. Amen."—She now gently awoke, and wondered to find she had been speaking. I mesmerised her a little, and she said how much good it had done her to come : all the weight and oppression had entirely left her. Seeing I placed my hand to my forehead, she asked if I felt anything, for she saw the symbolic flames : and I really had thought that my hand might be sensible of the glow. I read to her all that had passed, and while doing so, it was imbreathed to me that Isaiah had been the communicating agent. She was deeply touched with that part that had given me the choice of escape from my earthly tribulations.

I am to copy from my book of interpretations the opening piece referring to the picture of "The Shield" with which we commenced the above séance.

This drawing was finished on the 31st of December 1877, the anniversary upon which I completed the eighteenth year of my mediumship, and I have now been calculating the time that has been bestowed upon the work, for there have been intermediate (bespoken) drawings, so that it has been necessary to go with great accuracy through the various dates, as I strongly feel that this has been the most important work of which I have been permitted to be the mortal agent. It has closely occupied me for 32 weeks, and during the last fortnight the work was at the most intensely high pressure I have ever felt. It seemed as if I had scarcely time to draw breath. I had long had an impression that it was to be finished by some specific date (but as it had been begun on the 3rd of July 1876, many anniversaries of one kind or another had passed on unnoted), thus I sometimes realized that when commissions did *not* come to me that it was for the purpose of continuing this drawing, which finally was thus manifested to me, for in the middle of December I received orders for three small monograms, which were not allowed to be commenced until after the completion of this especial drawing: by which means it was so arranged that on the New Year's Day of 1878, I began a fresh picture without having a single unfinished one on hand, which has *never* been the case since my hand has been guided by my invisible friends —I mean with reference to beginning a *new year without* any incompleted drawing, for I used generally to prefer having two or three in hand, to work at in different stages according to the amount of daylight. So far it seems also as if that had been the concluding work of that character, for I have not since then commenced any of those symbolical representations, although it may yet prove that this has only been another interregnum in my artistic labours.

On that New Year's Day I went to an afternoon séance at Mrs. Guppy-Volckman's; but it was not for the exercise of her own mediumship, for she had long been very seriously invalided, partly the result of rheumatic fever, when her life had been almost despaired of, and nothing but the tenderest and most devoted nursing could have restored her to her friends. Although then to a certain extent convalescent, her system had nothing to spare of superfluous aura, so that her powers were completely in abeyance as far as regarded manifestations in circle, but she is always generously liberal-hearted, so she often engaged professional mediums; to satisfy the prejudices of those persons who prefer séances at other persons' houses rather than their own. There was rather a large circle, Mr. Williams as the medium, and the manifestations were of the usual class:—the direct voices, and the shadowy glimpses of two of the spirits, Peter and a female, but they could not appear with much distinctness. I must confess that I prefer a more select circle: I do not mean as to worldly position, for in that respect it was composed of rather the élite, but I mean as being more spiritually minded, for the larger proportion of those present only seemed to look upon it as a variation in their usual course of worldly dissipation, without any higher thought whatever, and I really should not have felt surprised to have heard any of those very mundane enquiries propounded that one hears suggested by outsiders whose minds do not rise above the level of the stock exchange and the race-course. A lady sat near me whose first experience it was of a spirit circle, and the flippant style of the chief part of the converse with the gone-beyond ones rather shocked her, but I assured her that most of those present were not to be termed Spiritualists or even enquirers, so that she must not let it deter her from seeking more deeply into this grandest of all subjects. Mrs. Volckman knew it was not the class of séance I affected, but she kindly invited me as being so close to the day we used formerly always to commemorate, and I did of course have the signals of my own special friends who were around me; and I also believe that even in such a séance as that, there are benefits accruing both to the spirits and the mortals; so that I would not have them utterly set aside, for I am certain that *all* things will eventually be worked in to fulfil God's purposes.

On the 7th of March I accompanied Mrs. T. to the meeting of the Psychological Society, established chiefly by the energy of Serjeant Cox, who was their very efficient President. He read a long letter published in (I think) New Zealand, telling of some very extraordinary manifestations, which, although not called Spiritualism, could not really be placed in any other category. After the meeting was over, I had a few genial words from him, and laughingly enquired how "psychic force" was to account for all that? I wish I could recollect the exact words of his answer, for I know it was to the effect that that theory was only as a *name* to satisfy the prejudices of the world in general, who might be willing to accept even of Truth, if it should come to them under a veil.

Mr. Enmore Jones is always striving to stir the somewhat stagnant and sluggish elements that constitute a large proportion of humanity, he volunteering his own efforts without calling upon others to contribute pecuniary aid, and he now took Grafton Hall for the evening of April 17th in commemoration of the thirtieth anniversary of Modern Spiritualism; the proper date being of course March 31st, but other exigencies had to be taken into consideration as to what night it could be held. He warmly invited all persons, whether believers or sceptics, to be present, and advertised the meeting largely beforehand, with the information that several good speakers had promised to deliver certain addresses on the subjects assigned them. The admission was to be quite free, the only difference would be that the Spiritualists were to occupy the body of the hall, while the others were to go up to the gallery. Unfortunately it proved a dreadfully wet evening, with a seriously heavy thunder-storm:—but black as it looked, I would not be deterred, and hurried through my dinner so as to get there before the worst should come on, and in that I succeeded —but—the doors of Grafton Hall were closed to me, as I was so much in anticipation of the appointed time : however, I took the opportunity of calling (at two or three doors off) upon Mrs. Welton, the clairvoyante, whom I had not seen for some years, and who was very glad of the friendly chat; and I had just reached that refuge when the stormy downpour came; but there was fortunately a little intermission when the proper time had arrived for me to adjourn to the Hall, to which she promised presently to follow. Mr. Jones greeted me most cordially; and he was still very busy with the decorating department, having brought the chief part of his own treasures in the shape of Spirit drawings, photographs, &c. &c., as well as a nice collection of flowers, which were ranged along the front of the platform. He told me that Mr. and Mrs. Jencken (formerly Kate Fox), with the two children, were to be there, and also the other sister (Margaret), Mrs. Kane, who were the two little girls through whom the original manifestations came, on the date now being commemorated; and they all duly came, as well as the promised speakers. But alas ! the Hall was desperately empty, and yet, if the outside public could have realized the treat that was in store for them, the place would have been thronged to suffocation ; and it did get to *look* better, for the gallery public gradually crept down to join the ranks of the believers, so as to convince themselves that what they were hearing was a reality, and not a delusion of the senses. For that cluster of powerful mediums were seated together at the right-hand side front corner of the platform, Mr. and Mrs. Jencken each with a child on their knee, those children likewise being strong mediums. Scarcely had Mr. Jones commenced his first exordium, when rap, rap, rap, came with assenting force on the platform beneath their feet. Then the sounds came from the other parts of the platform, every one on it being clearly in sight, and the feet on a most convenient level to the eyes of the beholding audience, so that even the most suspicious could watch every movement. The platform, too, is so arranged that it can be examined to the very back, and I was much amused by watching the movements of a lady whom I know to be an arrant sceptic, creeping round, and peering in every direction for some possible method of trickery, but alack! for her peace of mind, for nothing fraudulent could she discover, and what conclusion she finally came to I know not—for the sounds were so strongly detonating, as well as discriminative, that they evinced both power and intelligence. All the party on the platform of course took the responsive raps of the spirits as a most natural thing, and beyond an occasional smile of amusement made no demonstration. But it was a kind of jubilee for the invisibles, and when Mr. Jencken himself did his ten minutes' talk, they gave an extra amount of applause. The two pots near the centre (in front) of the platform, were fine specimens of the Calla Ethiopica,— known by the various names of the Lily of the Nile and White Arum; and on several occasions, these flowers were seen to bow forwards, as if in assenting compliment, immediately resuming their upright position; which was certainly a most wonderful manifestation, and I am half afraid I gave more attention to watching that phenomenon than hearkening to the discourse that called it forth. It was a pleasant evening, for each person understood the point upon which they had to speak, and I can but regret that there were not more listeners.

CHAPTER XX.

On the 13th of May Mrs. T. wrote to me from St. Leonards: "I saw you some little while since in your drawing-room, which had been *newly decorated*, and some one said, 'This is The Lord's House.' Then I saw that the house had a new look everywhere inside, and some one spoke as before, saying, 'It has been done to further The Lord's work.' Is it possible that some fresh opening may be coming to you?" When I was at the Albert Road soon after her return home, she asked if she had given me the *date* of her dream, when she had seen me in my renovated house, and she wished she had written it all out at the time, for that it had been so very vivid; and while she was speaking the whole beauty of it seemed to come before her again—there had been a border of roses and lovely flowers most exquisitely painted all round the ceiling, and every part looked delicately perfect. I said that her letter had been dated May 13th, but she had not mentioned when she had had the vision. She pondered very deeply for some little time, saying that it had occurred very shortly after they went down to St. Leonards,—then she said, "Oh! now I remember,—it was on the Saturday after Good Friday." "Then it was on my birthday, the 20th," I exclaimed. And so it had been, but she had scarcely realised dates at that time, for there had been so much to do and to think about, as her young son was on the eve of going away to New Zealand for the sake of his health, to be absent a twelve-month, and there were preparations to be made, as well as juvenile friends staying with the children, so that all her days had seemed to pass in a kind of maze.

In the evening of that same day, June 18th, about half-past nine, she turned towards me in the midst of our con-versation, as if about to speak, but hesitated; I then saw that

T

she was gradually passing under influence; fortunately I had some paper in my pocket, which I had been *told* to take, and which proved to be exactly the right quantity. She appeared to be earnestly noticing something, and said:— "A spirit kneeling, but poised in air; her hair seems *alive*, and she says, 'I am this night appointed to be a messenger twixt *her* and *thee*.'" [Who is it?] "She is called Mary, but that is not now her name; and in her hair is much strength, and it comes through nestling now against *you*:— it makes it alive; it floats and doesn't rest; it is alive, waving about, glistening with vitality; and it is shewn me that by folding it in a mantle, to wrap it up carefully, she can carry it away, and give it to the other one called Mary, and Mary will receive it, and its use will be to lubricate the passage through which the spirit ascends from her mortal body: and the more strength, or life, or power she can receive from this source, the fewer will be the parting pangs: —and *she* is called 'Comforter,' the one who gives the messenger the strength." [Do you mean *me*, dear?] "Yes." [That is a new name for me, then.] "Let the name rest with thee, for thou hast earned it, so I am allowed to say. So, dear Comforter, if you feel a nestling cheek, and even this living hair, be not alarmed, for the messenger must come quite close to your life to get needed power, and from this hour the separation will begin." [Shall I write this to her sister?] "Nay—but keep the record." [May I know the full name of the messenger?] "She is one who sinned, but she loved Her Lord." [Mary of Bethany?] "Thou hast said . . . Wouldst thou that He should raise the sick one to this life again?" [I would only *His* will, whatsoever that may be.] "Then the messenger will do her appointed work, and God's will be done on earth, even as in Heaven." She was silent for some little time, then made some movements, when again she spoke: "No, no,—that is not as it should be, let me shew you the way." She then gave clear and explicit directions how the invalid was to be mesmerised, so that I should write them to her husband, who used to do it for her every night, and she concluded thus,

"When the last contact takes place, on the soles of the feet, the operator should pray, mentally pray that The Lord may be pleased to release her from suffering, and if he can,—pray—'O Lord, release my companion from her suffering body, and let her spirit go free.'

"It is foreseen that he *can not* use this form, so you may give it to the strongest heart near her, and let it be repeated while the movement is made: *he can not* do it; so then she will be helped, but the one who says the prayer must feel it in the very heart, that The Lord may be pleased to remove her from her body. And ye who have felt to pray that she might be spared suffering, must now pray that The Lord may be pleased to remove her from her suffering body, and so may His will be done." I was here influenced to make a few passes, and she again turned towards me, saying, "The messenger has already gone. . . . She can get this help and power through you which could not so well come directly from those in spirit life, but given through and conjoined with your own power, including the tie of relationship, an actual substance is imparted, and she can be helped. Power as great could be *brought* to her independently of you, but it would not have affinity with her, therefore she could not be helped. So, dear heart, when next you despond, remember that your name is *Comforter*, and may The Lord be with you and bless you." Here she quietly awoke, and was surprised to hear all that had passed. We had much interesting talk about it, especially with reference to the fact that the hair of Mary of Bethany, with which in mortal life she had wiped the feet of The Lord Jesus, should now be permitted to be an agent in giving aid to the suffering one. While still in conversation, I felt the symbolic glow on my brow, as did also Mrs. T., while a few words were given through me with great force :—" I am the resurrection and the life. He who believeth on Me shall never see death :—the death, yea, of the mortal body, but not the after-death of suffering anguish.—He who *believeth* in Me, not the vain belief of mere intellectual affirmation, but he who sheweth forth that belief by treading to his utmost in My footsteps, and seeking to relieve his fellow-beings; *that* only is a living belief, and they who carry it out are Mine even for evermore. Amen."

In the course of our talk after the trance, Mrs. T. had asked me whether the monogram could be done of one who had very long ago passed away, and as the answer was in the affirmative, she said she would wish to have that on Mary of Bethany, and she *felt* that she was afterwards to have that of Lazarus. Not till the next day did I connect the opening words spoken through me with any thought of Lazarus; for my fullest feeling as to them is in the funeral service, when they have ever touched my heart with a deep thrill of hope; but I was reading the account to Miss Pery, who reminded me of the circumstance.

I wrote (on June 23rd) to Mrs. T., telling her that each evening, at the hour we had had the communication, I had felt the nestling cheek and floating hair of Mary of Bethany —each time receiving also the symbolic glow: but that yesterday morning, from about eleven till twelve, I had felt it strongly and continually, and it has since come to me at frequent intervals. Her answer came to-night (25th), in which she says, "What you tell me of your experiences is very curious and interesting. I too have felt the hair, and I have been reminded by it that I must say the prayer for dissolution. It seems so strangely sad and yet so grand to feel as it were made to help a sister spirit throw off her bonds. I seem to be learning a good deal of death and what we call life during these last few days. For one thing, life and death exactly correspond, I am told, to day and night, and if we *fully* understand the latter, there will be for us no mystery in the former. It is such teaching for me, and quite out of my own thought."

I saw the dear invalid on the evening of July 9th. She was then evidently near her end, and she passed away quite peacefully at six o'clock the next morning with only a sigh.

I had the pleasure of fulfilling the commission for the two pictures spoken of, and as rather fuller explanations were given than was usual with those miniature productions, I will here transcribe them. I was much struck with the fact that in Mary's monogram nothing of the character of resting surface was represented : it seems to float, in like fashion as did the spirit herself in Mrs. T.'s vision.

Tiny monogram of Mary of Bethany. . . . We have represented the ⌂ somewhat in the same manner that we usually sketch the spirit homes in these small drawings, as Mary is always identified by the name of her dwelling-place, but we have defined no ground, poising the monogram as it were in air, its only stay and shelter being heavenly wings. —Predominating characteristics, as typified by the colours employed in the work. Gamboge, faith : violet carmine, religion : cobalt blue, truth : crimson lake, love : chrome No. 2, gratitude : dragon's blood, sympathy : smalt, strength of friendship : carmine, tenderness : cadmium, courage : Indian yellow, probity.—In working the colours, the first lines of cadmium were brought down from the point of Glory, shewing that courage could only come to her from the loving words of The Lord—S. Luke, vii. 48, 50. " And He said unto her—Thy sins are forgiven : . . . thy faith hath saved thee ; go in peace."

L. Typifying in the Initial, the Crown gained by Lazarus. The letter was but small in the commencement of our work, expressing what had been formed during his first earth-life, but it was increased tenfold in the years granted to him *after* having been recalled to mortality by His Lord's loving words, " Lazarus, come forth," St. John xi. 43.

The silver cord having been *entirely severed*, Lazarus, during the four days in the " beyond," was enabled to be taught the grandeur and the responsibilities of mortal life, and rejoiced in the opportunity to redeem the past, bearing everywhere the Standard of The Lord ; which we have symbolized as almost the ground-work of the letter, Isaiah lxii. 10, 11 : " Go through, go through the gates . . . . lift up a standard for the people. Behold, the LORD hath proclaimed unto the end of the world, Say ye to the daughter of Zion, Behold, thy salvation cometh; behold, His reward is with Him, and His works before Him." It is unnecessary for me to enumerate the colours of which the typical letter was composed, but, with reference to smalt, signifying strength of friendship, allusion is made to its having been granted to him that The Lord should have spoken of him as "His friend." The new life bestowed upon him by that marvellous Friend had to be consecrated to Him and to His service with every fibre of that renovated existence, and he thenceforth became one of the most active but most unobtrusive of the followers of The Lord, a glance of Whose eye was sufficient to indicate to him the direction he was to pursue, and wheresoever there was sorrow or sickness he was to be found, strengthening and comforting many hearts with the details of the glories of the future life. Most especially was his work among children, joining with them as it were in their play, but instilling principles of uprightness in every joyous word that he spake to them. They knew not his name, but always alluded to him as the "Sunbeam." It was the Standard of Love earned by righteous dealing that he had come back *through the gates* to unfurl before the world, therefore he strove to plant the needful seeds into young hearts, so that they should take such strong root therein that no place would afterwards be found for the growth of untoward elements.

I think it was at the April soirée of the B.N.A.S. that I had the pleasure of making the acquaintance of Mrs. Gordon, whose eyes were just being opened to the realities of spiritual existence, which to a woman of her fine intellect soon became a joy indeed. Hitherto she had limited her horizon to this poor earth of ours, and although that had not sufficed to her *soul*, her *mind* had resisted the idea of anything beyond its own powers, especially as those powers were rather extensive, and her strong faculties had made her somewhat of a leader among the non-believing ranks of the present day. But her noble nature enabled her fully to receive the new truth when it had proved itself to her to be a truth, which conviction came to her both through the physical and the mental phenomena, for she spared no pains in seeking the evidences on all sides; and richly was she rewarded, for life presented to her quite a new aspect when she found it was but the preliminary step towards a future eternity becoming more and more full in the hereafter, when the powers that have had their birth upon this mundane plane shall gradually expand to their uttermost, and her grand soul realized that her fullest aspirations will have a scope far beyond any limit that she could have assigned to them. As it happened, on that first evening I sat behind her during the music, and may I be forgiven if I say that I fell in love with her hair, which is of the most exquisite chestnut tint I ever met with. My appreciation of true colouring is an integral portion of my being, and I indulged myself by watching the shifting lights and shades while there was no conversation going on to call my attention. But it was only later on, in the cloak-room, that I accosted her, for we happened to be up there together making our preparations for departure, and I then learned that she was but a novice and a sincere enquirer into Spiritualism, so of course I said I should be happy to give her any information on the subject that I could if she would like to call here; and it then turned out that she was living in the next street, and I had a visit from her on an early Wednesday. It became curious to note how often I afterwards met her during my little needful outings, and it was invariably in consequence of the spiritual directions I received, as to where I should cross the street, or perhaps to return home instead of proceeding on another small errand, and such-like minor details, which were each time proofs to her that she was the specific recipient of watchful care, as it also was to me that her assured conviction was a matter of importance. She gradually obtained a complete certainty, and has since devoted her great talents to the cause of Spiritualism instead of materialism. She was wonderfully struck with the spirit photographs, and selected a good variety of them from my remaining stock, but she was much grieved that no chance then existed for her to have a sitting herself, for she thought that her own personal evidence on the subject would carry yet stronger conviction to her immediate circle of friends than any others that she could shew to them. In this emergency she gladly availed herself of the suggestion made to her by an amateur photographer, who had been a friend of long standing in India, that he should bring his apparatus to her house, and there make an experimental trial. She engaged the services of Mr. Williams, while Mrs. T. and I were also most anxious to aid with all our powers, although I must confess that my hopes were by no means so strong as my wishes. On the 2nd of August, when we two went in there, we found Colonel Gordon busily engaged in hanging up a curtain for the background that was also to do duty as a kind of dark cabinet for Mr. Williams, and the upper room had been densely darkened for the operator, who was going to use the dry plates which are so sensitively rapid in their action. That gave another shake to my faint hopes, for I have great faith in the help given by mesmerising the plates before collodionising them, and was disappointed that I could not give that assistance. In due time we were all assembled; Mr. Williams took his place in the improvised cabinet, where he speedily became entranced, and several plates were patiently tried, but not the vestige of anything but ourselves appeared upon them. We had afterwards a séance in the back drawing-room, which she had for some time kept darkened for the purpose of holding circles there, having at different times engaged most of the professional physical mediums, to give her friends the opportunity of witnessing some of the phenomena that she had told them about. On this occasion very little of importance took place, for Mr. Williams was somewhat fatigued and exhausted when he arrived, having already held a séance that day, so that there was sure to be lack of power: still I do not believe that even if he had been fresh there would have come anything with regard to the photography, the operator, apparatus, and negatives being all new to the subject of spiritual apparitions.

I had been at Mrs. T.'s on the Sunday before the photographic attempt, and in a communication then given we three (including Mrs. Gordon, who was not with us) were exhorted to unite in a prayerful effort for a specific purpose, and the names then bestowed for that work were, Faith, G. H.—Hope, A. G.—Love, M. E. T. I only mention it because it became Mrs. T.'s custom to speak to me of Mrs. Gordon by the name of Hope. She wished her to be present at a séance with Mrs. Gray, so we arranged that it had better take place here: accordingly on August 12th, at about half-past two, we were seated near the window where my easel stands, as it was decided that we should not take our places at the table; so I only had the small one in front of me, with paper and pencil, hoping to take down what should be given, but the little Indian "Daisy," who speaks through Mrs. Gray, is such a rapid little talker, that I found it impossible to follow her after the first few sentences; I must therefore trust to my memory, and record it as I may recollect. Addressing Mrs. Gordon, she said:

"You will be very happy in India, much happier than you have ever been, and I think you will remain there longer than you expect; more than the three years. You will have much to do, and it will be what you like. You love much *brain* work: you *must* work your brain, and you will teach about Spiritualism, but you are not content to take a thing as people shew it to you, you must turn it about, and work it in every way, and when you have got it very sure, you hold it quite fast, and then you do the same with the next, and so on till all is complete." She then said a good deal about three little girls they have adopted, whose parents are both dead, all of which I omit. . . . "But you will be very happy. You love to conquer difficulties, and to *do* things. You must *lead*, you are a born leader. You can take up the reins, not for one thing only, but for a great many: then you take up the rein for *this* thing, and for *that* thing, holding them all, and governing right royally. You are a medium yourself, and you will have writing, different kinds of writing, done through your own hand from different spirits, and it will amuse you to see the different hand-writings. And you will see the spirits and flowers, and *pretty* things, for you like what is pretty, and you like *variety*, not to be all one thing. You will write, not novels, nor tales, but something of what you *know* and want other people to know. You will make a book." Mrs. T. then said that "they" had been shewing her a book, and to me came the impression that she would make concentrated and condensed articles respecting the various phases of Spiritualism that she will have studied and witnessed shewing the different bearings of them, and that those articles will be interspersed as it were with visions. Mrs. T. then passed under influence, and said what I suppose is given as the idea of the title:—"This book will be 'on the relation between mind and matter, with illustrations from my own experience.'— If you have an hour to-day, I will help you with the preface." [Who are you, dear friend?] said I, feeling sure that I recognised the speaker: but the only reply was, " I see I must go away. I thought I could introduce colour, but it does not do in this book; it must be mind and matter, and she will be helped by another." [Is it Sir Peter Lely?] The laughing response was, "I thought I should not be found out: but I must not help with the book." Turning towards Mrs. Gray, and shaking hands: "Well, Daisy, I have great pleasure in meeting you here." After a few more words he began to plead with Daisy for a pinch of snuff, about which he was rather urgent, and a little more talk went on between them about her own personal matters, and Daisy was much struck with his large and handsome snuff-box, of which he bewailed the emptiness. . . .

Daisy again addressed Mrs. Gordon, describing a spirit whom she saw near her, whose side face resembled her own very strongly, but who was not so like when looking fully: she had dark hair and was young (she was her mother), but her thread of life appeared to have been snapped suddenly (she had died at Mrs. Gordon's birth). She would be enabled to write through her daughter's hand, and might probably give her many details of her own earth-life with which her daughter was unacquainted. She then described a fine-looking man (her uncle), who seemed to be endowed with the same energy and power that she is herself, and the same talent for leadership. Daisy then turned to Mrs. T., and said:

"You, too, do a great many things, and a great deal of work, but you do not do it as a leader. You work and work, and set a wheel going here, and another there, to make things go smoothly, and other people think *they* do it all: they do not see the machinery that is always busy, a little oil here, and a little turn there; and the one who is always trying to smooth matters, and to help away all burthens, is not seen, nor known, nor noticed:—it just seems to people as if matters smoothed *themselves*, and they do not realise the continual thinking and fitting that thus make the things come smooth. You are like a person who arranges a number of figures, and then, while he is hidden, he pulls the strings, so as to make them move about, and do what is best for them to do. You work the Oracle. . . . But you must take care of yourself. You must not go away; the spirits are trying not to let you leave England; it is not good for you to go about, and they are trying what they can to keep you here. Ah! there is *another* little Daisy: she does you good, she pours something down your back to strengthen you; she is *your* little papoose (a baby she had lost *before* the time for its birth), and she is with you a great deal. There are many spirits round you, and oh! there are so *many here*, such bright ones." Then turning to me, she said: "I see that young man whom I have so often seen before, the one who was drowned." [My Charlie.] "Yes, Charlie, and he says he is with you a great deal: he can make the bird whistle—sing, I mean." Her saying that was curious, for Charlie has always claimed my cardinal as his bird, while the Dove belonged to my dear little sisters, and now has her dwelling in their home. Daisy now described Zilla, Papa, Mamma, Katie, Mrs. Osborne (whom she had seen before), and by her side she described a tall handsome lady, with a remarkably beautiful complexion and auburn hair, whom I recognised as her eldest daughter. Likewise my small sisters who were strewing quantities of flowers about me. It seemed to her as if my troubles could not continue much longer, but that at any rate my needs will be supplied, by varied little helps. She said there were many bands of spirits succeeding one another (I think she must have meant the ten septs), and that all did something for me. That there were always fresh and fresh people coming to me, each to gather what they could receive, and that in some way they would all contribute towards my requirements. More was said, but somehow I can less retain what was said to myself, than to the other two; I suppose because it is unnecessary to record it.

At about five o'clock we went into the back room for a little refreshment, after which we resumed our places, and I got out the coat of many colours, and the white one, to shew to Mrs. Gordon and Mrs. Gray. Then somehow, our thoughts reverted to the subject of the Sunday communication, and a great deal was spoken about it through Mrs. T. After which Mrs. Gray stood up, and with much dignity an address was made to each of us: the Spirit saying, "I am he who seldom gives his name." But it came so unexpectedly that I was not prepared to take it down, so that nothing remains to me, but that a name was given to Mrs. Gordon, referring to her work in India, that of the "Pioneer."

Mrs. Gray remained later with me than the others, and when I returned to her (where she was sitting by the window) after seeing Mrs. T. and Mrs. Gordon off, she told me she had seen a lady come out on one of the balconies, who had given her a certain impression, and she said she sometimes saw beautiful lights from houses when she knew nothing about the people, so I asked her what she thought of the shut-up house. "Oh! that is a very sweet influence: it belongs to one who has a very kind nature. She would like to help every one and to make them all happy; but somehow her nature has been cramped in her youth,—cramped and warped. But she would wish to make everybody happy, only she would like to do it in her own way, for she cannot bear even the slightest interference: she must to a certain extent dominate wherever she is, and is apt to be (shall I say?) displeased if at all contradicted; but notwithstanding that, hers is a charming nature, and the house is filled with very bright spirits when she is at home. I had not mentioned whether it was a lady or a gentleman who inhabited the house, nor that I knew the inmate, but the delineation of her character was very accurate.

Mrs. T. came to me on the 23rd of October, and as she had been some time absent from home, we had much to talk over, among which we touched upon the prophecy (published in the last *Medium*) given through Mr. Colville, of the changes which may be expected in 1881, which is similar in many respects to much that has been inbreathed to me, and also in later times given through various mediums. I said something about our quiet talk between ourselves, going into space, perhaps to rest in other minds, all unknown to us. She then seemed to listen, and I asked if she heard anything, while at the same time a sentence came into my thought, to which I did not give utterance, but *she* spoke it, saying, "Although they have neither speech nor language, yet their voices are gone forth even unto the ends of the earth." In looking back upon this, it seems to me that while *she heard* the voice, it must equally have gone to my inner senses, although not to my consciousness, and that it may be *thus* that I receive the inbreathing, only with spirit rapidity, for I appear to gather such a fulness of ideas all at once.

On the last day of October Mrs. Gordon called here to say farewell, but as I happened to be out she left word for me to go round to her, as she would be too fully engaged to come in again, which I accordingly did, so as to have a final peep at her before her departure for India; and it seems that Daisy was right in her prevision, for the three years are nearly expired, and I hear no word of her return, although her name has been prominent as an energetic worker for Spiritualism in that distant land of *ours*.

One evening in November, Miss Pery was with me, and was anxious to have some messages about her mother's health, as she had had while with me on the previous evening, but she only received a few raps, with nothing decisive, but presently she said, "Oh! what a very uncomfortable influence I feel! it makes me quite shiver with intensity of cold: is it F——?" No, it was not. "Or old M——?" Still no, so she placed her hand on the little table for the alphabet. A letter was given, then another, but they made no sense, so she asked for a recommencement, but the same two were given, and we then realized that they were the initials of a double name, and we received communications on the subject of the spirit, who had not very long passed from earth; but when the messages were over, Miss Pery could not recover from the intense feeling of cold, which seemed to pierce her through and through, although she sat down on the footstool, turning her back to the fire, for the spine appeared especially to suffer. She said she had had the feeling of being surrounded by icebergs, even seeing their cold, jagged, shining points rising up on all sides. It was one who had been utterly and selfishly cold, except to his own personal belongings, and we were told that this is his retribution, also that the ice cannot be melted from the *out*-side: his heart must warm towards others, and thus only can it be dissolved, but *our* prayers and kind thoughts may reach him and in some degree kindle an answering glow; and we are both doing our best in that direction. It was a singular lesson, and one that all may do well to lay to heart. At intervals we have occasionally had a few words, and they were each time of an ameliorated nature.

CHAPTER XXI.

ON the 18th of November Miss Ingram came to see me, and later on Miss Pery likewise came in, which was their first introduction to one another, and we had a small séance of which I have nothing special to record. Miss Ingram went away about eight o'clock, and after she had left I told Miss Pery that her stone was the diamond. The idea of an appropriate precious stone was new to her, and she asked what mine was? "The Opal," and she then wondered what *hers* might be. The answer, however, did not come to me, but to herself, that it was the sapphire (meaning truth), of which the corroboration came to me, and it led to my telling her about Mrs. Ramsay, and that while they were in India, they were robbed of (I think) plate and jewellery to some considerable extent, so they sent for one of the Indian seers (or discoverers of stolen goods, though I am not sure of the name by which they are called), and he noticed on her finger a large sapphire which she usually wears, and said to her :—"You will recover your *rings*, because you still retain that one, which is your own stone." His prediction was fulfilled, for the rings were recovered, all tied together, but none of the other articles. Having discussed that matter, we talked of other things, and presently she complained of feeling a disagreeable influence, and wondered who it might be, but we received a negative to all our suggestions; when suddenly that Indian flashed into my mind, and I was told that it was he, and that he had come to seek for Light. Miss Pery wondered how we could help one who was as it were so far out of our range, so I said we must not only pray *for* him, but strive to teach *him* to pray ; so I placed my hand on the table, and asked him to unite with me in what I was going to say. I then commenced The Lord's Prayer, and at each petition he tipped the table three times in assent. When I came to, "Give us this day our daily bread," there was a hesitation, until I explained that spiritual food was also typified, when he assented as before; but when I said, "Forgive us our trespasses as *we* forgive them that trespass against us," I received a positive refusal; all my talking and persuasions were unavailing, he would *not* be induced to forgive the injuries he might have received; that Christian grace is at present beyond his grasp, and we then learned that he was gone. Presently Miss Pery was impelled, as she often is, to give me caressing touches on the face and head, asking *who* it was, and after some mental questioning on my part, I found that it was Jim Ramsay, and that the mission was then given to him to work among those Indian spirits (a multitude of them being in the same radius as the one who had communicated), and that he is to strive to bring them to Christianity, being to some extent prepared for that labour during his earth-life by his sojourn in India (where both his birth and his death took place), and his knowledge of their language, which is a need in dealing with spirits of a low grade; but that he will also be strengthened and helped in the work by prayers from this side, so I wrote to Mrs. Ramsay about it, and to ask her to give her aid, which will of course be all the stronger from so much of her own life having been passed in India.

Mrs. T. came to me on the 2nd of December, when I read to her the above account; and while we were discussing the subject, she passed under influence, so gently that I was scarcely aware of it at first, when she said: "His was the kind of brain suitable for the reception of impressions, more so than some that might be looked upon as more intellectual, and he could thus be made available for the higher directing influences, to serve as a medium for them among those Indian minds which had been as yet unprepared for a true knowledge of The Lord Jesus Christ. Through this medium, therefore, those directing influences could come within reach of those who have never heard of the Kingdom of The Lord Jesus, which is now being drawn from all the ends of the earth and from the Heavens in which He is to reign. So with this explanation it becomes easy to see why this man has been chosen for this work, and by it one is helped to understand how and why sometimes men seemingly unsuitable are chosen for special missions. It is necessary that a man should be suited to, or have some special relation with, that work to which he is to be called, but it is still more important that he have a brain which can be acted upon and through by wiser beings than himself,—indeed, those wiser ones left to do the work by themselves would be like men without hands; they *could not* do it. No man, no spirit, is so high as to say to any other, 'I have no need of thee,' so we learn the great lesson of reciprocity, and to include charity as the greatest of all gifts.

"There was a purpose in this man's life, nourished by his tender mother: there was a greater purpose in his death. For by his life he was fitted for this great work, and she may continue to greatly aid him. Let her be sure that his death was a needed step in the great plan of his whole life . . I am permitted to say that through and by what he has already done, many even now rise up to say—'Let the sunlight smile upon her:—let the moonbeams gently touch her:—gentle mother, she is blessed.'" She said these latter words very tenderly, and then awoke.

I had a curious book lent to me, entitled "Modern Hieroglyphics," consisting of coloured illustrations, as interpretations of the Apocalypse, combined in a manner with the revelations discovered by Professor Piazzi Smyth in the measurements of the Great Pyramid. Both she and a friend who was then staying there, were much interested, and the prophecies led to considerable discussion. Towards the end, when it came to the 144,000 who were sealed, Mrs. T. heard the numbers frequently repeated to her, and she said to me, Were the 144,000 to be all? I said, No, they were to be the *first-fruits*, but all would eventually belong to Christ's Kingdom, for that is to be *universal*.

Then she seemed to be seeing, and gently murmured

that many who *made sure* were *not* among the sealed ones, and many also there were *among* them who had not deemed themselves worthy, and she saw their looks of glad surprise coupled with humility. Gradually she passed quite under influence, and said: "Some there are in this present day who must take heed. Let them take great care in this respect, that they do not repeat history in ignoring the messenger who precedes the Coming New Dispensation:—or else their attitude to this New Dispensation will be precisely that of the Jews to the Christian Dispensation now drawing to its close." [May I ask who it is that gives this message?] "One who sat and listened." By which I well understood that Mary of Bethany was implied, but something disturbed her, and she awoke.

She came to me on the evening of December 30th, in the thought of the anniversary of my mediumship, which would take place the next day, but that being *Tuesday*, she would be engaged at home. After a time she asked for the little table, having an impression to place her hands upon it, and we agreed that it was quite in accordance with the idea of her visit, as it had been bought for the express purpose of my development, so I put it in front of us, with a supply of paper and pencils. . . . Mrs. T. gradually passed under influence, and said, "Let the living voice testify of Me. Thy *works* are sufficient for the time, but now, in the fulness of time, let thy voice be heard. Many will hear and believe that thou art taught of The Lord.—It is His work, and good in His sight, so fear not, Comforter." . . . (I omit here a portion of what passed.) For a little time she was silent, but then resumed, "When the power returns, give it voice, and it shall tell thee what is true, and direct thee in thy shaded path, and thou shalt avoid every stumbling-block, for thy feet will be guided." Here was again a long pause, and the expression of her countenance lost its solemnity and became smiling, as if in response to friends: then she said, "Who is William? He gives thee greeting." I thanked him cordially. "Many of us greet thee, and would fain have speech, but the power is lacking."

I greeted them all in return, and it reminded me of another 31st of December that she was with me, when almost in her normal state, she saw so many of my friends, and said it seemed like a family gathering, and that they were all strewing flowers around me, and now, when she awoke, she said she smelled the perfume of flowers. Presently she again passed into trance, and said: "The Lord shall quicken whom He will, and none shall say this is the work of man: behold, all things that are alive shall be made new. Let the dead bury their dead and pass away. Ye who are called to newness of life must in no wise pause to look back. The Lord's work claims thee, and by it ye shall live and not die, and those who are dear to thee, for thy sake they also shall live, and all will be gathered into the Kingdom of The Lord, Who now speaks by the mouth of His messenger." [May I ask the name of the messenger?] "Even he who announced the birth of Our Lord and Saviour Jesus Christ." [Dear Gabriel?] "Even so. Many signs will follow those who believe, and, as of old, it will be for the simple to see and to comprehend: the worldly-wise are shrouded in their own wisdom, and cannot see the Light now dawning in the world. None may speak of these things except by and through The Lord (here she clasped her hands together): The Lord gives the power, He may also take it away. Let The Lord's name be blessed. (Rising, and spreading her hands outwards), Now to The Father, The Son, and The Holy Spirit, be praises evermore, world without end, Amen." She here awoke for a time, and we were again in quiet conversation, when a new power came upon her, causing her to speak more rapidly than she is wont, and in a rather plaintive and imploring voice:

"Dear Hope is talking, and she says—'How is it? and why all this turmoil? Do write and tell me how things are, and tell me how I stand, explaining all these dark things to me. Comfort me, and let me know all there is to be known, and whether all is fraud, so that I may learn to know my own mind. I reach out—I reach out to you in spirit, and you will help me, and not turn my hands empty away. What is true? and what is right? Who is truthful? I seem to be on the sea without rudder or chart, and I know not where I am drifting. I thought I had an anchor, but my rest is gone; so help me, comfort me; shew me what is true and what is stable, and do not leave me, for I shall sink without help." Here she awoke, and she saw Mrs. Gordon standing as it were between us, so I read to her what had passed, and we thought that possibly dear Hope might have come to us in her sleep. The circumstance referred to was something that had been published in the Spiritualist journals some time previously which we had thought at the time might be a worry to her, but which had now passed out of our own minds. Mrs. T. had been wishing to write to her, but had not her Indian address, which, however, I could give; so we agreed that I should copy the communication, and also write her a letter, which Mrs. T. would forward with hers. We had another communication referring to the omitted portion, which I likewise withhold; so I will now give an extract from Mrs. Gordon's letter, dated *February* 19*th*, 1879. " It seems rather a strange coincidence that I only heard of the case in question at the date or thereabout you mention as having been sitting with Mrs. T. It must have been about the 29th of December that I saw the account in the *Banner of Light*. We only arrived in Calcutta on the 22nd, and my husband after Christmas went and called on Peary-Chand Mittra, and brought home some papers he lent him. I was *really* distressed, but even more astonished at what I read, but it did not *in the least* shake my faith : I *knew* there was no fraud in my house, and no exposure can affect me in that way. My distress was for the cause, and a feeling that it weakened one's arguments when a sceptic could bring the very men, who had given the séances by which one admitted one's conviction, forward as accused of imposture. I felt as though I should be unable to fight so well against scoffers and sceptics if they knew this." It seems to me clear that in the very first moment of her distress (which it must have been at the time of her appeal to us), she felt it even more keenly than she afterwards remembered, for I know by my own feelings in such matters, how one exaggerates the fear of the mischief to the cause that they may occasion, and how fully one learns to realise that that which is God's *own* work, cannot permanently be injured, and that it is indeed safe in His Hands.

Mr. Joseph returned from Melbourne towards the close of the year, wonderfully renovated in health, although still somewhat of an invalid. He had now most entirely accepted the Divinity of Christ, and was essentially a Christian, but I never urged him to any open acknowledgment, for I think that in such cases a man must act according to his own judgment; besides which there are such diversities of sects in the Christian Church that he would need to weigh well all the different considerations ere he should decide to which he would unite himself:—to say nothing of the pain he might give to his family, especially to his tender, loving mother. Not that such plea was ever put forth by him, for the question was never in the slightest degree mooted between us. He used to go on the Sunday to different places of Christian worship, and doubtless gathered benefit from each and all. But his inner questionings were all brought to me, and I could always answer so as to give him conviction, help being given to me to make my words simply clear. His visits here were generally on the Saturday, and we often passed over a great variety of ground in our talks. He was a fairly good French scholar as far as understanding the language went, but he was not very secure as to his pronunciation, and he once asked me if I knew any Frenchman who would be willing to make a mutually advantageous arrangement, by taking an English lesson in reading from him in exchange for a French one. I certainly did not, nor did I quite think such a plan would be practicable, but I offered to do duty as a Frenchman by giving him the reading lessons myself, *without* the exchanged benefit, and I agreed that he should come every Saturday morning at eleven for about a couple of hours, also suggesting that the best book for his purpose would be the New Testament. He had made himself thoroughly conversant with it in its English form during his long absence in Australia, so that he would have no difficulties as to translation, although I did have a good deal as to the pronunciation of some of the sounds, and we would have a word repeated over and over again until he got it with tolerable accuracy; but it reminded me of the test as to tribe which was devised by Jephthah; see Judges xii. 5, 6. "And it was so, that when those Ephraimites which were escaped said, Let me go over; that the men of Gilead said unto him, Art thou an Ephraimite? If he said, Nay; then said they unto him, Say now Shibboleth: and he said Sibboleth: for he could not frame to pronounce it right. Then they took him, and they slew him at the passages of Jordan." For it really seemed as if he could *not* "frame to pronounce" some of the combinations correctly, and the effort in straining every muscle of his face was to me very remarkable, for there seemed to be a kind of physical disability. They *were* French lessons, but yet more decidedly they were theological ones; for we began with the Gospel according to St. John, and the elucidation of those divine words, which *we* seem to have drawn in with our mother's milk, had to be shaped into words that should make clear explanations to one to whom all was novelty, and the one chapter to which we limited our reading would give rise to endless thoughts. First, I would read a verse or two, and he would then read the same until he had mastered its obstacles, when we might perhaps branch off into its theology, so that the two or three hours we might thus spend would be in every way valuable to him. Our talk was interspersed with the narration of some vision that he might have had in the interim, of which he would either receive the interpretation himself, or perhaps I might give it. He used to term me his mother No. 2, because I had originally developed his mediumship. He was still very much out of health, and resolved upon going down to Hastings for a time for the benefit of the sea-breezes in the hope of thus gaining strength, and on his last visit here, we exactly finished St. John's Gospel, when I said we had better wait until his return before deciding upon which Book we would go to next, but I little thought that such return would never be in mortal form, for while at Hastings he was attacked with something of the nature of English cholera, and one of his brothers was summoned down just in time to be with him during the last few hours. That same brother afterwards called upon me to communicate his death and the manner of it: he said he seemed to fall off into a peaceful sleep, with scarcely even a sigh.

He had fully realised since the first renewal of his visits here that a great mission was before him; in fact the visions of his childhood, to which I have already alluded, were premonitory in the same direction, and his predominant feeling was that it would be among his own nation, to lead them first to Spiritualism and through that to Christianity, in the same course that he had pursued, and he expected that health and strength would be given to him when he was ripe for the work, so that he should therein be an active labourer, although he waited with the utmost patience until the right moment should arrive, when his field of action would be made plain to him. Since his departure I have learned that his mission has indeed a far larger scope than even he had anticipated, for it is to the countless generations of his nation who have passed *out* of mortality that he is to teach the high truths that have been revealed to him here, so that it is a parallel case to that of Jim Ramsay. To touch the Jewish prejudices, still strong as ever in the beyond, it was needful that there should be the powerful national affinities, and he has been in every way prepared for the work he has to do, even those French lessons being as a type that every muscle and fibre of his being was to be rendered more supple so as to enable him to be in harmony with each tribal division. To me it had been vouchsafed to be the means through whom the first gleam of the true light should be shed upon him; thus the Christian element was contained within the first small stream that was poured in upon him, and rested gently within his soul ready to amalgamate with all that should be in harmony therewith until the mighty Truth flooded his entire being, and then he was prepared to be summoned to his real sphere of action.

I wrote to tell Miss Ingram of his, to us, unexpected death on the 12th of July (the 2nd had been his 47th birthday), and I was so much struck with what she said on the subject, that I must transcribe it. "I am much startled to learn that Mr. Joseph is called to the other side. He has been made ready here for a life of important action on the other side, and had he been called thither sooner, however loyal and ardent he might have been, he could not have gained the needed instruction and experience so rapidly and effectively there as he has done here. He goes to swell the hosts of The Most High—which all who pass from this side certainly do not, for they are not ready. But there can be little doubt that Mr. Joseph has been made ready, and what is *equally important*, he has made himself ready. They who are to compose the hosts of The Lord are more numerous in the spheres than on the earth—the conflict will be a terrible one—the issues stupendous—and this little Earth the battle-ground. Men,—mortals, will have to decide. They will find no hollow talk about God or the Soul will avail them. But a direct recognition that God is a living God, very near to all of us, that HE IS LORD, that He rules in the affairs of men, and that His government has reference always to the right-doing and the good actions of men. Hideous greed is not easily abandoned. Most Englishmen have been acting as Lot did. They have been eagerly choosing the good things even when these led them to associate with Sodomites. Though some of them even like Lot, who 'vexed his righteous heart every day,' have grieved much at the evil they have witnessed; yet they have kept the good things, and not withdrawn from the evil associations. Think of the frailty and contradiction of life in a good man, '*vexing his righteous heart daily.*' Yet the seductiveness of riches—of good things—

must be great : they must drug the sensibilities. There is not the faintest intimation that Lot ever contemplated changing his place of residence so as to escape from those evils that vexed his righteous heart: Lot was a materialist, and had not a vivid mind to grasp the truth of things in actual life."

I have alluded to my difficulties, but they have taught me many lessons as to what those of my own class may have to suffer in mournful silence when external supplies fail them. I had a variety of little trinkets that I loved for remembrances attached to them, but even some of those had to go. One of the earliest, for it had only been my own purchase since we came to *this* house, was a small gold chain for the throat on which to suspend a locket, and for it I had paid 18s. I do not think I had worn it a dozen times, so that it was as fresh as when new: and for that I could only obtain three shillings! I tried in two different shops, painful as was the feeling in so doing, but the result was the same, and as even that tiny amount was of importance to me, the sacrifice had to be! Many many such trials were mine! Some things there were that I *could not* part with, so I resolved to try the other expedient of which I had heard, and to pledge them. I knew their value was considerable, but all the jeweller would give me upon them was £3, on which a monthly interest was to be paid that did not sound so very much, but that in the year mounted up to twelve shillings. It was not nearly what I needed for my then purpose, but, thank God! the remainder came to me from another source. I had hoped to be able soon to redeem them—but I was not. When the month's interest was due, as I should be in the neighbourhood (for it was at some distance from here), I suggested to my counsellors that I should call and pay it, which they negatived, and still did so on each successive occasion until nearly the expiration of the year, when I went to pay the amount due, and then how thankful I was that he had not given me more upon them, as the drain would have been so much the heavier : but then I learned that even in that particular, my unseen teachers were wise beyond my knowledge, for the law permits that at *each* payment they give a fresh pawn-ticket, price one penny:—if therefore I had paid monthly, as had been my original thought, the cost would have been an additional shilling in the year! When the next twelve months had almost rolled round, I was in a real agony of mind, for I had not the money to spare, and even should the shillings come in, I thought—should I dare to part with them? had I not better let my treasures go!—for thus in five years I should have to pay *all* I had received, and might still be unable to redeem them! The thought was bitter indeed!—But then came a commission for a tiny monogram, and the curious sum proffered for it was twelve shillings! But I was immediately given to understand that it was so fixed for me to realise that it was expressly intended to meet that especial difficulty, and that therefore I was to have no qualms about thus appropriating it. The commission came through the interposition of a friend who generally comes up to London once a year, and always calls upon me during the time of her visit. Although these sort of troubles are generally deeply hidden within one's own secrecy, I could not help telling her how great had been the relief she had been the means of bringing to me. The next year she was again in London at about the same season, and called upon me with her friend of the monogram, who bought a pair of little socks, and other things that would again help me through the trouble. Then she took me aside, and whisperingly asked me if it would be any comfort if she should lend me £2, to redeem a part.—Oh! would it not? for my fear always was—suppose when the moment came it should be impossible to meet the emergency! In a day or two she brought me the money —telling me that I could make the small payments that I should have done as interest, which were to be in gradual liquidation of the debt!!! Her means are narrow, but may I point out to such as are wealthy that that is a class of help they might sometimes give? *She* did not need the security of my jewels, and they were to be in my own keeping. She is indeed a true and sterling woman, and will find her path in the hereafter strewed with countless blessings. Of course I immediately redeemed a portion of my belongings, most thankful once more to have them in my possession, and towards the close of the year I was able to pay the other sovereign so as to reclaim the remainder.

In the October of the previous year, Mrs. T. had told me of her anxiety about the health of her youngest child, the one who spiritually may be considered as partly mine, according to various messages both before and after her birth, and through me an intimation was then given that it referred to her future development into trance mediumship, and there were also directions as to treatment. She then heard the words—" Think of Anna the prophetess; have her much in mind." Now Anna had greeted Our Infant Lord in the temple ; and may have to help this child medium. . . . She presently passed under influence, and said :—" Out of the mouths of babes and sucklings thou hast perfected praise (here she pressed her finger on my brow with much force), and to *thee* I say that the eye of faith may penetrate beyond the veil, that veil which is impenetrable to mortal sight. I likewise enjoin upon thee to let thy thoughts dwell much and often upon this child, for *thou* art her prototype, and she will know that I Am, and I shall reign throughout all the kingdoms of the earth. Fear not—all will be well." She then awoke, and we had a little more conversation on the subject before she left. I met her the next evening at Langham Hall (for the Recitations of Miss Ella Dietz and her brother), and she then told me that the child had that day had the very worst attack she had ever had ; but that she had herself felt quite calm through it all. That was the very last instance, for there has since been *no* repetition.

Mr. Green came to see me on the 29th of October 1879. We began with some little talk, and then I shewed him one of the drawings, but while he was yet examining its beauties and admiring it, I was impressed to mesmerise him, for he had been somewhat detained in coming, which had flurried him. It was the *heart* that was mesmerised, and he almost immediately said how much his *head* was relieved. Then he asked; "Who is that tall lady standing behind you? she is tall and slender, and the name 'Anna' comes to me." I could not at first think of any Anna till he said: "She seems to have been a very long time in the spirit world, and her hands appear to be enveloped in a kind of blue atmosphere." I then at once understood that it was Anna the prophetess. I was telling Mrs. T. about this when she came to see me the next evening, and she related to me that when she had taken the child on her knee on the previous afternoon, she had exclaimed at seeing her surrounded with a blue light, and one of those present had thought that perhaps her eyes were dazzled by having just come in from the sunshine,—but it was a soft beautiful blue atmosphere, such as that described by Mr. Green, and it must have been a signal to her of the presence of Anna, which she will understand if she should see it again.

It was our first meeting since her return from America, so that naturally our conversation had ranged over many subjects, and something was said about the many changes in the course of life, especially in the long years ago, and she said (although she afterwards wondered how she had ventured to put such a question), "Which part of your life do you think has been the happiest?" To which I replied, "Oh! *this*, beyond all comparison, notwithstanding all the pressure of my pecuniary difficulties. The absolute certainty of realising God's continual Presence is beyond all other happiness, besides that of being always surrounded by those whom I have loved in the past, so that I feel a joy and a peace far beyond all the pleasures of my former life."— Then in a dreamy way she said, "I see a bird,"—and I found she was passing under influence, so I got paper and pencil, and she repeated the words, "I see a bird, coming up quite close. It has got a twig in its mouth. It isn't very green, and it means peace." [A twig of olive, is it?] "It is holding it up for you to see. It has a berry on it: I see the berry, which is a much deeper green than the leaf. It shews the fruit, but it means peace. It says—Peace I bring with Me—My peace I give unto you." [May I ask the meaning of having a fruit in the emblem of peace?] "It symbolises the DAILY BREAD which The Lord promised to those who loved Him if they asked for such sustenance." [Has the form of the symbol any reference to the olive being a tree of my own land?] "In order to reach you, it has been needful for the Dove to watch the waters lest at any time they might overwhelm you; and *now*,—at the moment when these *begin* to subside, lo! this bird of promise is able to gather the branch of promise, and it is brought to you at the earliest moment. It is an indication that from a *very near* point of time the waters have commenced to subside, and you will be able to feel your feet on The Lord's earth. This tender spirit whose outward symbol has brought you comfort." [May I ask what Spirit?] "The Holy Spirit—The Comforter, Whose peace passeth understanding. It is expected that you will see this branch; it will remain with you, and when you faint,* it will be right to ask that Our Lord in mercy grant you the power to see this token. It will even go before you as the light passed before them of old.—It will go before you to shew you the way, and when it rests you may safely repose. There was one who in the olden time received the blessing, the sweet assurance that the waters had begun to abate; the same blessed Master sends to you by the same message the same blessed assurance in all its spiritual significance. Receive, dear sister,† this sacred sign, and treasure the symbol now sent FOR THE SECOND TIME, to signify that the world *will* be saved." Here she awoke and was much struck with the

---

* The word *faint* shews me that I may still expect a season of struggle and anxieties. Psalm xxvii. 13, "I had fainted, unless I had believed to see the goodness of the Lord in the land of the living." Prayer-book version; 15, "I should *utterly* have fainted."

† There was a kind of hesitation before the word "sister" was used, which led me, upon thinking over the séance afterwards, to enquire who had been the communicating spirit, and I was informed that it was Anna the prophetess.

fulness of the promises given. We then talked about my Whit Sunday Dove, which I had received as a symbol of The Comforter, and Mrs. T. wondered whether it might be the spirit of that very bird that had been enabled to bring me the emblem of Peace, and she was answered that it was.

In the earlier part of the evening I had spoken of Mr. Harrison Green's visit to me on the previous day, and of his having been like myself an amateur photographer; also that he had some years ago purchased a large new camera and other apparatus that he had never yet used, and I thought that perhaps at some future time he and I might try for the spirit photography—but we were not thinking of the subject, when she said, "Just at that moment I had a glimpse of that photographic apparatus that I saw here before, long ago. [See First Series, page 340.] It was just behind you, where your easel stands, and it seemed to be pointing towards the door. I saw a man with his head under a black cloth looking through it. I do not know whether that would be the right place for the camera to stand, but perhaps it would have to be placed there at first so as to be filled with power, as that is the most sacred place in your room, being the one you occupy while engaged upon your drawings."

CHAPTER XXII.

I WENT to see Mrs. T. on the 6th of November, and was much struck with a beautiful tiny wheatsheaf on a table near the window, when she told me that she had been impressed to unpack it that morning, and to place it on that particular spot. It had been laid on the coffin of a beloved relative, deceased during her late visit to her girlhood's home. We established ourselves in front of the fire, and talked away to our hearts' content for some considerable time. She suddenly gave a slight start, and began to rub one of the fingers of her right hand, saying that it was like the burn from a spark of fire; but the fire was burning very gently, moreover the feeling was on the side of the finger nearest to me, and *away* from the fire, which led us to talk of St. Stephen's signal, and the various occasions upon which we had both felt it, either together or apart. I had with me the two little books into which I copy her visions, and read to her the one she had had the week before, about the Dove and olive-branch; and also, in connexion with the death of my Arthur's week-old baby, the beautiful vision she had had of children floating, that I had copied, and sent to Arthur in his trouble. I afterwards spoke of an earlier vision that had occurred on the 18th of February 1870, which I read to her as follows:—"I have been looking at what I supposed to be little globes of light, but when I look more closely I find that they all enclose a little form, very tiny, like the first beginning of the child; one part is larger than the other, and it curves and tapers. The air is full of them. These are children of the brain: they are *thoughts* which can be sent to receptive people from the spirit world. The ball of light which seems to enclose the tiny shape forms the atmosphere by which it can be carried from one place to another."

I told her that that vision often recurred to my mind, and that I expected the idea would some time be elaborated either to her or to me, and that something of the kind has been represented in one or two of my later symbolical drawings, but of which I have not as yet received the interpretations. Even while I was yet speaking, it *came* (inbreathed) to me that these thoughts must, in the first instance, rest in a brain sufficiently elevated to be in affinity with it; there it, as it were, germinates and developes, then passes out again, still in a thought-form, but having acquired something of earthliness by which it may be received by a somewhat lower mind, where the process is repeated. It thus continues to descend, becoming more and more material, or it may be called *tainted;* but only by such means could it at all reach the lower levels of humanity.

It was also symbolised to me as a long-suspended thread, having on it different beads at intervening distances; the *upper one* being dazzlingly white and transparent, the descending ones becoming gradually *coloured* by the thread, or *mind*, whereby they have travelled, of which the higher ones may still retain glowing rainbow tints which become muddied in their transit, until at length they appear opaque and almost black; but the downward shading is so gradual, that by carrying the eye upward, it may be seen that all is in harmony, and hope may be felt that the clouding may be cleansed away, and the pure thought, although apparently almost annihilated, may eventually be able again to spring into life.

All this came fragmentarily during our conversation, and then Mrs. T. passed into trance, and said:—"They get first into the sphere where it is possible to apprehend naked Truth. Then we shall do well to bear this truth in mind, that sometimes what we take for falsehood or error is because of its clothing, or what is put on to it by passing through various minds, when it gradually gets encrusted, and the form of the essential truth is changed by these encrustations. So we say, it is false; it is an imposture, and no truth is covered here. But Our Lord, and many who are less wise, *could* find in these *malformations* spiritual truths disguised; and we who can be wise enough to examine what is meant by each presentation, may gain much wealth. In Our Lord's plan of the universe all is conserved, and nothing is *common* or *unclean*. In all humility, from highest to lowest, we may take this lesson into our hearts; thus The Lord's name will be praised."

She sat silent for a few minutes, then pointing to the miniature wheatsheaf of which I have spoken, she said :— "*She is here.*" [Who?] "She who was gathered in the fulness of time, and whose work is fitly represented by fruitful corn." [You mean your beloved relative; but has her presence anything to do with what has been said?] " No. But it means that she could not see that some things were true that were not according to her own perception of truth. She is listening, and what we have been talking about has been said *for* her, for since her change of state she has not been happy; she could only see things in her own way.

" It has also something to do with this burning (pointing her fingers towards one another). You must be pricked on the right hand and on the left to open the body to a perception of The Lord, and if one had not been pricked in body and in spirit one cannot see ; and in some way it has now been given to her to feel the importance of what has been here said, and in God's mercy it has been her *first* help in understanding *her* place in the plan of life. She is stroking my hand. It is the first time I have had the apprehension of her presence, but I have had with respect to her a feeling of sadness, as if there had been disappointment to her, but without any detailed causes. Her life was outwardly full of good work—of good and useful work— but so. full that she, as it were, suffered interiorly by being drawn surfaceward, and by the external life being too active and made of such paramount importance. There must, for a time, be for her a period of repose ; she must wait upon The Lord, and be content to see others take up her accustomed routine. She dwelt too much in one groove of thought and action, and was unable to see that on

x

either hand might be branching side-walks as efficient, and enlightened by as much truth as the path whereon she herself trod. Things more necessary to her happiness will gradually be unfolded to her as the equilibrium between the inner and the external bodily life is adjusted, but that will not be for many days. For the present this interview will help to comfort her, and will aid her in the way of attainment." Here she awoke into her normal condition, but she still felt her relative's presence while I read it to her, and we continued talking.

I went to see her again in about a month, and after dinner I read the communication to her, for she scarcely realises the fulness of them in the first instance, as she may be only partially roused. I offered if she liked, to copy it out for her sister, who was anxious to know anything that might come in reference to their relative. She made some scruples as to giving me so much trouble, but those I overruled. Then she said, but more as if enunciating what came to her from some other mind: "Do you not think it ought to be published? I think it is meant not only for her, but for a number of others: (passing more under influence): it could be called—A Lesson—A needed Lesson." [Do you mean the whole? from the beginning?] "About the *thought*? Yes—but it will be more instructive without personality—no—not *more*, it will be *as* instructive." [I could write it for the *Psychological Review*,* and perhaps *you* would send it.] "Yes, I can send it, and say that I think it should be read by more than first listened to it. It is a thought, and that is all; and we intended it to be circulated." Just then I was startled by a flash passing at about a yard's distance before my eyes towards her, and although I could not have defined the *shape*, the feeling was so strong that I exclaimed, [The Dove flashed before me!] "Yes, I felt its head *here*, (touching her right cheek), and it is the harbinger of peace and plenty. Peace—*this* is *peace* (raising her left hand and placing it as if covering her right, which she held very much cupped), and the

* It was published in the last number of that series.

other, *plenty*, and there must be much room to hold it. Peace *and* Plenty (here she held her hands as if filled to the uttermost). It cannot yet rest, because the water still covers the earth : it will come again and often. But when the waters subside, and the earth is left dry, then the Dove will take its flight, and go perchance to give comfort to the one who works in the West." I put some questions, the answers to which were to " rest in my own heart." Then was said : " When your feet take firm stand, such other change will be. . . . When you *rest* in *strength*." [Ah! *that* I think *may* be a long time.] " And it may be only a short day." [Any way, a little bit of firm ground would serve me.] " The Lord who knows your need will give you support." After a minute she shook my hand with her left one, and in a changed voice, said briskly—" Good-bye, Georgiana," and immediately awoke, feeling a pressure as of great weight in her right hand, which was the sensation of my promised " Plenty" that she still retained, and she remembered having felt the Dove's head against her cheek.

We afterwards learned that the spirit who uttered the last three words was my cousin Mary, and indeed if the change had not come so unexpectedly, I should have recognised her immediately, for the manner and the farewell intonation were essentially characteristic, and it is those kind of small evidences that people are so apt to overlook, and yet they are truer tests than any that can be planned beforehand as what ought to be required.

On the 31st of December Mrs. T. came to spend the day with me in honour of the twentieth anniversary of my mediumship, and in the afternoon she told me about a special circle she was attending at Mrs. Billing's, for the enunciation of some spiritual theories by the direct voice; but she did not know much of what was said, as she was usually in a kind of quiet semi-trance. After tea we had a séance, when she took up the pencil, and some curious writing upside-down was done, so that it was in the right position for me to read it: also, under influence, messages were given from several of those dearest to me, one of which was spoken in a sort of poetical strain, and although I cannot say much for its value as poetry, yet that, too, was a test, as the speaker was one who had once filled a page of my scrapbook with original verses, and was the only person who had ever done such a thing for me, also it was his only effort. She had been occasionally suffering from acute pain about four inches below the collar-bone on the left side, for which she had consulted a physician, who had attributed it in some way to diet, and had recommended care; and while we were still amusedly talking over what had passed, she said, while placing her hand on the spot; "They are shewing me about that pain. It is power taken for helping those voices, and last night I had it again, only not so severely." Even as she spoke, she passed into trance, so I enquired, [Ought she to go?] "There is something the matter with the left lung; hence the pain, which is caused by obstruction, otherwise no pain would attend the abstraction of such power." [In that case is it right for her to go to the meetings?] "No." [Can she in some way retire from these séances without any worry as to the cause?] "Perhaps— But she probably may not be able to go again, but if she goes, she can be taken care of, for it is not a necessity that she suffer." [Could I help her in any way? for instance, by prayer on the Thursday evenings, on which the circle is for the future to be held?] "Yes,—by centering your thought *here*" (pointing to the spot). Here she awoke, and I explained to her what had passed, and how desirable it was that she should if possible give up attending the circle, which she then told me she had only joined for the sake of making up the number (in a pecuniary sense, I think, so that that was settled), and that the unexpected change in the evening of the week upon which they were to be held, might compel her absence, because of other engagements. There was something more given upon the subject, but this has been sufficient to shew that it is necessary to be extremely cautious as to the especial state of health of the sitters when forming a circle for a series of séances, and that any one who suffers in consequence should withdraw immediately, at any rate until the ailment shall have been subdued.

She again passed into trance, and said :—" Be not forgetful to entertain strangers, for thereby some have entertained angels unaware.—The Angel of The Lord encampeth hereabout, and on *this* spot will be fixed His tent (pointing upwards with much solemnity). When He fixes His tent, it will be on the rock, and it will stand, and no flood will overtake it; and *in* the tent some will be succoured, some will be strengthened, ere they go forth to the battle of the forces; and these can return and be again strengthened for the work's sake.—Now, Faithful, what wilt thou ask in the name of The Lord?" [I know not *what* to ask—whatsoever The Lord wills to send.] "But The Lord wills to be enquired of, concerning the gifts thou wouldst receive." [I fain would receive my sight.—That mine eyes may be opened to see the spiritual beings around me, as was vouchsafed to the prophet's servant.] " . . . . If thou hadst asked for thine hands to be filled, and the way of thy life lightened, even this would have been given thee. Thou shalt receive thy sight, and all these other things will be added thereunto. But the time waits.—The sun will *surely* shine on thy pathway, and its light will brighten all thy way, and so, God's will be done on earth as it is in Heaven." There was a long pause, then she resumed, with strong emphasis. "The earth is The Lord's, and the fulness thereof; the world, and they who dwell therein. Shall He not do as He will with His own? Is there any to bind or to loose save The Lord Only?

"There be those who say—A *stone* was my father, a *stock* was my mother. I came *from* the earth, *to* the earth I return :—there is no will save *mine*, there is no power.—

"The Lord is about to lift His right arm (here she raised hers with a powerfully threatening attitude), and *when it falls* (she here brought her hand down on the table with a vehement blow), these children of stocks and stones will be crushed to powder: it were better for them that a millstone were put around their necks and they were drowned in the sea." Further denunciations were given with yet more vigour, and when she finally awoke, she was troubled and awe-stricken with the prophecies of woe that I had to read to her. She then asked for the Bible, and in the same forcible manner that is usual with her, it was opened, and the fingers of each hand pressed on opposite pages. The first she read was still denunciatory, Isaiah xix. 1 to 10. But the second ends more tenderly: Isaiah xvi. 1 to 5, which says—"And in mercy shall the throne be established: and He shall sit upon it in truth in the tabernacle of David, judging, and seeking judgment, and hasting righteousness."

She was again impressed to take up the Bible, which was turned several times in her hand; and as it was opened, she said, "This is for *you*." The words were *towards* me: the first was, Isaiah xxx. 20, 21. "And though The Lord give you the bread of adversity, and the water of affliction, yet shall not thy teachers be removed into a corner any more, but thine eyes shall see thy teachers: and thine ears shall hear a voice behind thee, saying, This is the way, walk ye in it, when ye turn to the right hand, and when ye turn to the left." The second text was from Isaiah xxviii. 29. "This also cometh forth from The Lord of hosts, which is wonderful in counsel, and excellent in working." Thus the year ended for myself with words of comforting promise.

I accompanied Mrs. T. on the afternoon of the 16th of January 1880, for a séance with Mrs. Billing, and afterwards went home with her, and in the course of the evening I mentioned that on the previous Sunday afternoon, I had been sitting in deep thought, and when I looked up I saw, just above my worked chair, a spirit light in the form of a small hovering bird, which rested quietly for about the time that I might have counted three. "At the moment you spoke to me," said she, "I was seeing the Dove." So we had no doubt that it was my impression of the Dove's presence that induced me to mention the vision I had had. I have already told of the first glimpse I had of her, so that this was the second, and I have had none since, but on *both* those occasions the fruitful branch was coming *across the waters* to me, in the shape of a remittance from my two dear boys in succession.

I will endeavour to give the substance of our séance with Mrs. Hollis-Billing, for I may only now and then remember the exact words. It was a densely heavy, rainy day, coming after the previous evening's snow, so that it was neither wholesome nor pleasant for any one. We found that Mrs. Billing was not very well, for she had been out to give séances on the two previous evenings, so that she was fatigued and otherwise poorly. I asked whether she would like me to mesmerise her (for mediums do sometimes object), and she said she should be glad, if I felt the "impression" to do so, and that had necessarily preceded my offer. At first the mesmerism was entirely to the throat; the lungs were next worked upon between the shoulders, and finally the spine, especially the lower part, and in each case my "Friends" had of course found the seat of mischief.

We all three then went into the completely darkened back drawing-room, where we sat for some little time in quiet conversation, when suddenly a brisk clear voice exclaimed, "How are you, Squaw T——?—glad to see you, Soh!"—It was the Indian, Skiwaukie, usually greeted and spoken of as "Ski," who then said a few cordial words to me, expressive of pleasure at my visit, which would make us mutually acquainted. He talked to Mrs. T. about "Chief" T——, and his present improved state of health, and various family matters. He then spoke to her about another person, saying that there was nothing spiritual *there*, for that the groove in which he dwelt had money only as its end and aim. The phrase he then used had reference to something in the earlier part of the conversation, when we had been talking of the narrowness of scientific men and such-like, who will receive nothing out of their own channels, and as Ski said, "would wish to cut a narrow path for other people to walk in." He spoke of some one she had had to do with, who was not of a very warm-hearted nature, and Ski said she was like a sponge, wiping up everything and keeping it. All at once he said, "Well, Squaw Houghton, what about the photographs?" [Oh! I have one in my pocket, done some little time since by Mr. Hudson, of Dr. Friesë.] "Yes—of Paulina, *I* told Dr. Friesë to go to him, and that he would get Paulina, and he *did*." [I have one of you;] said I—"Oh! I know you have, you have had it a big, *long* time." Which was true enough, for it was the one done stereoscopically in 1873: and I spoke to him of its close resemblance to the photograph lately given in the *Medium*. We then had some considerable discussion as to the probability of the photographic work being resumed, and Ski said, "One special person was appointed from the first for that work, and *you* are the one selected." How or when it was to be resumed was not clearly told, and perhaps Ski does not know, but we did not *question*, for I do not think it well to *seek* any information beyond what is volunteered. "I have been to your house, and seen your pictures," said he, so I asked what he liked best. "Oh! those beautiful lines and colours." [Did you see the one I was shewing to Mr. Hudson on Wednesday?] "No: what was it?" I then explained to him that it was the monogram of the Queen of Wirtemburg, which I had shown to him because a Russian gentleman had been about London a good deal with Dr. Friesë, and perhaps on some future visit to England they might come to see me. Ski expressed a great desire to see the picture, so I made an appointment with him to come to-morrow (Sunday, January 18), at two o'clock, when I will establish it on the easel, and I have no doubt I shall have some intimation of his presence. . . . Presently he said, "Squaw T——, St. John is by you: he always comes when you are here." This led to our talking of St. John in conjunction with us both, and also to a great deal about Spiritualism in a religious point of view, and Ski said that his chief aim was to lead people into higher thoughts on such matters, and out of the frivolous excitement seeking which resulted in such painful affairs as one that had lately taken place. "I see a spirit by your side who is always with you; do *you* see him?"

No, I told Ski that I had not yet the happiness of the gift of sight, but looked to its coming to me somewhen. Mrs. T. asked about the health of a friend she was anxious about, and Ski said she was better, but must not tire herself with too much talking; and some observations were made about her "Chief," when Ski told of a lady who said that the worst she wished for *her* Chief was that he would go to Heaven. He then said he would retire for a little while and try to help some one else to come. Shortly I heard a very faint whisper of—"Mary—Mary—I am so glad, Georgiana, to speak to you here." Mrs. Billing asked if I recognised the spirit, and I told her it was my cousin, the wife of Mr. Pearson, who has been once or twice at her public circle, and she knew him very well, but had no idea of our relationship. Mary spoke a little more, but nothing of special import. She finished with a warm "Good-bye, Georgiana; God bless you." After a short interval came another whispered voice, yet closer to me. "My dear, I am here." [Who are you?] said I, not at all realising it as a test.—"Waiting, waiting, waiting." Still I did not catch the idea, till Mrs. Billing said, "Is there any spirit who might use that phrase to you as a test?" When the rhymes spoken through Mrs. T. on the last day of the year, of which those had been the opening words, were brought to my recollection, so I recited them all, and he repeated them after me, but being the first time of his exercising a voice, he could only add a final "God bless you."

Then a spirit friend of Mrs. T.'s spoke with her for some little time, and after he had taken leave, Ski again conversed with us upon the expected changes. . . . He told me with much pride, that he had a portrait of St. John, a photograph in a frame that had been presented to him by a lady, on his birthday fête, December 29th. Mrs. Billing shewed it to me after the séance, and it is from a beautiful piece of sculpture, and I do not wonder at his pleasure in its possession. At last he said he had done all he could for us, and was glad we had been able to have so good a séance, which could not have been expected. [Because of Mrs. Billing not being well?] "Ah! no, my medium being poorly makes no difference, but because the weather is so bad that with some sitters they might scarcely have been able to get a word." [Did we bring the brightness with us?] "*Yes*, you brought the sunshine in your pockets. Good-bye, Squaw T——: good-bye, Squaw Houghton. I am very glad to have seen you both." And thus ended our very pleasant séance. The voice of Ski was clear and bright, and I was much amused by his continual use of the interjectional Soh! either beginning or ending a phrase, and sometimes both, with wonderfully varying intonation. Mrs. T. afterwards said that she thought my having mesmerised Mrs. Billing made one chief element of success in the séance.

January 19.—Skiwaukie kept his appointment yesterday, and at first he interested himself in reading a letter I had just written to Mr. Hudson, after which he noticed many things about the room: he then accompanied me to the portfolio stand, whereon I had already placed the portfolio containing Queen Olga's monogram, which was to be looked at there instead of upon the easel as I had expected; and thus Ski had a steadfast look at each drawing as we passed through it. Some I had to take out, and hold up for more perfect inspection, and the O. R. was thus held for him for a considerable time. When the contents of the portfolio had been thoroughly examined, I had to close it up, and he seemed much interested in the careful arrangements to protect the drawings from any possible injury. I then fulfilled a promise I had made on the previous day, when I sent to Mrs. Billing, as a gift for Ski, a photograph of "The Eye of The Lord" (No. 2), of which I said I would shew him the original on his intended visit to me. He contemplated it a long time in steadfast stillness, and afterwards inbreathed to me that he had learned from it many spiritual truths that were new to him. He took his leave at ten minutes before three, having to keep another engagement, but he was sorry to go away. While I was copying the foregoing into my book,

I received a note from Mrs. Billing. "*January* 19*th.*—
DEAR MISS HOUGHTON,—Ski is much obliged for the Photo
you so kindly sent. I think it most wonderful, and feel that
I shall often look at it with pleasure. He has paid his visit
to you as he promised, and was much pleased with what he
saw. Hoping you are quite well; with kind regards, I am
sincerely yours,   MARY J. BILLING."

I went on the 23rd of June to Mr. Burns's soirée at the
Cavendish Rooms, and while talking to Mr. Hudson, Mr.
Towns tapped me on the shoulder, and said that he had
been wanting to get at me, for that he had seen a *very*
ancient individual standing by me, with his breast all written
over with Hebrew characters—a great deal of writing. I
asked if he could give me the name, and he said it was one
of the sons of Jacob. "Is it Ephraim?" said I, feeling
that son and grandson would be synonymous, especially the
one from whom a tribe was named. "Yes, you are right."
So I told him my belief that the English are the descendants
of Ephraim, also some of my specific feelings with respect
to him. He went on to say that in the coming changes in
this new dispensation, those ancient ones would be prominent workers, as they had not been able to be in the former
one, and that they were peculiarly linked with me. Much
more he told me of my approaching work, when I shall be
one of *three* who will have to bless the other workers. He
said he had been *obliged* to tell me all that, and was very glad
of the opportunity of my moving down to that part of the
hall.

Mrs. T. came to me on the evening of December 13th,
when there were many things of different kinds to discuss,
more especially the next evening's Council meeting at the
B. N. A. S., when the secretaryship question would be
finally concluded, although it was already virtually so, for
the financial gain would be a certainty, and that was a
necessary consideration with us; but we feared there might
be some present who might raise obstacles. During our
talk she passed under influence, and some fresh light was
thrown on an important point. There was also a prophecy,

ending with these words . . . "and a great support may drop from you." [We can only trust in The Lord's help.*] "But at the proper time The Lord can again engraft this useful member, and the work will be no more hindered. You will be led to say, 'All can now be made right.' . . ."

On the 14th the attendance of members of Council was large, but notwithstanding the universal expectation, all went off amicably, and I think spiritual power had been at work to still the troubled elements. Curiously enough, after the members had dispersed, I had a conversation with two gentlemen, one of whom did not belong to the Council, when every bit of her revelation was corroborated in all its details, and alas! early in the following year the prophecy was fulfilled, although not by the *will* of the "great support!" but I trust the time may come when he will again be engrafted upon us.

Mrs. T. came to me on the closing day of the year 1880, and I will make one or two short extracts from my records. Very denunciatory texts had been given from the Bible, and after we had discussed the sad prophecies we sat silent for some little time, when she said to me, "What is the name of the prophetess?" I saw she was passing under influence. [Do you mean Anna?] "Yes, I hear some one calling *you* Anna the prophetess." [I wonder why.] "Because thou speakest by power that is given thee." Again there was silence. . . . Her hands were resting on the little table, but presently she raised her right hand pointing upwards, placing the elbow on the table, the fingers slightly bent forwards as if to attract mine, but I found I had to raise both hands in conjunction with hers, forming a kind of tent, and it came to me to say, "The hand of The Trinity as a tent enfolding the faithful." . . . A great deal passed, but her final *personal* words for me were—"There is more, but I cannot catch the rest. It is going to be a *very full time for you.*—I think for a good while."

* Even at that very moment the feeling came to me that it was M. A. (Oxon) who was alluded to.

CHAPTER XXIII.

I HAD for some time past seen in *Spiritual Notes* occasional observations as to an association of some kind that was in contemplation or formation, under the title of the Guild of the Holy Spirit, but it had not struck me to enquire into it, as there had been *other* combinations of Spiritualists with which I certainly would not have connected myself. But on the 1st of November I attended the Discussion meeting at our rooms in Great Russell Street, arriving there very early, as I like in such cases to see the most I can of my friends. Very soon after I got there the Rev. Dr. Davies came down from the little upper room (which I of course knew that he was renting from us), and was very glad to find me there, as he wanted to tell me all about it. He then explained that he was the Founder of the said Guild, and had had his first small gathering that afternoon (All Saints' Day) at four o'clock. He entered into full particulars of his views and wishes, being well assured that they would be in accordance with mine. His plan was to hold sittings there twice a week (or more often, if the numbers grew), commencing with a short service for the administration of the Sacrament, and that then the circle should sit in a sort of stillness, waiting for what might come. There was to be singing, and whatever else might be deemed expedient, either in the dark or the light according to directions received at the time, but his desire was thus to give them a religious character and to prevent them from degenerating in any way into frivolity and trifling. He wished them to resemble as closely as might be the assemblage in the upper room on the Day of Pentecost. The thought had been for some time in preparation, and he had had a number of letters from deep thinkers in many parts of the kingdom who had already enrolled themselves as members of the Guild, and who, wherever they might be, would unite in prayer at the hour appointed for the meetings, thus to be joined in spirit with those who were present. The hours fixed were to be, four o'clock on the Monday afternoons, and eight on the Thursday evenings: the latter I could manage, and promised to be punctual and constant unless anything urgent should supervene to prevent my going. I then accompanied him upstairs to see his arrangements, and found that he had fitted his room up quite as a little oratory, and it already had the feeling of a place appropriated to praise and prayer. They were very happy little meetings, rarely exceeding a dozen, but the elements were harmonious, and the fact of Dr. Davies donning his surplice tended to give sacredness to their character. The manifestations were never very powerful, and were chiefly mental, but it was not excitement that was sought, so that what came sufficed for the few who formed the steadfast nucleus, while there were some who perhaps only came once, and some who were irregular, but that might be in a degree from the force of circumstances. After a time, contributions were made for the purchase of a harmonium for use during our services of prayer before and after the sittings, one of our members being kindly the instrumentalist.

On my second occasion Mrs. T. had come here towards the close of the day, and received a strong impression to accompany me, which she did: (and oh! what a pouring night it was, so that I was fortunately sheltered with her in a cab, instead of walking the weary length of Gower Street from the station). She was influenced to *place* the various sitters, and those who were then present were as far as possible always to retain the same seats; and other directions were likewise given through her. I also was spoken through, which indeed was frequently the case, especially when our circle numbered the fewest. Around the walls and on the mantelpiece were photographs of friends who had passed away, as well as memorial cards; all of which would be likely to serve as links to draw them towards us, thus to swell our small congregation into a large one on the invisible side. There was also on the little altar-table a good-sized cross, I should think about a foot and a half high, which had been prepared with the luminous paint, so that it had a sort of moonlighted look when we sat in the darkness.

On the 6th of January a gentleman came, whom I had first met at the rooms in Sloane Street, and occasionally since, and we were great friends in that sense, but he knows nothing of me in my home : he was accompanied by his wife, to whom I had been introduced at Langham Hall, after a public meeting held there by Mr. Enmore Jones. She is a trance medium, but passes a life fully occupied in family affairs and suchlike, so that it was very long since she had been in any way influenced. But very soon after our séance commenced, in the harmonious stillness she began to see the spirits around her, and gave a communication referring to some friend of Dr. Davies who was not present, and afterwards had a few words from a relative of the lady who was seated next to her. She then said, "There is a spirit belonging to Miss—Miss—oh! help me to the name,—I mean the lady who paints." Her husband said : "You mean Miss Houghton." "Oh ! yes—Miss Houghton. It is her mother." Of course I made some little response. Mamma spoke through her of the extreme beauty of the spirit world, details of which it used to be her great desire to learn, and she was always disappointed that no descriptions of it were ever given to her through me. The medium then came close to me from the opposite side of the room (we were in total darkness), and began caressing my arms and exclaiming, while she seemed to be searching and feeling about me—"The token—*the token!*"—to which I could give no kind of help, for I did not know of anything she could consider in that light, but she seized my left hand very strongly (she appears always to be controlled with great vehemence), moved the one ring away so as to take a firm hold of her own slender wedding-ring, then lifted my hand to her lips, kissing the wedding-ring with great warmth and fervour. Of course I gave the interesting explanation that it was the ring that had been placed on her finger fully 76 years ago (in 1804), which I had worn ever since its removal from her hand in 1868. She spoke some loving words of blessing and tenderness; but this is just the bald statement of the circumstance as I noted it down the next day. When the candles were afterwards lighted I shewed the ring to those who were present, none of whom had ever noticed that I wore it, for the thicker ring almost hides it, besides which in those meetings we were none of us likely to trouble ourselves as to what the others might have on; but this incident was of value to them all as a test of such an unexpected character.

On another evening, in the dark stillness my hands were uplifted to make mesmeric passes, and always with a kind of feeling as if I were gathering something into the room: then gradually arose a sensation as of a dense multitude flocking towards that upper chamber—a host as it were, and yet not of bright ones:—it gave me almost a sense of oppression, as if they were an imploring host—but all that then came to me was that they were Assyrians, and I explained something of what I was experiencing to the other members of the circle. As I afterwards walked quietly along Gower Street, it was revealed to me that they were the hosts of Sennacherib, slain in one night by the angel of The Lord (2 Kings xix. 35,) who had ever since then lain in a kind of torpor, from which they had only now been roused by the mesmeric fluid poured *through* my hands and afterwards converted into a species of magnet to attract them to that small church, whose chief duty was to help the ignorant and suffering ones in the beyond. On the following Thursday I was powerfully spoken through, to urge all those who were present to give their aid to these "Assyrians wandering Home;" entreating them, at any time of day when the thought should arise, to utter a prayer for *an* Assyrian wandering Home. From that prayer would issue a beam of light, which would be as a beacon to *one* poor soul, inducing him to look upwards, until by degrees he should gain more and more light, to enable him to apprehend truths, to which in his long ago life he could not have attained, but which in these wondrous days of 1881 will be bestowed upon countless myriads who have been lying supine—therefore not mischievous—until the fulness of time, when there is as it were to be a literal fulfilment of the prophecy of Ezekiel (xxxvii.), when the dry bones shall become living beings (through the aid of the sons of men), and shall be brought to sing their rejoicing praises unto The Lord.—Oh! ye who may read these pages, and who believe in the inspired word of old, may I beseechingly implore you thus to contribute your quota to aid in The Lord's work, and to breathe an occasional prayer for the benighted ones of ages, thereby bestowing upon them the help they need. It may give a *first* light to one soul, or it may be as another beam to one who is already soaring, but be assured that it will *not* come back unto you empty. I have learned that this was the especial purpose for which that Guild was instituted (all unknowingly perhaps by its Founder), and although its meetings are now at an end, the Spiritual Church simultaneously established still flourishes, and the work then commenced continues its course with vigour, and I know that this assurance (only *now* given to me) will be a comfort to that Founder, should these words ever meet his eye in his distant home.

After the first few meetings Miss Godfrey joined us, and was constant in her attendance except when professional engagements prevented her from coming; and her presence was a great acquisition, especially to those for whom the whole subject was a novelty, for she often had very beautiful visions which she would describe as they gradually unfolded themselves, but I do not remember any of the details, and I had by that time become too fully occupied to make even the slightest record; but I know that in one instance a sadly unhappy spirit came seeking aid, and Miss Godfrey's guardian spirit permitted her to take possession of her *because* our little tent was to be a haven of refuge for such. She began very scornfully, but by dint of questioning I elicited that she had murdered her new-born

Y

illegitimate child—and the dire trouble that appeared to render her callous, was the belief instilled into her here upon earth that that innocent one was condemned to eternal perdition because of its death in an unbaptized state, and I had to argue long with her before I could shake that deeply rooted conviction. She had searched in the *depths* for that poor infant, but hitherto without success, but I uged upon her that she had sought in the wrong direction, and that she must strive *upwards* to have any chance of meeting with it. My Zilla was there, and told me she would keep the poor wanderer in view, and would give help from time to time, when such assistance could be administered. I was in hopes that at a future sitting we might have learned something of her progress, but there was generally some fresh thought touched upon, which probably would be the best suited to meet the needs of the circle in the flesh.

On the 17th of February Miss Cook came, having been invited by Dr. Davies. She was quite alone, and our circle was an unusually small one. I do not think we numbered more than ten. My usual place was on the left hand of Dr. Davies, and as we sat round the room, Miss Cook might perhaps have been about facing me. When our service was over, and the lights were extinguished, raps were almost immediately heard, and the first question Dr. Davies put, was whether we were seated properly for those manifestations, to which a very decisive No was the answer, and by dint of further enquiry it was found that I was to change places with the sitter on Miss Cook's right, so I seated myself by her side, and held her hand *during the whole* of the séance, for the chief part of which she was completely entranced, placidly leaning back in her chair in a gently breathing slumber. Almost from the moment that I had sat down by her side, I had felt the spirit-touches in more material character than they come to myself; and gradually first one and then another of the circle exclaimed that they felt the touch of spirit hands, which to most of them was an utterly new experience. The gentleman on her left felt busy fingers undoing his necktie, which I think was then laid on his wife's lap. Then the hands that touched became more and more substantial, and they all felt them as palpably as human hands : one was quite a baby's hand, which allowed itself to be tenderly clasped by more than one of the party. I felt dear Môtee's, giving me the various familiar tokens, and placing itself, according to my old request, to my lips to be kissed. We also heard the voice of the spirit Lillie, and I think we saw her light, but in that respect I may be confusing in my own mind with a later séance when she was with us; but at any rate it was most interesting, and I can bear the strongest possible testimony as to the genuineness of the whole, for, as I said before, I held her hand firmly during the whole time, and Dr. Davies and I were the only persons in the circle whom she had ever seen before. I must also own that the tales I had heard circulated made me doubly watchful, and therefore I am the more solicitous to make my evidence in her favour unmistakably clear. On the next Thursday she was again with us, but the rumour of the successful manifestations we had had, brought us such an accession of visitors that our little room was quite crowded, some of the new-comers being quite strangers, and the result was— almost a failure—there was scarcely anything! Our little church was *not* for the curiosity-seekers, so they went away at the close with disappointment instead of wonders to tell of. About three months later she was with us for another séance, but we were chiefly the *habitués*, and then again the manifestations were very good, and the spirit Lillie came amongst us in bodily form, shewing her delicate little face by the aid of her spirit lamp, from which emanates a light white as alabaster: also she stood on the platform behind Dr. Davies, and we saw the substance of her arm as she held it up in front of the luminous cross.

That 5th of May was the last sitting of our little band of Christian worshippers, who had gone along in our quiet way for six months, but it had not grown into the strength that Dr. Davies had contemplated, and another step had been urged upon him which would give him promotion in his own profession, besides which an offer was at the same time made (in conjunction with the other) for a class of work for which he is most especially fitted, where there would also be openings for his very large family. So, after many prayers for guidance, he resolved upon making the change, but—as he told me—he would never have withdrawn from this especial effort if it had grown according to his own sanguine expectations. But clearly, that very stagnation was the evidence that another field of labour was to be opened to him, and that the establishment of this for Spiritual purposes was all that was needed: its fulness of work will be carried on on the other side, and I, for one, do not feel that the Guild is dissolved because we no longer hold our terrestrial meetings—I believe that we are still all linked together, going on in our several departments with the duties then entrusted to us.

A farewell soirée to bid him God speed was held by our Association on the 20th of May, and at the close of the evening the members of the Guild, accompanied by many of the other friends, adjourned once more to that upper room for a final service of prayer and sacred song: and thus I concluded my ten years anniversary of the Private View day of my Exhibition.

A few days since, I was reading in *Light* the report of the discussion by the Church Congress at Newcastle. It would be out of all chronological order if I were now to touch upon that meeting, about which I have nothing to say, but I find therein a charge which I most unmitigatedly repudiate.

"But further, we cannot accept that degrading view of the body which seems to be an element in the highest Spiritualist teaching. It is represented, not as an instrument for the acquisition of knowledge, and as being, no less than the Spirit, the work of God, and consecrated to His service, but as a foul obstructive. Vegetarianism, and of course teetotallism, are essential to every one who would reach the higher knowledge; his very residence must be a place where no blood is or has been shed."

Among Spiritualists there are as many varieties of opinion upon the question of diet as among all the rest of the world, and I have come to the conclusion that there is no sort of general rule, and that the old adage of "what is one man's meat is another man's poison" is most essentially true. The one great law is that each person shall find out the system that shall keep his body in the state of highest health; not coarse, bloated, apparent health, but real vigour, so that every faculty of body, soul, and spirit should be in fullest power to work harmoniously, and to make the very utmost of the years granted to us here below, so as to carry all the completion possible into the beyond. My aim has always been to attain the very highest that I can, and, having ever found my advisers invariably correct on all points, I have very frequently taken counsel on that matter of diet. When Mrs. Hardinge came to England many years ago, she rather inveighed against the Spiritualists in our land for their consumption of pork in its varieties of ham, bacon, &c., saying that no American Spiritualists would thus contaminate themselves. Of course I at once enquired of my dear friends whether I should renounce it, and I was told that, on the contrary, for me it was especially beneficial,—and I am led to wonder wherefore there should be the prejudice against what she termed swine's flesh: some say that it is because pigs will eat all manner of food, but in that they only resemble poultry, and who, among the most fastidious, will reject chicken, unless they are total vegetarians, whose numbers I find are much on the increase? and wheresoever that system agrees best in *invigorating* the individual, it ought undoubtedly to be pursued; but in many cases I look upon it as a reaction from, and a protest against, the very high living which I consider a sin, both towards their own bodies and the poverty-stricken ones of our land, who suffer in consequence of the waste elsewhere. And under the head of over-feeding I class the unnecessary number of meals, each as it were a kind of dinner, in which so many people indulge, until they fancy they are absolutely indispensable—

whereas I find that two are quite sufficient (and *no driblets* in between), breakfast—without meat—and then dinner. Formerly I used to take an intermediate slice of bread-and-butter, but for the last year or two I have dispensed even with that. I do not mean to say that I make myself a slave to any rules, so that if I chance to be out, I just take what other people are having, and at their hours, and my health is so perfect that any change one way or another would not affect it. The question to me always the most anxious one has been whether by any method of diet, or abstaining from special things, I should the better fit myself for the gifts of clairvoyance and clairaudience, but the sense of the unfailing answer has been that our mortal bodies during our earthly sojourn should be looked upon as the temples of God, therefore they must be kept in pure health, thus to become the more worthy recipients of His varied blessings whensoever He may deign to bestow them.

I have heard much upon the food question as to the experience of others:—one gentleman can only eat plain boiled rice, *without any addition whatever*, even a pinch of salt causing nausea: another has lived for many years upon only bread-and-butter: others, who are vegetarians, include eggs and fish among the permissible articles. Through Mr. Spear directions used often to be given as to the best diet for *individuals*, and that is the real thing to be learned. For me, he prescribed any amount of refined sugar, and I also feel that I must take my tea fully sweetened.

I *am* a teetotaller, but, as I have already said, I did not become so on Spiritualist grounds, but on economical ones; and I had really thought that a small amount of stimulant was a necessity for the system, especially when growing into years, but it has been even then that I have made the change, and have found no ill effects from it; and I would warmly advise all my readers to do the same, and to *set aside* the sum they would have spent therein to the purpose of helping their fellow-creatures, which will give a glow to their hearts far surpassing the previous warmth to any other portion of their being. Besides which, I have instanced the effect produced upon Mrs. Marshall by the smell of my breath after having taken but a half-glass of wine, so I feel that by our own self-denial we may give strengthening help to the struggling ones beyond.

A soirée was held in the Cavendish Rooms on the 5th of January 1881, for the benefit of Mr. Burns, and at it I met Mr. Towns, who, as is always the case, had some communication he was required to make to me; and as I had been *advised* to take my slate-tablets with me, I was able to write it all down. He said, "I see a very ancient spirit standing by you, of the time of Joshua, and he says you are to read the first five verses of the 4th chapter of Joshua, and afterwards you are to go to the 17th chapter, and read from the 16th to 18th verses. I think you are to have a vision about them, or something that will come to you at a future time. . . Those who live in this coming time will not only see, but understand; and there is a new spiritual unfoldment coming to you. This is the beginning of the first year of the new pentecostal season. Seven years of the outpouring of the Spirit to all who will prepare themselves for its influx, so that they can go in and out of the two worlds. You are going to have a change of condition—to pass into a new condition. During this pentecostal season, all must prepare themselves as vessels for the out-pouring and in-pouring of the Spirit, and it will *rest with you.*" There was some interruption from those around, after which he resumed, "They term you a sister of mercy, because you survey things in a merciful way. You will hear birds chirping and singing; you will hear them about you, and it will be a preparation for hearing voices.—You are to go on as you commenced, and as you are going on: you are not to let the *old* part of religion be pressed out,—you are to hold fast to it *all.* As you sow, so shall the harvest be apportioned."

There had been some bits of intervening talk, and now a great deal was said as to the late changes in the arrangements of our Association, which he was strongly impressed would be beneficial. He gave me a long message for a friend, referring to circumstances which I alone could know to be true. Then he added that I had had some home trouble that had given me a great deal of anxiety and annoyance, and that it had caused much discord and inharmony at times. I answered that it was very true, and that it was from an old cook who had lived with us for upwards of six and thirty years, and who I found had always been robbing us in every way she could. But I had freed myself from her, and that she was since dead.—"Oh! but she is here now :—I cannot see her distinctly, for she is so *very dark*,—but she is not very tall and stoops her head a little. She has a great deal to do in *your* home, and you will have to help her. There is still something to be found out. —She has to clear and scrape away all the bad influences and dirt of one kind or another that she has left there—oh! she has indeed a great deal to do." I told him it was very curious that he should give me this communication now, for that that same afternoon, while Elizabeth was dressing me, she had told me of a dream she had had the last night. She had dreamt that Preston was come back, and that *in* her dream she could not make up her mind whether she was glad or sorry. (She had made the girl's life miserable by her temper.) She did not see her face, for she had her back turned to her, and she was doing a thing that surprised her, for she was *scrubbing the kitchen floor*, and was down on her knees for the purpose; she had on the old black gown she was accustomed to wear. The kitchen was all as it is *now*, but she did not know whether Preston saw or noticed any alteration, she was just busy with her *cleaning*. Another theft was afterwards "found out."

On the 14th of January I had a visit from Mrs. Dr. Fuller-Baldwin, with an introduction from Mrs. Cooper, with whom she had been staying while at Brighton. She was a pleasant genial woman of Welsh birth, but whose parents had emigrated to America when she was only five years old, and now she had come back to this country about some business for her brother, and had been stranded here from want of means to take her home, and she had gone through considerable difficulties during the last few months. She was a powerful healer with a magnificent physique, but was unknown to English fame and therefore had no patients, and she gave me many of the details with the frank openness of a true nature. After a time she spoke in a half-dreamy sort of tone, but still in her normal condition, of a something concerning me and the character of my work, which she felt she could not at all understand although she said it. I did, however, comprehend it, for to a certain extent it represented the working and *intention* of my drawings, and was given with great depth of insight but with peculiarity of language. I did not attempt to write down any of it, from a sense of delicacy, because it was quite out of my power to offer her anything in the shape of even the smallest fee, and she was well aware, too, that such was the case. She then gave a description of a bright, active, energetic little elderly gentleman near me, whom it was some little time before I recognised. He was my grandfather, Alexander Warrand, who has never before been described to me by any medium, but as a child I was very fond of him and he of me, and it is only *now* while writing this out (for my only record was, "described Grandpapa"), that the full force of the circumstance comes to me, for he is alluded to in the beginning of these memoirs, which I then had no idea of being able to compile for many long years.

A special council meeting was held in Great Russell Street on the 25th of January, for necessary regulations consequent upon the changes that had taken place, and I found Mrs. Dr. Fuller there when I arrived, and she was still in the reading-room when the meeting was over, having remained for the purpose of being introduced to some of the members, to whom Mr. Blyton had spoken about her at the board. Finally, when all had left except Mr. Pearson, Mr. Blyton, and myself, she settled for a small séance with us, and after a good bit to the other two, she took hold of my hand, and said :—" I do not know what it is—but there will be a something in you, or of you this year, that will bring crowds to you. They will come rushing to your home, and it will be quite unexpected to you:—some great change that you now know nothing about. . . . (Slowly and impressively) The wheel goes round—and then the changes come—it has been very low down indeed with you, and now you are rising to the very top. . . . Oh! you are going to have Joseph with you:—Joseph and his coat of many colours—those colours all mean character—or qualities:—and you will see them. But what has gone forth from you, will come back into the coat—to make it.

"Oh! there is something so funny that I scarcely like telling you about it. There are quantities of horns—horns and baskets. Horns of plenty, and baskets full of everything you can want: and everybody seems to be crowding to bring you things."

When she had finished speaking, I told them about the séance when the materials for the coat of many colours really had been brought to me, which interested them all very much, for even my cousin Mr. Pearson did not know anything of it, for these home sittings have been very little known beyond the immediate circle who composed them, besides which it was only the *pieces* that were brought, and the after-formation of the coat, with the interpreted signification of the colours, had been only between Mrs. T. and myself; and just a nine days' wonder and nothing more, to any one who may afterwards have heard of it; so that the parallelism between the two explanations was to me very striking and a strong evidence as to Mrs. Fuller's mediumship (see page 45). I promised to take the coat with me the next time I went to Great Russell Street, so that they might see it. The latter part of her vision reminds me of Job, when all his many trials were at an end. May it be God's will that mine, too, may be drawing to a close, but I also pray that I may never forget the lessons taught me in adversity.

CHAPTER XXIV.

How drearily commenced this year 1881.—There was frost so severe that most of the upper-service water pipes in the houses were broken, and I shared the fate of my neighbours, for it had taken us by sudden surprise: in some houses there was no water at all, and one lady at the "Guild" told me that for her baby's bath she had been obliged to use melted snow,—for there was early snow,—then darkness and fog— and on the 18th of January such a snow as London has never known within my memory—it was a fine, drifting snow that blocked up every place, rising fully two feet against these drawing-room windows, and yet allowing a glimpse in parts of the balcony itself. Thus in the open roads there were high drifts, even smothering up carts, so that horses and men were frozen to death, not exactly in London itself, but within easy distance of it: traffic to it was necessarily suspended from all parts of the kingdom;—the milk-supply was utterly stopped, and but for modern inventions matters in that respect would have been bad indeed, but fortunately the condensed milk was to be had, and as the disaster was not of many days' duration, the stock in the grocers' shops did not become utterly exhausted. Even the underground trains were compelled to stop running on that Tuesday night in consequence of the snow. A circumstance happened in my very kitchen on that self-same day that never even in the far-back years has been known in my experience, for, absolutely, the supply-pipe from the cistern to the boiler got frozen, so that the boiler had to be carefully attended to by its upper lid, or that would have burst. I was without professional work of any kind or description, and my prospects appeared as much closed up from all external hope as London herself.

"*The hour that is darkest is the hour before dawn.*"

On Wednesday the 19th, a friend came to see me, and as it were completely overwhelmed me with the subject of his conversation, saying that it was a matter that he had for some little time had in consideration. He knew that at some distant period I hoped to formulate my records into book shape, but the thought was too far away for me to have fixed a *when*, even at the lapse of ten or twenty years, for it would be an impossibility without surplus funds, and I had not even the indispensable ones. What was my astonishment when he suggested that I should begin at once! and that he would provide the needful means and undertake all risks. It was like a thunderstroke of joy! But yet fuller and fuller became that joy from the intense delicacy with which he made the proposition, saying that he wanted a history of this new development of spiritual life as it had risen in our land, and that he felt it could best be understood by individual experiences, and that as I had taken part in most of the external movements of importance during the last twenty years, the outside history would naturally be interblended with my own, and would thus be carried on upon one continuous thread. He questioned as to whether I had any special ideas or plans. Oh! yes, the names of the books had long ago been given to me (and he liked them both), also that my thought had been to illustrate the photographic work, and he acceded to all my wishes:—then went at once into the consideration of type and such-like details, which were all a novelty for me to think upon, for although one naturally finds some books nicer to read than others, one scarcely realises the why. He suggested a book, the type of which he thought I should like, and that I could examine it at the Great Russell Street rooms and decide. What I wished was to make my work as full of substance as possible without rendering it too heavy to hold comfortably, and yet I wanted to pour my whole soul into it, and after counting lines in a page, and words in a line, I found that the model thus suggested would give me free scope for all.

He had intended speaking to me on his previous visit,

but some one else had come in, which had deprived him of the opportunity, but I said that even that had been in *order*, for that I always feel that the 20th of each month belongs to me, and the 19th as *leading* into it—"the evening and the morning were the first day"—that I should begin at once that very night the *griffonage*, and the fair copy the next morning: and at that very time I set my heart upon the dates when each and all of the MSS. should be finished. No amount of close work would daunt me, and I wrote on with my entire being, singing one continuous pœan of rejoicing, and what it was to me few can conceive. How little could I have anticipated that the prophecy given through Mrs. T. on the closing day of 1880, with which my 22nd chapter concludes, should within three weeks be in intense realisation—"It is going to be a *very full time for you* —I think for a good while."—Full to the brim it has indeed been,—what with writing, proof-correcting, photograph-preparing, &c., &c. It has literally been "rising early and late taking rest," but it has been to tell of God's Love in its greatness and in its minuteness, and to chant my hymn of praise all the way through. The year continued dark and foggy, so that, notwithstanding the cold, I had to sit close to the window to be able at all to see to write, but the sunshine in my soul made the outward obscurity of little account.

There have been three great epochs in my annals, divided into decades. In 1861, came the drawing mediumship, to open into all the rest.—In 1871, the exhibition of those ten years of work.—And now, in 1881, this most comprehensive labour of all!—I cannot but speculate—what will the next decade evolve? what shall I do in 1891?

My friend gradually smoothed all the details for me, consulting with me as to each separate item. It was he who suggested the monogram of Christ to grace the back of my book, as being the most consonant with my feelings, and at once expressive to all the world of my standpoint, and I owe him another bit of gratitude for the thought. The outside garb of a volume is likewise an important consideration: it should not only be a suitable cover for what it is to contain, but should have a kind of personal distinctiveness, not only as to ornament but *colour*, and I feared that the one I wanted might be difficult to meet with in these days of muddled tones, for I wished for a *living* tint, in the freshness of God's creation—that of the orange-leaf green, and three leaves were gathered from my own tree for the purpose of being matched—and I have been happily satisfied. In one particular on which I have not been consulted, it is clear that there has been the supervision of the invisibles, for now that my first book is *out*, I see that the cover is lined with a delicate jessamine pattern, and I have in this volume mentioned that the jessamine is my flower of flowers.

Spiritualists are not bound to be Greek scholars, and some of my lady friends have enquired of me the real signification of a symbol they know well by sight, but have always hesitated to ask of learned men the meaning, while the unlearned do not know it, but just pass it by as a mystery. My own exact knowledge, too, was incomplete, so I wrote to a relative, a very erudite clergyman, asking him to give it me in clear, concise form, and what he kindly sent me has the charm of combining Christianity with a Spiritual manifestation, making it doubly appropriate as the Standard under which I fight; I will therefore transcribe it in its entirety, and I am sure that others will be grateful to him as well as myself.

The monogram ☧ is made up of the two letters X and P which are the two first letters of the sacred name.

        ΧΡΙΣΤΟΣ *Christos* = Christ
        Χ Chi pronounced like ch hard
        Ρ Rho   ,,   ,,   r
        Ι Iota   ,,   ,,   i short, as in *fist*
        Σ Sigma   ,,   ,,   s
        Τ Tau   ,,   ,,   t
        Ο Omicron   ,,   o short
        Σ Sigma   ,,   ,,   s

This monogram is sometimes called the labarum,—a name which properly signifies the military standard adopted by the first Christian emperor, Constantine the Great, just before he defeated his rival Maxentius at the battle of the Milvian Bridge, A.D. 312. The military standard (together with the reason of its adoption) is fully described by Eusebius in his *Life of Constantine*. Eusebius was Bishop of Cæsarea and a friend of Constantine for many years, so that the story rests on contemporary authority. The following is Eusebius's account. (*Life of Constantine*, Book 1, chap. 28) *Chap.* 28 : " Accordingly he (Constantine) called upon God with earnest prayer and supplication that He would reveal to him who He was, and stretch forth His right hand to help him in his present difficulties. And while he was thus praying with fervent entreaty, a most marvellous sign appeared to him from heaven, the account of which it might have been difficult to receive with credit, had it been related by any other person. But since the victorious emperor long afterwards declared it to the writer of this history, when he was honoured with his acquaintance and society, and confirmed his statement by an oath, who could hesitate to credit his relation, especially since the testimony of aftertime has established its truth? He said that about mid-day, when the sun was beginning to decline, he saw with his own eyes the trophy of a cross of light in the heavens, above the sun, and bearing the inscription CONQUER BY THIS. At this sight he himself was struck with amazement, and his whole army also, which happened to be following him on some expedition, and witnessed the miracle."

Chap. 29. " He said moreover that he doubted within himself what the import of this apparition could be. And while he continued to ponder and reason on its meaning, night imperceptibly drew on; and in his sleep the Christ of God appeared to him with the same sign which he had seen in the heavens, and commanded him to procure a standard made in the likeness of that sign, and to use it as a safeguard in all engagements with his enemies."

Chap. 30. " At dawn of day he arose, and communicated the secret to his friends : and then calling together the workers in gold and precious stones, he sat in the midst of them and described to them the figure of the sign he had seen, bidding them represent it in gold and precious stones. And this representation I myself have had an opportunity of seeing."

Chap 31. " Now it was made in the following manner. A long spear, overlaid with gold, formed the figure of the cross by means of a piece transversely laid over it. On the top of the whole was fixed a crown, formed by the intertexture of gold and precious stones, and on this TWO LETTERS INDICATING THE NAME OF CHRIST SYMBOLISED THE SAVIOUR'S TITLE BY MEANS OF ITS FIRST CHARACTERS—the X (Rho) being intersected by P (Chi) exactly in its centre : and these letters the emperor was in the habit of wearing on his helmet at a later period. From the transverse piece which crossed the spear was suspended a kind of streamer of purple cloth, covered with profuse embroidery of most brilliant precious stones, and which, being also interlaced with gold, presented an indescribable degree of beauty to the beholder. This banner was of a square form, and the upright staff, which in its full extent was of great length, bore a golden half-length portrait of the pious emperor and his children on its upper part beneath the trophy of the cross and immediately above the embroidered streamer. The emperor constantly made use of this salutary sign as a safeguard against every adverse and hostile power, and commanded that others similar to it should be carried at the head of all his armies." *

I have in some instances heard another term applied to the symbol, so, as I like to obtain certitude on all points that I can, from the very best authority, I again applied to my clerical relative, and here subjoin his answer. " I have never heard the monogram ☧ called the Pax, and I can see no

---

* The translation followed in this extract is that published by Messrs. Bagster in 1845.

reason or sense in such a name for it. At the same time, as the two letters of the monogram look like the Latin or English letters X and P, it is possible that workmen (sculptors or painters) may (in the slang of their craft) call it the Pax —but I never heard of it."

It reminds me of having once heard a respectable woman explaining the Christmas decorations in church to a companion, to whom she pointed out the letters I.H.S. on a cross, interpreting them as "I have suffered."

I had often had a feeling that I should like to have Mr. Towns for a séance here in my own home, and Mrs. T. kindly smoothed the matter for me to be able to do so. The appointment was made for the 28th of February, and she was to come as early beforehand as she could; so we had a bit of talk, and she remained in the drawing-room while I went down to dinner, as I make arrangements for her more in accordance with her usual hour. When I returned here, she said she had had such a very strong impression during my absence, that *crowds* would be coming up my stairs. It was quite a new feeling to her, for that she generally has the sense of such a calm stillness here, and she wondered what it might portend. I then reminded her of Mrs. Dr. Fuller's similar prophecy about a month previously, that there would be something that would bring crowds rushing to my house.

Little Mr. Towns duly made his appearance punctually at the hour I had fixed, and while we were taking tea he told us some very curious interviews he had had with people, whom he had as it were turned inside out.

When we had settled at the table after tea, he asked as to our usual course of proceedings, and I said that I was on the point of telling him that I should wish to begin with The Lord's Prayer, and that then we would wait for whatever might come, and that was quite in accordance with his own feelings. I had no idea that the raps came to him, but I was glad to hear the three strong raps after each clause of the prayer, shewing that the invisibles were uniting with us.

He then said, " How very curiously you two seem to

belong to each other : knit completely together as it were. I can scarcely explain the entire *one-ness* that there appears to be,—it is so wholly harmonious and perfect, but my words are weak to express the full unitedness."

He now suggested that mental questions should be asked, to which the responses should be given by blows on the table with his *right* hand, and that sometimes explanations are given with his left hand. He thus answered a good many of Mrs. T.'s silent enquiries; I did not ask any questions. He then passed into trance, and said, in rather a shrill female voice—" Good evening, ladies,—I am glad to make your acquaintance, I like to come into the society of *true* people ; allow me to shake hands with you : " which was accordingly complied with. She then spoke warmly to Mrs. T. about some charitable action she had performed (of which I had never heard), giving many of the details, which were all true. Then turning to me she said, " We would speak to you upon a momentous question, for we know that you have been thinking a great deal about this year 1881." I pleaded for slower speech, so that I might write it all down; but although I did so, the prophecies were not clear enough to be shaped into form, so I will only extract a few bits here and there. . . There will be earthquakes and great heavings of the sea, and there are days coming in which there will be great darkness for the time being ; and we see before us more troubles, such as warfare, political disturbances; and there will be great floods between now and May 1882, and after then you will see the old condition of the earth will be on a new basis : there will be a re-awakening of the intellect of the great human family. There will be also mighty changes—mighty reforms. . . There will also be in this coming year a great increase of the death-rate, because of the influences of the passing planets ; but we can congratulate you both that you will see the end of 1881, when many around you will be called away ; you will be left to rejoice in the new year. . . . This is a great purifying time, and in 1888 will again appear the Star of Bethlehem.

Another influence now spoke through him :—" Here is a

very old gentleman—with a long white beard. He wears a robe all dotted with gold and silver stars: he has got a girdle round him—he is evidently one of the old patriarchs. You must have had a message at some time from Elijah, for it is *he* who now comes again to you. There is a new unfoldment going to be given to you, and a new interpretation."

To Mrs. T.—"There's such a pretty little girl coming here, with curls: she is presenting you with some flowers."

Turning again to me—"Who's Bertie?" [Oh! Bertie!! (my Arthur's baby) bless him!] "He says, Bless *you*. He is floating about here with a wreath of flowers, and he is trying to fix it on your head:—oh! he is trying to tickle your ear, and he is trying to shew himself to you—he is trying again at your ear, so that you may feel him." [Then I *am* feeling him, and have been doing so for the last three or four days, and I have wondered about it, for I thought it was the signal of a baby friend, only it was so much stronger than she gives, spreading over all the upper part of the ear, as if coaxing and caressing it, while she only touches just the tip.] "He came floating about in a nice white light, and he has his teacher with him. He is so bright and merry. I think his eyes are blue." [Can you tell me the flowers that are in the wreath?] "It is bound round with forget-me-nots, and there are moss-roses, and a lot of flowers, primroses, violets, and two such fine lilies at the top, and some blue-bells, and lilies of the valley. It is a pity you can't see them! He is pushing them into a bunch in his hand, and he says—'Good-bye, Auntie.'

"Who's Aunt Sarah?" [She is my very dear aunt.] "She is only come to give you a blessing: she says she is often with you.—Now I see a lady who looks like somebody the medium has seen. She is holding a letter that she wrote to her husband, and she tells him not to be so depressed in his spirits, she is always near him." [Mary?] "Yes—Mary."—"Who is Uncle Ben?" [My dear Uncle Ben! he is Papa's brother, as well as my Aunt Sarah's.] "He is very pleased to be here: he is a very nice-looking old gentleman, and he always likes to come to you. He was very glad to give me his name." All those things were curious tests. Mary was my Aunt Sarah's daughter, and before her death she did write a letter to her husband, because she thought it would be a comfort to him if she told him her wishes upon a variety of small details. As for my uncle, it was his literal name, for he had been christened Ben Oakes, after his mother's brother, but he did not exactly approve of it while a dweller upon earth, and always signed himself Benj. Houghton.

"Now shall I tell you something about your home in the spheres?" [I shall be very glad if you can do so.] "I will tell you anything you like, and will say it as slowly as you please, so that you can write it down, for I could go into a thousand houses and not be able to hold my medium in the way I can here.—I can hold him as long as ever you please.

"As soon as you pass over the river of life—when the spirit leaves the body, then it begins to live.—I see a magnificent terrace with several steps all ascending to a beautiful porch with many pillars, and between each pillar there are such gorgeous flowers, and wonderful plants and evergreens, all representing everything that is most beautiful in a tropical land. As you ascend this porch it widens and widens with a lot of arches like a long vista of these magnificent porches, till we come into a splendid place like a temple. It is known as the sphere of love and mercy—oh! and within it are such sparkling fountains and lovely borders of flowers, such as no eye could conceive, and there are gold and silver fish which leap and play and rejoice the moment the angelic eyes are upon them. Those beautiful borders and flowers and fountains go up in such order, and the porches on each side are so splendid. They are all set as it were in golden crystal: then each seems to project a reflecting light, each representing the seven rays of colour according to their order, and as you look up this grand and magnificent building, no tongue can describe its beauty, its grandeur: no hand could paint it! the decorations so perfect that it must lift up a spirit almost to the highest degree to be permitted to enter into that beautiful sphere.—And as we pass on we see the multitude of those beautiful angels as they walk with such exactness that it seems but one movement—their dresses all in order, though there are thousands of them all seen at once. Everything is order as if the eye were the moving feature and all obedient to its rule :—all is harmony—all for one united happiness and joy.—Then I see flying between the pillars birds of the most gorgeous plumage : they also fly all in harmony, and all sing together. All is harmony, all joy, all beauty, all love, all sunshine.—My dear loving sister, I have only given you a very faint description of your future home, for it is far beyond the power of my words :—therefore work and have faith, for thy crown is what thou hast formed for thyself, and thy Father to Whom thou hast lifted up thy soul so many times will claim thee as one of His own— God bless you.—

" Do not fear about the medium, but he will take some time coming out; but do not be alarmed, for he *will* come out. He has been far deeper than he has *ever* been." [Do you mean higher?] " Higher in *spirit*, but *deeper* in sleep : —we have numbed the conditions to raise up the spirit."

There was a pause of some considerable duration, and then it was clearly Mr. Towns's own inner self that was speaking :—" I don't know *where* I am :—oh ! where *have* I been ?—I seem lost :—I can't get across *that* river—oh ! they are bringing a boat : oh ! what a funny river, and they are such pleasant people, all smiling : (Then in a tone of dismay) Oh ! I don't want to go on that bank,—I don't want to go up that dark road : (imploringly) oh ! let me go back with you. (Plaintively) They have gone away and left me here in the dark :—I don't know where I've got to now : —oh ! I've lost my head : I've been away somewhere, and I've lost my way. Oh ! I don't know where I've been to, I'm sure,—oh ! dear, I hope you'll excuse me (yawning very much)—it seems very rude.—Dear me ! I shall never get awake again, I think.—Oh ! dear me ! . . . I feel better now—at last." By this time he had come to himself, and I proposed his moving round to sit by the fireside, where we had more talk, and he presently exclaimed, "Who is Charlie? for he is here now!" My Charlie—of course he was: so I pointed to Arthur's photograph, and told him he was his brother and the uncle of the dear little baby Bertie whom he had seen in his trance, which he remembered nothing about. It was singular that Charlie should thus be the *last* to come, instead of the first, according to his usual preference, for I had been telling Mrs. T. that I thought my first series of Evenings at Home would *end* with all the long account of Charlie as crowning the work.

That has been the only occasion of my witnessing the unwillingness of a spirit to return from the ecstatic state to the earthly condition, although I have heard and read of such being the case. It certainly was a very curious experience, and his miserable tones when left on this dark side of the river of life were very lamentable; when, however, he was really *with* us again, he became quite comfortable, and said that he had never felt more brisk nor in a pleasanter atmosphere, and he was really sorry when the time for departure had absolutely arrived.

I seldom write out any of my own little conversations, but the following one amused me so much that I did, and I give it as a kind of sample. I had had a letter on the Saturday evening (May 7th) that had given me much happiness, for it referred to the publication of this work; and while writing two or three letters on the subject the next day, I had several times felt dear little Bertie's signal, to which I only paid the heed of a few loving words. When I afterwards established myself to read, he came again, going on very persistently with his small sign. I asked if he had any message for me. "No." [Are you crowning me with flowers?] "No." [Anything for me?] "Yes." [*Not* flowers?] "No." [Fruit?] "No." [Feathers?] "No." [Birds?] "No." [Drapery?] "No." [Something in the way of dress?] "No." [Jewels?] "No." [Are you *sure* you have anything? for I cannot think of more.] "Yes."

[An ornament?] "Yes." [A ring?] "No." [A necklace?] "No." [A chain?] "No." [A crown?] "Yes." [Such as are described in my drawings?] "No." [A golden crown?] "No." [Gold with gems set in it?] "No." [Any gold?] "No." [What is it then? must I go on trying?] "Yes." [Opal?] "Yes." [Is that all?] "No." [Something bedded in the opal?] "Yes." [Precious stones?] "No." [Flowers?] "No." [Fruit?] "Yes." [Like our earthly fruit?] "No." [Fruit of my life?] "*Yes.*" Then the description was fully inbreathed to me of an opal crown, exquisitely and delicately carved, like ivory carvings, as of beautiful clusters of fruit, with changing tints, brilliant and glowing, formed of the opal only, about eight inches in height. There seems to me now, while I write it out, a something that is difficult to catch—oh! it refers somehow to the radiant gleams which shoot from it, and seem to fly to distant spots, piercing into hearts, sometimes with a soft glow, and sometimes like sharp needle-points, wounding to heal; and there seems to be no limit—as to the distance where they may make themselves felt. . . . They are trying to make me conceive some notion of its wondrously delicate tracery, almost as if the touch even of infantine spirit fingers must crush it, yet really having a strength that Samson would have been powerless to fracture. . . . I have written out all the questions as I put them, for I had had no idea of anything special, and went on because Bertie was so persistent. He says his little fingers retain all the varying tints, and sparkle beautifully.

That which was a mystery to me as I wrote it, is now to be explained in this, my closing chapter.

"Those fiery gleams have at this time work to do in the world, going forth as it were in search of hearts that may be touched, whether to the strengthening of a pure life or to the awakening unto repentance where the life may have been sullied. We would fain write strongly on this most important point.—Conjugal life is God's ordinance,—twain beings are born to form an ultimate one-ness;

and blessed are they who here below are conjoined with the partner for eternity. But let each man and woman examine deeply into their own souls ere linking themselves in matrimony, for that tie should be indissoluble, and all mistakes must be borne with. Through *this hand* we may not give the fulness of our meaning, but we make no distinction between woman and man,—God's law for the one is even the same as for the other, and that law is <u>*absolute purity*</u>— from childhood until the dissolution of the mortal form; and the human race will not rise to full perfection until such law is universal. Fathers and mothers! look to it how ye train your babes! remember that the earliest impressions are the most permanent, especially when day by day the same sweet reticence is inculcated. Our language is necessarily vague, but none the less it may strike home to the innermost soul, and wheresoe'er it strikes, *there* will be sheltered a ray from the opal crown. Some there are who take refuge in The Lord's words, utterly misconstruing their import. S. Matthew xxi. 31, 32: "Jesus saith unto them, Verily I say unto you, That the Publicans and the harlots go into the kingdom of God before you, for John came unto you in the way of righteousness, and ye believed him not: but the Publicans and the harlots believed him: and ye, when ye had seen it, repented not afterward, that ye might believe him."—What *is* belief?—A leading into repentance. What is repentance? A turning from sin.— The ground of hope for sinners is the henceforward walking in the path of righteousness; not a mere *belief*, but a newness of life evincing that belief. But sin, however much repented of, has still tarnished, and it is long ere the foul spots can be cleansed away: repentance is but the first step thereunto. Oh! ye preachers of the Word! see ye to your flocks, whether they be the sheep or the lambs.

Ye must understand also how pure was the tiny hand commissioned to place that crown on its destined brow. The baby Bertie inherited perfect purity from three generations, parents, grand-parents, and great-grand-parents, and we, who *know*, could carry the spotless thread yet higher and higher. It has already been explained in the earlier pages that the opal gem symbolises purity."

My work went steadily on, and even as I proceeded, fresh evidence of watchful care seemed to come to me almost daily, so that at the exact moment that I was writing on any special subject, a fragment that would dovetail into the thought and give it fulness of completion would be apparently casually spoken while I was in Great Russell Street or elsewhere, perhaps reviving some byegone memory, or teaching me an argument or a point that I had overlooked. My first manuscript I finished on Maundy Thursday, and wrote the preface on Good Friday—and to this final volume of the three I shall be able to affix the date (not yet arrived) that I originally planned.

Mrs. T. came to me on the 10th of June, and after much conversation on all that I was doing, we spoke somewhat about my full portfolios of drawings, and in the midst of our talk she passed gradually into trance, and after a few opening words on the same subject, she added:—"You won't have *time* to draw any more, not that you *could* not. . . . You have been so diligent.—You have done what your hand found to do with your *might*, and so you compress much work in a small measure of time." (Compressing her hands together.) After that, some prophecies were given respecting the books, of which I must patiently await the future fulfilment.

The last proofs of my intermediate work, the photographic chronicles, came to me for correction on the 24th of September, and the publication has been delayed for the illustrations, which are not yet ready, somewhat to my disappointment; but now I can see how providential has been the hindrance, for by this morning's post I received a letter from His Most Serene Highness, the Prince of Solms, (in answer to one I wrote to him some time since), giving the highest testimony to Mr. Hudson's integrity, with a most gracious permission to make whatever use of it in my book that I may wish; therefore I can insert it in the as-yet unwritten preface. If my own impatient desire had been fulfilled (and at this *very* moment the necessary illustrations have been brought to me by post), the weight of this additional evidence would have been lost. Another fact also the preface will contain, which is that on Thursday, October 13th, Mr. Hudson came here for a photographic experiment, under rather unfavourable circumstances, for our dark closet can only be contrived in the underground department, so that our journeys up and down stairs are very lengthy, but on the seventh plate we did obtain a something. It is a manifestation that the outsiders would scorn, but *we* hailed it with joy as containing a future promise to be in some way worked out according to The Higher Will.

Thursdays were the original photographing days. On Thursdays I attended the Guild of the Holy Spirit.—On a Thursday I was born, and on a Thursday I believe that this manuscript will be delivered, with that date appended to it, into my friend's hands——may God grant His Blessing upon it to work to His Glory.

Thursday, October 20th, 1881.

END OF SECOND SERIES.

PRINTED BY BALLANTYNE, HANSON AND CO.
EDINBURGH AND LONDON.

www.ingramcontent.com/pod-product-compliance
Lightning Source LLC
Chambersburg PA
CBHW030744250426
43672CB00028B/391